Advance Praise for 118 Days

"Like a tapestry woven with all the colours of life, this book weaves together the many details of the difficult story of kidnapping. The events are portrayed, but more importantly, the people are portrayed. So many people live the story and are changed forever by that living."
~ *Rev. Dr. Karen Hamilton, General Secretary, Canadian Council of Churches*

"*118 Days* contains a magnificent story, rare in our tormented world, of Christians taking Christ seriously, acting as though the truth were true."
~ *Daniel Berrigan, S. J.*

"There is no greater love than to lay down your life for your friends," the nonviolent Jesus said. Tom Fox did just that. He and his Christian Peacemaker teammates obeyed the commandment to 'love our enemies' by journeying to Iraq, befriending the Iraqis, and practicing nonviolence. In these pages, we hear their testimony, share their behind the scenes anguish, deepen in faith, hope and love, and receive a rare, authentic witness. Their story will inspire you to be a peacemaker, a follower of the nonviolent Jesus who works for a new world without war."
~ *Rev. John Dear, author of* Living Peace, The Questions of Jesus, *and* Transfiguration

"Christ never promised it would be easy. That is, Christ did not say the work of peace would be without conflict. So we are fortunate to have this wonderful book and testimony to the pain, loss and elation it takes to do the work of peace. These honest and sobering reflections help all of us committed to the work of peace better understand the world in which we live. I hope this book will be widely read."
~ *Stanley Hauerwas, Professor of Theological Ethics, Duke University*

118 DAYS

Christian Peacemaker Teams
Held Hostage in Iraq

Edited by

Tricia Gates Brown

Christian Peacemaker Teams

Chicago

Toronto

Published in the United States by
Christian Peacemaker Teams,
Chicago, Illinois USA/Toronto, Ontario CANADA
www.cpt.org

To order copies of this book, contact CPT at (800) 318-2843,
or visit www.118days.org or www.amazon.com.

Cover Photo by CPT At-Tuwani
Cover Design by Darryl Brown

118 Days:
Christian Peacemaker Teams
Held Hostage in Iraq

Edited by Tricia Gates Brown

ISBN: 978-1-438-20243-3

Contents

Editor's Acknowledgments

The outpouring of support for Christian Peacemaker Teams (CPT) from Arabs and Muslims during CPT's Iraq hostage crisis inspired awe. It prompted Christians around the world to call attention to the plight of detainees in Iraq. Add to these voices a global choir calling for the release of *all* captives and you will sense the flood of peacemaking occasioned by the CPT hostage crisis. This book includes many stories from the crisis— stories of this reaching out across cultures and faiths, stories that subvert the voices calling for division, stories of hope in the face of grave loss. Stories people need to hear.

As important as these stories are, getting this book to press has presented extraordinary challenges (see chapter "Why We are Self-Publishing"). In light of this, I wish to thank the book's authors for their steady devotion to this project and to telling all of the stories that need to be told.

I also wish to thank the following: Doug Pritchard, Anita David, and Gene Stoltzfus—the CPT reading committee; Zoe Mullery, for serving as liaison between me and Watani Stiner; Joel Klassen, for translating the chapter by Sandra Rincon; Anita David, for sending the Arabic statements translated into English; Esther Kern, for gathering the list of support statements; Jan Fox, for responding to my inquiries so graciously; Harmeet Sooden, for providing the text of the interview included herein; Norman Kember, for permission to reprint his article; Darryl Brown, for designing the book cover.

I will never forget the exact moment, 3:20 a.m. PST on March 23, 2006, when I received the phone call informing me that Norman, Harmeet, and Jim were freed. The same overwhelming joy and ineffable sadness I felt at that moment reverberates throughout this book, beneath every voice and story. Thank you, the reader, for listening in.

Tricia Gates Brown, 38, has been a CPT reservist since 2003. She holds a PhD in New Testament Studies from the University of St. Andrews and is author of the play about CPT entitled *Whatever Kindles* and the book *Free People: A Christian Response to Global Economics*. She is editor of the CPT collection *Getting in the Way* (Herald Press, 2005). Tricia's poems have appeared in *Rain Magazine*, *The Portland Review*, and *Geez Magazine*. She lives with her teenaged daughter on the northern coast of Oregon where she works part time as a museum curator and freelance editor, and writes. She recently finished a book of memoirs and started a novel.

Foreword

Iraq runs throughout the life of Christian Peacemaker Teams (CPT). In our faith tradition, it is the site of the Garden of Eden and the home of Abraham and Sarah before they followed God's leading to Hebron. In our work, it is the destination of CPT's first-ever delegation on the eve of the 1991 Gulf War. It is the location of our first death where a CPTer died in a car accident. It is the place where a CPT delegation was kidnapped and a team member killed (our second death). And it is a place where we have continued to work.

The kidnapping is like a rock thrown into a pond. This book describes the ripples set in motion by that rock. Ripples in the lives of CPT teams and the communities in which they work. Ripples among the families and friends of those taken—Tom Fox, Norman Kember, Jim Loney, and Harmeet Singh Sooden. Ripples across the world in faith communities, prisons, the media and their audiences.

The crisis, as we sometimes call it, tested CPT in a way that we had not been tested before. We walked through the valley of the shadow of death where so many of our project partners and friends have walked before us. We hope that this testing has refined and purified us for the work yet to be done. Scripture says, "Consider it all joy …when you encounter various trials, knowing that the testing of your faith produces endurance" (James 1:2-4 NASB). We have been tested, and we have endured as an organization, but it was not all joy.

The murder of Tom Fox was a devastating blow. We grieve for him. We ache for his family and friends. We continue to reflect on the meaning of his life and death.

We cannot forget the sleepless nights of that long winter crisis. We remember our fears of a ransom demand or a violent rescue attempt. We recall the false reports, the misinformation, the broken promises, our frustration at never being able to contact those who took our colleagues. We still do not know who they were or why they did this.

Despite this not knowing, Harmeet, Norman, and Jim have forgiven those who held them. In a public statement made eight months after they were freed they said, "We unconditionally forgive our captors for abducting and holding us. We have no desire to punish them. Punishment can never restore what was taken from us. What our captors did was wrong. They caused us, our families, and our friends great suffering. Yet we bear no malice towards them and have no wish for retribution."

Jesus' call to love our enemies was lived out in a powerful way during the crisis. CPTers were among the few foreigners in Iraq without a gun or an engineering contract. Dozens of Muslim leaders who knew our peacemaking work courageously called for the release of our delegation. Christian leaders in turn called for justice for the 14,000 Iraqis who were being held at the time by the Multi-National Forces in Iraq without charge or access to their families. Our efforts to gain the release of our colleagues were supported by the work of hundreds of CPTers and friends and by the prayers of hundreds of thousands around the world. People in despair at the cycles of violence saw hope in the witness of our brothers to another way of being in the world. We are delighted to have our three friends restored to their communities after an operation that apparently injured no one. These are all enduring legacies of this crisis. This does bring us joy.

This book gives a window into many people's witness during 118 days of crisis and beyond. To some these choices seem foolish. To others, they are challenging and inspiring. For CPTers, "God's foolishness is wiser than human wisdom, and God's weakness is stronger than human strength" (1 Corinthians 1:25).

—Doug Pritchard, *CPT Co-Director*

Why We are Self- Publishing

Publishing this story has been its own challenge. Even before the kidnapping was over, a church press approached CPT hoping for a book. When we were at last able to take a collective breath, after the release of Jim, Harmeet and Norman, and memorial services for Tom, we considered carefully what part of the story was CPT's to tell, and how it might be told. We proposed gathering into one volume some accounts of the many ripples set in motion on November 26, 2005, the day of the kidnapping.

One of the lesser-known ripples of the kidnapping was how Jim's partner, Dan Hunt, and the community of which they are a part, made the heartbreaking choice to become invisible in order to protect Jim's life. We were aware that same-sex love is a highly charged issue for many churches. Therefore, we wanted to make sure the publisher would not silence any author by editing out aspects of the story concerning sexual orientation.

The publisher and CPT agreed that the book would portray "significant things that happened in the Muslim world, the Christian community, and in those immediately affected," and in that context, there would not be "any kind of censorship" around Dan and Jim's relationship. The publisher also confirmed their readiness to face the critique this might bring as a result. Tricia Gates Brown, working closely with the publisher's staff, compiled and edited the collection.

On the eve of going to press in February 2007, the publisher demanded that we cut the paragraphs in Dan's chapter that spoke most tenderly of his love for his partner Jim. The publisher had received negative feedback from church leaders, one of whom characterized Dan's chapter as "a pro-gay apologetic." When we refused to make the cuts, the publisher withdrew from the project.

We found a second church press who expressed interest in the book. We provided them with the full manuscript, including Dan's chapter, explained how and why the book had been pulled at the last minute, and confirmed that the new publisher's proposed "house wash" would "not include an editing out, in any way, of the queer element in these stories." They agreed and a second launch date of March 23, 2008 was set—the second anniversary of the release of Jim, Harmeet, and Norman.

Again, just a few weeks before the book was to be published, the second publisher informed us of concerns raised by an external reviewer. They asked for the removal of sections "describing Dan and Jim's courtship and details of their personal relationship, which readers will infer in any case." We refused. The publisher cancelled the book.

"It seems that the final breaking point of this project concerns one chapter out of twenty-three," the second publisher wrote. "[We] hope that some reflection might enable CPT to consider how a decision to focus on a particular detail has damaged a project with an enormous global canvas."

Sadly, what neither publisher seems to recognize is that their editing requirements are part of the same system of homophobia that threatened Jim's life while he was in captivity, and subsequently condemned Dan to invisibility.

The many circles of action and response rippling out around the kidnapping continue. Its impact on diverse people and communities is still important. These are stories that will continue to change lives and open pathways to peace. So, we have decided to publish the book ourselves.
—Christian Peacemaker Teams

1

Unless a Grain of Wheat Falls:
A View from the CPT Crisis Team

Doug Pritchard and Carol Rose

(Doug) Saturday, November 26, 2005, 9 a.m. EST. My wife, Jane, was in Edmonton, Alberta, helping our future daughter-in-law, Jasmine, shop for her wedding dress. I was home alone in Toronto and had just picked the newspaper off the front porch, ready for a leisurely read in bed. Then CPTer Greg Rollins called from Baghdad. "The whole delegation has just been kidnapped. Don't tell anyone yet. I will call you when I have more details."

My stomach sank. I took a deep breath, thinking, "We all knew this could happen. We have been through emergencies before. We know what to do." I prayed for a quick release for the delegation and for strength and wisdom for all of us in the days ahead. Then I took the subway to the CPT office, where I would work, pray, weep, hope, eat, and sleep for the next four months and beyond.

(Carol) On Thursday, November 24, my husband Duane and I had digested Thanksgiving dinner with my extended family. On Friday I'd spoken about CPT's work with an enthusiastic group in Fresno, California. On Saturday the twenty-sixth I woke early to the most brilliant of fall days in the comfortable home of a CPT supporter—ready for a transition. A bus ride would take Duane and me to the heart of Los Angeles, where we would visit a courageous and compassionate congregation in one of that city's most troubled neighborhoods. But nothing had readied us for the transition announced by the early ringing of my cell phone.

Doug's tone spoke of crisis before his words: efficient, accurate, clear, holding back the storm of emotions so as to do what needed to be done. "The Iraq delegation has been kidnapped. Crisis Team call in 60 minutes. Need to be off the phone to get further information from the team in Baghdad." I hung up and began the waiting of an Advent that took four months instead of four weeks. My heart echoed with the prayer it had learned decades ago, "Lord Jesus Christ, have mercy on us."

Flame-colored leaves carpeted the ground, canopied the sky, fell around me.

(Doug and Carol) Greg phoned back with more details. Doug immediately called together a Crisis Team. This initial Crisis Team consisted of us as the CPT co-directors, Delegation Coordinator Claire Evans, Training Coordinator Kryss Chupp, Canada Co-Coordinator Rebecca Johnson, Colombia Project Support Coordinator Robin Buyers, and CPT Steering Committee Chair Brian Young. This Crisis Team never met face-to-face. It carried out its work of coordinating CPT's response to the situation through daily telephone conference calls. This team maintained an amazing unity, focus, and energy level through the constant stress of the crisis. This was a gift from God.

We had been through serious crises before. CPTers had been held prisoner. Chris Brown and Kim Lamberty had been severely beaten and hospitalized in Palestine. George Weber had been killed in Iraq in 2003 when the new SUV he was riding in blew a new tire and rolled several times. Yet this current crisis was on a whole different level. Eventually it would extend across four continents and last four months.

From that day on, we in CPT began juggling two new priorities along with the rest of our work. One priority was to support the extended families of the four who were missing: Tom Fox from the United States, a full-time member of the CPT Iraq team; Jim Loney, the other CPT Canada Co-Coordinator based in CPT's Toronto office and leader of the short-term delegation that was kidnapped; and the other members of the delegation, Norman Kember from the United Kingdom and Harmeet Singh Sooden from New Zealand.

The other priority was to do everything in our power to secure their safe release.

Members of the Crisis Team contacted the immediate families of the missing four to break the news, then stayed in close contact with them for the months to come. Each family had its own concerns, complexities, and needs. Extended family members from around the globe also became involved and the team contacted them too. In some cases, CPTers were able to visit the families. For example, Fr. Jerry Stein flew from Texas to northern Ontario to stay with Jim Loney's parents for the first month until their other children were free to come.

The families and CPT also called on the wider support networks of the missing four. These were phenomenal groups in each case. Tom's Quaker and Mennonite communities. Jim's Catholic Worker community. Norman's extensive networks in the British peace movement and his home church. Harmeet's friends in the New Zealand and Australian peace movements. They spoke extensively with the media and were tireless in organizing appeals and vigils, supporting the families, and seeking contacts who might influence those who had taken the CPT delegation.

The team in Iraq had the most access to avenues of action, avenues that might lead to the safe release of the CPTers. They contacted everyone CPT knew in Iraq and sought their assistance in gathering information and making contact with whoever was holding our friends.

At the outset, diplomats who were experienced with Iraqi kidnappings insisted it was best to avoid publicity for the first 72 hours to give the best chance for a quick release. Thus we said little to anyone beyond the delegation's families, despite the growing number of leaks and pointed media inquiries. This secrecy was a heavy burden for those of us who did know. It cut against the grain of CPT's culture of trusting, open teamwork. It inhibited the prayers of CPT's wide network of supporters and the actions they were ready to take on CPT's behalf. We now see this initial silence as a mistake.

Ironically, the release of the first video on November 29, on the Arabic television channel Al Jazeera, was in many ways a relief. It showed the CPT Four alive and well. It allowed CPT to tell its stories publicly. It allowed us to tap the source of CPT's strength in its communities of prayer.

It was also distressing to see our brothers confined and accused of being spies. CPT appealed to the world for statements of support to counter this accusation and to call for their release. Hundreds of statements came in the next few days, from senior religious councils and from school children, from political leaders and from those organizing for justice and human rights, from friends in distant nations and from strangers near at hand.

Most significantly, prominent Muslim leaders courageously called for the release of these Christians, two of whom were citizens of countries with troops in Iraq.[1] This resulted from generosity beyond measure and

---

[1] The following statement by the Al-Quds conference of Muslim scholars is just one example of the statements collected by CPT during the captivity of the CPT Four. For a full listing of groups and individuals who issued statements on their behalf, see Appendix. —*Editor*

Muslim Leaders Demand the Immediate Release of Kidnapped Peace Activists in Iraq:
Press Release, December 5, 2005
> We, the undersigned, call for the immediate release of the four western peace activists who were kidnapped in Iraq last week. We have been saddened by the kidnapping of these peace activists whose only mission in Iraq has been to express solidarity with the Iraqi people and see for themselves the devastating effects of the U.S. invasion of Iraq. They were intending to return home to inform the public in their own countries about the destruction and havoc brought about by the invasion of Iraq by the United States of America and its allies.

3

We have come to learn that the Christian NGO to which these four activists belonged is a peace-loving organization that is well-known for its support for the just causes of oppressed nations around the world and particularly for its sympathy with the Palestinian and Iraqi peoples and its support for their struggle for emancipation from the shackles of occupation.

Such peace activists should have been welcomed into Iraq and treated as honorable guests instead of being kidnapped and used as a bargaining chip. Neither the hostages nor the organization they represent possess the means of forcing the occupation authorities to free the Iraqis held in its detention centers across Iraq.

While fully supporting the right of the Iraqi people to resist occupation with all legitimate means, we denounce as illegitimate any act of aggression against innocent civilians irrespective of their religion or nationality. We therefore call for the immediate release of these four hostages and of all other western civilians kidnapped in Iraq, and urge whoever has the ability to play a role in securing their release and their safe return to their countries to spare no effort in this regard. All illegitimate acts of aggression against innocent civilians, including kidnappings, indiscriminate killing, or other forms of harm inflicted upon noncombatants, only harm the just cause of the Iraqi people and their legitimate struggle for freedom and independence.

Signed, Sheikh Yusuf Al-Qaradawi, chairman of Al-Quds International Foundation
Sheikh Faysal Mawlawi, secretary general of the Islamic Group in Lebanon
Sheikh Harith Al-Dari, head of Association of Muslim Scholars, Iraq
Khalid Mishaal, head of Hamas Political Bureau, Palestine
Musa Abu Marzuq, deputy head of Hamas Political Bureau, Palestine
Maan Bashur, secretary general of the Arab Nationalist Congress
Hasan Hudruj, Hezbollah, Lebanon
Mahmud Al-Qumati, Hezbollah, Lebanon
Father Antwan Dhao, Lebanon
Sheikh Abdulhadi Awang, Islamic Party, Malaysia
Professor Aleef-ud-Din Turabi, Kashmir
Dr. Mohamed M. O. Jamjoom, businessman, Saudi Arabia
Dr. Khalid Abdurrahman Al-Ajami, university professor, Saudi Arabia
Dr. Muhsin Al-Awaji, Islamic writer and thinker, Saudi Arabia
Dr. Abd Al-Quddus Al-Midwahi, Yemen
Muhammad bin Ali Ijlan, Yemen
Dr. Abdullatif Al Mahmud, Islamic Society, Bahrain
Abdulmunem Jalal Al-Mir, Palestine Solidarity Association, Bahrain
Dr. Muhammad Al-Sheikh Mahmud Siyam, former imam of Al-Aqsa Mosque, Palestine
Khalid Mahmud Khan, Pakistan
Dr. Zafrul-Islam Khan, India
Dr. Azzam Tamimi, Muslim Association of Britain
Haitham Yassin Abu Al-Raghib, Jordan
Saud Abu Mahfuz, Jordan
Engineer Boulafaat Abdulhamid, Algeria

from CPT's years of respectful work with Muslim partners in Palestine and Iraq. We hope that bridges of trust between our two faiths strengthened during these months will be a lasting legacy of this crisis. Supporters organized hundreds of prayer vigils and continued to do so for the duration of the CPTers' captivity. We believe that these prayers and statements kept our four friends alive and led to the eventual release of three of them.

CPT also got hate mail. At times it was frightening to see the depth of fear and anger in these thousands of bilious messages, many instigated by right-wing bloggers and talk-show hosts like Rush Limbaugh. CPT Canada office assistant Scott Albrecht took on the ugly task of sorting these e-mails from other inquiries and messages of support, thereby sparing the rest of us the emotional distress of reading them.

In the second video released on December 2, those holding the CPT Four threatened to kill them unless the U.S. and the U.K. released all detainees and withdrew their troops from Iraq by December 8. In a subsequent video, this timeline was extended by 48 hours, to December 10, which is, ironically, International Human Rights Day.

Here the Crisis Team experienced a shift. This was not solely about CPT and our colleagues. Addressing the widespread abuse of human rights in Iraq was an important part of CPT's work. The world's spotlight was now on our four friends. The Crisis Team felt the Spirit's call to let that same spotlight illuminate more clearly the plight of 14,000 Iraqis held by the Multi-National Force in Iraq. They were being held without charges or access to legal processes or family. Many of them had been abused, as CPT's investigations and others' photos from Abu Ghraib had shown.

CPT was never able to make direct contact with those holding our friends. Our surest way of communicating with them, whoever they were, was through our website and through the media. So CPT's media work played an integral part in our strategy for release. The most important media for this purpose were in Iraq and adjacent nations. Therefore CPT focused its efforts on appeals, news releases, interviews, and actions for the Arabic media. This concentration on Arabic media was sometimes frustrating for media and supporters in North America, the United Kingdom, and New Zealand, who wanted more of CPT's time and attention at home for the "human interest" story of their kidnapped citizens. To monitor the impact of these efforts, we had a network of people following the Arabic and English media and giving daily feedback to the Crisis and Media Teams, but we wished we had even more.

Normally, CPT-related media work is carried out by our large network of CPTers and members of previous CPT delegations who develop their own media contacts in their home communities. We laughed when a reporter called and wanted to speak to our "communications department." Media coordination was initially managed by CPT's creative but overworked Colombia Project Support Coordinator Robin Buyers, who was joined by the volunteers on CPT's ad hoc Media Team. They met frequently by telephone, disseminated news releases and statements of support, monitored media coverage, worked to correct inaccuracies, and provided regular media guidelines to CPTers plus the hundreds of CPT spokespeople in the above networks. These spokespeople were accessible 24 hours a day and gave consistent, competent responses to the media across many time zones. Some journalists said that, in their experience, CPT was unusually professional for an organization of its size and that it should give "media seminars" to other small nongovernmental organizations!

During this crisis, partner organizations and the four men's support communities also took a great deal of initiative. As Pat Gaffney from Pax Christi UK writes, "Without a press office, without spin doctors or PR people, I believe we did a great job in maintaining the integrity of the witness and message of Norman, Tom, Harmeet and James. Perhaps our weakness was, in the end, our greatest strength."

After the December 10 timeline expired, there was a worrying and wearying seven-week silence before the next videotape. During this time, CPT was buffeted by repeated rumors of ransom demands, negotiations, executions, and imminent release. We received calls from people pretending to have connections. More foreigners and nationals were kidnapped in Iraq. Some were released. Some were killed. CPT continued its call for justice for Iraqi detainees through an Epiphany Fast at the White House and our Shine the Light Campaign in Washington, D.C., Chicago, and Toronto.

We also had to get back to supporting the work of the rest of CPT. Kryss Chupp was released from the Crisis Team to lead the upcoming training of new CPTers, which started on January 2. Robin Buyers was also released from the team to rejoin the Colombia team. CPT reservist Jane MacKay Wright replaced her. Brian Young had to leave the team for a few weeks to complete his seminary term and was replaced by Steering Committee Vice-Chair Ruth Buhler.

In the course of this crisis we experienced the power of adrenaline. The Crisis Team, the rest of the CPT Support Team, and the field teams ran on little else for the first weeks. But like all drugs, adrenaline has its limitations and side effects. As our exhaustion grew, we began to seek the advice of counselors who helped us establish more sustainable patterns for work, worship, meals, sleep, and breaks. The CPT offices in Chicago and Toronto were now supported by 100 volunteers who brought meals, maintained computers, answered phones, organized vigils and mailings, and provided hospitality. As the stress from this crisis accumulated, the Crisis Team made plans for the extensive stress and trauma care that would be needed once the crisis was resolved.

Throughout this time, CPT held true to its center. The core of CPT's work is living out Jesus' call to love God, love our neighbors, and love our enemies—living out nonviolent ways of being in the world. War zones are where CPT works. If CPT is not prepared for the risk of injury and death, we should not be there. This could have happened to any of us. Our teams are well prepared for violence reduction work in war zones—through our strong Christian commitment and through the work done in CPT training, on project sites, in developing creative nonviolent tactics and media skills, and in the ability to face danger and death.

Just two weeks before the kidnapping, the Iraq team had spent a day discussing the topic, "Why Are We Here? What Does it Cost?" They named their current goals in Iraq as: being a witness for peace and the power of the cross; telling the truth of what was happening; supporting and building bridges among local human rights organizations; and using CPT's power to assist Iraqis in gaining access to U.S., U.K., UN, and other authorities. They also counted the costs of this work: burnout; limited outlets for physical exercise; absence from family and friends; and daily risk of injury, kidnapping, and death.

Despite the costs, CPT-Iraq team members were unanimous in their commitment to continuing their work of Christian peacemaking. Tom Fox reflected on this discussion in a powerful way the night before he was taken, saying, "[We are here] to take part in the creation of the Peaceable Realm of God... to root out all aspects of dehumanization that exist within us. ...We are here to stop people, including ourselves, from dehumanizing any of God's children, no matter how much they dehumanize their own souls."

In keeping with Tom's words, which echo long-standing CPT policy, the Crisis Team resisted attempts by the media and government to demonize those who had taken our colleagues. We referred to them as hosts, brothers, and friends, and appealed to them as fellow human beings concerned about justice and the future of Iraq. We were confident that our captive colleagues were doing the same, seeking to show their own humanity and reaching out to the humanity of those who were holding them.

From the beginning, we knew that an armed rescue operation was a possibility. In a hostage situation, CPT rejects all military or violent approaches. But others do not. On the day of the kidnapping, the Iraq team immediately told the governments involved, "We do not wish for either government or military intervention as we believe it may endanger [our colleagues]." The governments insisted that, while they too sought a nonviolent outcome, they reserved the right to use armed force, and they would do so without reference to the missing men's wishes, or those of their families, or CPT. The possibility of an armed assault that could lead to the death of the captives, bystanders, those holding our friends, or the soldiers themselves, hung heavy over us all. CPTers reiterated this concern repeatedly in our encounters with governments and in our statements to them through the media, but the governments were just as insistent that this was their call alone.

From the beginning, we also knew that a ransom demand was a possibility. Since the U.S.-led invasion, thousands of Iraqis have been kidnapped for ransom. Some of the political kidnappings of foreigners have apparently also led to ransom demands. We did not know who had kidnapped our colleagues and what their motives might be. We still do not know. CPT has a clear and long-standing policy against paying ransom. But now it was a real and immediate concern. These were among the most difficult discussions with the families of Tom, Jim, Norman, and Harmeet, and within the Crisis Team, as the team weighed our friends' lives against a possible ransom. We felt a heavy responsibility to be prepared in case we received such a demand. As we considered this possibility again and again, the Crisis Team and the Iraq team remained unanimous that we must not pay a ransom.

CPT enters war zones to offer nonviolent alternatives to war. That is our mission. CPT is founded on a commitment to Jesus and to his way of love for all, regardless of the cost. We believe that paying a large sum to support a violent group directly supports the ongoing violence of that armed group and would seriously compromise CPT's work of nonviolence. Paying a ransom would also set a dangerous precedent that would immediately put in greater danger the lives of other CPTers in Iraq and in other kidnap-prone project locations like Colombia.

Some told CPT that if a ransom is not paid and the hostages are held longer, the risk of a violent military intervention rises. While this is possible, we held that paying a ransom to an armed group increases the likelihood of their continuing their own violence against others. Some told CPT that if we do not pay a ransom, CPT is responsible for the deaths of our colleagues. We reject this argument. CPT is not responsible. Those who do the killing are responsible.

CPTers and delegates are all informed of CPT's commitment not to pay a ransom. Each of us, in joining CPT, takes this seriously—that there will be no ransom and no armed intervention to save our lives. Paying a ransom would betray the deepest convictions of our colleagues.

In the end, CPT received no genuine ransom demands. To our knowledge, neither did anyone else.

The long silence of those holding the CPT Four was broken on January 28 with the release of another videotape on Al Jazeera. We were relieved to see that our friends were still alive. However, an accompanying statement said that this was their "last chance" or "their fate will be death."

Through friends, CPT's website, and the media, the Crisis Team and the Iraq team continued trying to make contact with those holding our colleagues. We continued to hear conflicting rumors of contact, imminent release, and death. U.S. soldiers raided more homes and mosques in Baghdad in search of various kidnappers and even fired on Canadian diplomats in Baghdad's Green Zone, further raising the Crisis Team's fears of a violent rescue attempt by trigger-happy troops. The new Canadian foreign affairs minister, Peter MacKay, said he was "very optimistic" about a safe release based on "the most up-to-date information." He retracted the statement the next day, saying that there was no new information, and he phoned the families to apologize. Other hostages were shown on TV. Christian and Muslim groups issued new appeals for the release of all hostages.

At the same time the "Danish cartoon" controversy exploded around the world. The CPT Iraq team immediately issued a statement condemning these cartoons, which insulted Islam, and CPT circulated this statement as widely as possible in the Arab world. Soon after, the Shia shrine in Samarra, Iraq, was destroyed and the violence in Iraq began to escalate dramatically. Yet the CPT Iraq team continued its peacemaking work. They were heartened by a new group of Iraqi human rights workers who had heard about CPT's work and had now held their third public vigil calling for the release of the CPT hostages. March 5 marked the one hundredth day since the kidnapping, and special vigils were held around the world, especially in the United Kingdom, organized by Norman's supporters.

On March 7, the last video was released on Al Jazeera. Ominously it showed only Harmeet, Norman, and Jim. We in CPT had no idea why Tom was not shown, and we did not speculate publicly. But we were afraid. Two days later, on March 9, Tom's body was found on a street in western Baghdad.

(Carol) Friday, March 10, 1:30 p.m. EST. Our first hint of this news came twenty-four hours later when I got a call from the U.S. State Department asking for assistance in contacting Tom's daughter. It wasn't the first time I'd talked with this official. She didn't give me any information, but I sensed an edge of something different about this call. I was in Toronto at the time for the semi-annual meeting of CPT's Steering Committee, and so Doug and I were able to meet in person to speculate together about what the call might mean. Was it related to Tom's absence from the last video?

(Doug) A few minutes later I got a call from Canadian authorities saying that a body had been found and it was believed to be Tom's. I was numb. The worst had happened.

(Carol and Doug) After we called Tom's family and the team in Iraq, we gathered with those in the Toronto office for comfort and prayer. Through the months, we had kept those who had taken our friends hostage in a positive light and in prayer. Now we were taking a further step along this journey of enemy love. We remembered Tom's family and friends. Doug read aloud the Iraq team's Statement of Conviction that Tom had signed. We prayed the Lord's Prayer together. Then we gathered ourselves for the next frenetic round of team and media work. Needing to keep our composure for this work short-circuited our grieving. We shed some tears on our own; we shed tears at the subsequent memorial services and debriefings; we shed more tears working on this book. But there are more yet to shed in order to plumb the full depths of our loss.

At the time, the CPT Steering Committee was meeting down the hall from the Toronto office. They laced their meeting with prayer as this latest chapter of the story unfolded. U.S. authorities denied the CPT Iraq team the opportunity to positively identify the body. Instead, the authorities waited another seven hours before confirming from other sources that this was Tom. After the news was finally confirmed, the Steering Committee members phoned as many of the 190 CPT full-timers and reservists as they could to share the news personally and to offer their support and appreciation for the risks that we all take in entering this work.

CPT was determined to accompany our fallen comrade on his last journey home. The Iraq team had received promises from U.S. authorities that this would be facilitated. Despite several days of efforts by the CPT Iraq team, the Crisis Team, and Tom's support group, the authorities denied CPT the right to accompany his body. Instead we were limited to a send-off by CPTer Beth Pyles from the Anaconda military base in Iraq and a two-day vigil by CPTers Rich Meyer and Anne Montgomery outside the gates of Dover Air Base in Delaware, USA, until Tom's body arrived on March 13. Carol traveled to Dover to join Tom's immediate family and Rich Meyer for a viewing of the body and a brief memorial service before his cremation.

The Crisis Team continued its work for the release of the remaining three amid growing anxiety about their future. Yet we were heartened when two CPTers offered to join the Iraq team immediately, despite the increased danger. CPT directed its appeals to people and groups who might influence the captors, such as the captors' own families and associates. Iraqi contacts were sympathetic, but were also dealing with dozens of deaths every day in Iraq. Former hostages and negotiators whom

CPT contacted were increasingly pessimistic. March 18, marked the third anniversary of the start of the Iraq war. CPTers spoke at many rallies about the cost of this war and called for an end to the abuses and injustice feeding it.

The team in Baghdad continued to support the building of civil society in Iraq. On the day that news of Tom's body was released, they were preparing to host a gathering to introduce several Iraqi Sunni, Shia, and Palestinian human rights workers to each other. The team felt that Tom would have wanted this gathering to go ahead, and so it did. A week later a group of 88 Palestinian refugees fleeing Baghdad asked the team to accompany them to the Jordanian border. Tom had been part of a similar accompaniment in October 2005. Again the team felt that Tom would have wanted them to do this accompaniment, and so they did.

(Doug) Thursday, March 23, 3:30 a.m. EST. Jim Loney's partner Dan Hunt called me in the dead of night. "They are free!" he said. "I just talked to Jim. I don't know the details, but no one was hurt." My wife, Jane, had woken up a moment earlier thinking about Jim. I phoned Carol while Jane woke CPTer Scott Albrecht, who was asleep in the next room. This was the call for which we had waited and prayed for months. Finally. Good news. Thank God. But we had little time to absorb and savor it. After a brief hooray, we jumped in the car. Jane drove us through dark empty streets to the CPT Toronto office as I began to inform the rest of CPT, and Scott took media calls.

(Carol) The phone jolted me out of sleep—again. Heart pounding. What was it this time? Another hoax trying to get us to send ransom money? More news of death? Another reporter from a very different time zone wanting to know some detail—like, what high school one of the missing men attended? Another video? A CPT supporter intending to leave a message about an administrative matter? As I had done dozens of times in the past four months, I instantly rolled over, grabbed the phone, and turned on the light. Just in case it was—after all these months—"the call" from those who were holding our teammates, I took the tape recorder and guide questions in hand.

"They're free!" Now this was news worth waking for! I jumped. I danced, thereby waking my teammate downstairs. I hugged Duane, my husband. I squealed in delight. I called teammates. I dressed. Media calls started moments later. In the office that day my frenetic work of responding to the needs of the Iraq team, families, other CPTers, and the media was punctuated with outbursts in which I would whirl a volunteer or teammate into my dance of joy.

11

(Carol and Doug) At our offices, we first tried to find a centered place out of which to speak to media despite our very incomplete information. We were so thankful our three friends were free. We were thankful for all those who worked nonviolently and who prayed fervently for their release: religious leaders and soldiers, teammates and government officials, partner organizations, friends, family, children, women and men all over the world. We were troubled by the military nature of the rescue operation, yet grateful for its immediate fruits, and that no one was injured in it. At the same time, our gladness was made bittersweet by the fact that Tom was not alive to join the celebration.

The next hours and days were tumultuous. The Crisis Team encouraged the Iraq team in their frustrated efforts to support and accompany our colleagues home, and encouraged them as they consulted with their Iraqi partners about the future of CPT's Iraq work. CPTers worked with the men's support communities at home as they responded to media, planned homecomings, and prepared for Tom's memorial services. Together with trauma counselors, the Crisis Team made plans for extensive debriefings and healing work for Jim, Harmeet, Norman, the Iraq team, and all the others in CPT who were affected by this long crisis. All this was expected.

Somewhat unexpected was how quickly the media turned on CPT. Until then they had been surprisingly sympathetic to CPT, its goals, and its work. They had largely respected CPT's security concerns regarding the missing men's backgrounds (Tom's service in the U.S. Marine Corps band, Harmeet's former work for a New Zealand defense contractor, Jim's same-sex partnership with Dan), and CPT's protection of the Iraq team's identities and place of residence in Baghdad. The media had also mostly refrained from vilifying those who took the CPT Four while they were still in captivity. At the same time, they had repeatedly published unsubstantiated and wrong information as they sought to scoop each other on this big story. *Newsweek*, for example, insisted on printing that Tom's throat had been "savagely slit," despite CPT's several calls to them saying that Carol had seen the body and this was not true.

First was the accusation that CPT was not grateful enough to the military for their role in the rescue (for details, see the chapter by Simon Barrow and Tim Nafziger).

Then came the accusation that by initially using the term "release" CPT was denying that it was a "rescue." It is still unclear how our friends were freed, given that the captors fled 15 minutes prior to the troops arriving with another captor in tow. Was a deal done? U.S. and U.K. government spokespeople also used the term "release" in their initial statements, and we did not know then, nor do we know now, why the captors had fled. One U.S. talk-show host was so outraged at CPT's use of "release" that he urged his listeners to call the CPT Chicago office. They did so in such numbers that this harassment overwhelmed all the CPT Chicago phone lines for the next 48 hours. CPT was unable to receive calls at this office from anyone else.

Then there were the broadsides against CPT as a whole. For example, Toronto newspapers said that CPTers were "misguided, arrogant and foolish ...idiotic and churlish ...Christian zealots ...imprudent and foolish pacifists consumed with their own righteousness" (*Toronto Sun*); "Lenin and Stalin['s] ...useful idiots ...[with] aggressive idealism" (*Toronto Globe and Mail*); "pawns ...[who] put their loved ones through a nightmare" (*Toronto Star*); "callous or woefully naïve ...virulently anti-American ...zealot[s]" (*National Post*).

This turnaround in the media coverage surprised and embarrassed some in the media too. Tony Burman, the editor-in-chief of the Canadian Broadcasting Corporation, wrote, "I find these outbursts of media hostility toward the Christian Peacemakers somewhat perplexing. ...I suspect most Canadians have little patience for this. Most of us not only felt genuine relief and happiness about the rescue but, more profoundly, saw in these 'peacemakers' something that was quite admirable [and] courageous."

This whole story touched people at a very deep level, ourselves included. People are hungry for alternatives to the violence that has destroyed so much in Iraq. The media served to open a much-needed debate. They voiced the worldly wisdom that says only violence and armed force can bring peace and security. We had an opportunity from our direct experience of the world to speak of fundamentally different possibilities.

Many people, hearing about CPT for the first time, wrote to CPT about their concerns, questions, hopes. Many prayed who had not prayed before. Many wept at the news of Tom's death and then wept again at the news of the others' release. This kidnapping stimulated a vigorous public debate about the work of nonviolence. It provided an opportunity to lift up both the powerful writings and witness of Tom, Jim, Harmeet, and Norman, and the work of the CPT team in Iraq. An important public discussion was stimulated by this crisis, and it will continue long into the future.

Jesus said, "Very truly, I tell you, unless a grain of wheat falls into the earth and dies, it remains just a single grain; but if it dies, it bears much fruit" (John 12:24). Our delegation was kidnapped and Tom was killed. Yet this crisis has already produced much fruit. We have no idea of the full extent of this harvest.

Doug Pritchard was born in northern Ontario and trained as a chemical engineer. He is married to Jane, a family physician, and is the father of three sons. After thirteen years in the chemical industry, Doug took on the primary childcare role at home along with serving as Peace, Justice, and Social Concerns Coordinator for Mennonite Church Eastern Canada. In 1997 he was appointed as Canada coordinator for CPT and since 2004 has served as co-director of CPT. He lives in Toronto.

Rev. Carol Rose is the co-director of CPT, a poet, and a pastor. As part of the formation of the CPT Colombia project, she regularly served as a reservist until becoming co-director in 2004. Since that time she has also served on site in Iraq, Palestine, Arizona, and Kenora. An active peacemaker since the late 1970s, Carol has worked with Mennonite Voluntary Service, Brethren Voluntary Service and Mennonite Central Committee in projects around the world, including work in Central America, Thailand, and the Philippines. She pastored Mennonite Church of the Servant in Wichita, Kansas, from November 1997 through February 2004. Carol is married to Duane Ediger and lives in Chicago.

2

Continuing the Work in Iraq:
The Work of CPT and the Iraq Team

Peggy Gish

"We basically walk around looking for trouble," said my colleague, a member of CPT in Hebron, West Bank, with a straight face to the college campus audience after someone asked what CPT does in Hebron. I looked over at my colleague, watching for the grin that would indicate she was joking. "I'm serious," she added quickly, responding to the unspoken question in the room. "We live in the heart of the old city of Hebron, where about two hundred Israeli settlers live, surrounded by about 120,000 Palestinian residents and protected by about 1,200 Israeli soldiers. When we hear about or see trouble brewing, we go there to be a violence-preventing or violence-reducing presence.

"We say we are 'getting in the way.' When there is violence or injustice against a group of people, we try to block or challenge it. But this also refers to our attempt to follow 'the way' of Jesus, making ourselves vulnerable to evil as we confront it nonviolently using the power of love."

I recall the beginnings of CPT in 1986, during the Reagan administration, when missiles were called "Peacekeepers" and when the Iran-Contra scandal would soon be exposed. Two years earlier, Ron Sider, founder of Evangelicals for Social Action, challenged Christian pacifists to be willing to go into areas of conflict and violence with boldness and take the same risks in working for peace that soldiers take in making war. His challenge led to discussion in churches about doing more active peacemaking and culminated in a 1986 gathering of Mennonites and Brethren at Techny, Illinois, that established Christian Peacemaker Teams. Soon representatives of the Society of Friends (Quakers) joined this new organization, followed in years to come, by other church traditions.

Between 1990 and 1992, CPT sent delegations to Iraq (before the Gulf War), to Haiti, and to the West Bank. Out of those experiences, the organization decided to develop a corps of full-time and part-time trained volunteers to establish ongoing teams working to reduce violence in areas of conflict in countries around the world. In consultation and partnership with trusted local leaders and organizations, CPT began working in Haiti and inner-city Washington, D.C. As the need arose, they started teams in Chiapas, Mexico, First Nations communities in the United States and Canada, the West Bank, Colombia, Iraq, and the Arizona-Mexico border. At the time of this writing (December 2006), CPT has twenty-seven trained, full-time members and 159 reserve corps members, including a twelve-member support team working out of two principal offices in Chicago and Toronto.

Like all CPTers, my team experience started with a two-week delegation (in 1995 to the West Bank). Years later, after completing the month-long CPT training and working as a reservist in Hebron, I co-led the October 2002 delegation to Iraq. The deep love I felt for the Iraqi people compelled me to stay on and face with them the horror of the U.S. invasion in March 2003.

"One of the most important things we do is to listen," my colleague continued. "Listening is the first step toward lowering defenses and building trust. We try to understand all sides of the conflict. It often prompts us to report and document human rights abuses."

In Colombia, where guerillas, paramilitaries, and the Colombian army threaten farmers, CPT team members listen to and engage each of the armed groups in dialogue. In Haiti in the 1990s, listening meant documenting past and present human rights abuses suffered by rural Haitians, and telling the world their stories of insecurity, terror, and pain.

My colleague continued: "We also act as international observers. We say we have the 'grandmother effect.' There are things you wouldn't do with your grandmother watching you. Right? Well, there are things soldiers or people intending to harm others wouldn't do if international persons were watching. Often just standing and watching, without saying a word, prevents violence.

"We also do accompaniment work. Israeli settlers are often violent toward Palestinian shepherds when they take their sheep to graze on their own land. So CPTers live among these shepherds in the village of At-Tuwani, south of Hebron and go with them out on the hills. Since Palestinian children have often been beaten or terrorized by Israeli settlers, Hebron and At-Tuwani team members regularly accompany children to school."

I thought also of the team working in Burnt Church, New Brunswick, Canada, who during the fishing season went with the Esgenoopetitj First Nation people as they laid and checked their lobster traps. This became necessary because of violence against them by non-native local people and fishing authorities. With the Ojibway First Nation community in Grassy Narrows, Ontario, the work involved being present as the community blocked logging trucks employed by companies clear-cutting trees on Ojibway treaty land.

16

Besides accompanying and observing, we also take part in nonviolent actions that dramatize the truth about injustice or that confront and call on individuals or groups to change. Hebron team members will walk up to a soldier beating a Palestinian at a checkpoint, and tell him, "Stop that! Treat that person with respect!" In Colombia, the team holds prayer vigils on the tarmac beside helicopters used to dump poison on coca and food crops. Often one side of a conflict has little power, making effective negotiation unlikely. Nonviolent direct action can help to balance the power equation.

In situations of conflict, we try to remain neutral as we listen to and help people on both sides come together to work through their differences. In Hebron this means listening to the concerns of Israeli soldiers. On the other hand, we can't remain neutral when it comes to injustice, poverty, or violation of people. We often say that we "stand on the side of whoever the gun is pointed at." This means walking a fine line and having to continually discern how to be involved with local groups who feel unjustly treated.

"And we act out of a spiritual center," my colleague continued. "Our daily prayer and worship as a group and as individuals give us the strength to sustain our work and enable us to act out of calmness and love. Our tiny actions are 'watering the miracles' of peace and reconciliation that God wants to bring in particular situations."

My mind went back to the Arizona-Mexico border, where as part of a prayer service in May 2005, CPTers spray-painted white crosses on a wall to commemorate Mexican migrants who had died crossing the border.

As I contemplate my colleague's description of CPT's work, I think about our team's work in Iraq over the past four years.

We had no idea what lay ahead for the CPT delegation that left for Iraq in October 2002. This delegation joined with others from the Chicago-based Voices in the Wilderness to participate in the Iraq Peace Team (IPT). We were part of the larger worldwide movement calling for an alternative to war.

During those five months before the war started, we lived in Baghdad among the Iraqi people, listening to their experiences in this time of threat. We learned about and reported the violence and oppression they experienced under Saddam Hussein, but also under the U.S.-led UN economic sanctions. This took us to places such as hospitals, where we talked to mothers watching their children die of malnutrition, waterborne diseases, and cancers. Cancers among children had increased dramatically during the previous decade, largely due to depleted uranium dumped on Iraq in the 1991 Gulf War. Most Iraqis were unable to get basic healthcare because of the lack of medicine and up-to-date medical technology resulting from UN economic sanctions and the damaged infrastructure from the war.

17

The Iraq Peace Team held public vigils and carried out symbolic actions directed toward the international community. Banners reading "To bomb this site would be a war crime," were displayed at a water treatment plant, an electrical facility, a school, and a hospital. Across from the UN headquarters in Baghdad, where international weapons inspectors left each morning to do their work, our banner read, "Inspections, Yes, Invasion, No." During four days of prayer and fasting at the Iraq-Kuwait border in late February 2003, we prayed that the U.S. soldiers camped on the other side of the border would be able to return to their homes and families. We prayed that they would not suffer through a horrible war, doing things they would later regret.

When the war started, we spoke about what the common Iraqis were experiencing and about the destructiveness of war. Some of our group slept in tents at the Al Wathba water treatment plant, which serviced a nearby hospital complex. A part of that complex was a children's hospital where members of our team volunteered regularly, doing art projects with the children in the cancer ward. By sleeping in the tents, we kept a presence with families and organizations in that neighborhood and witnessed to the illegality, under international convention, of bombing civilian infrastructure.

We visited civilian sites that had been bombed. We went to hospitals full of wounded men, women, and children. The horrors of war became very real to us.

After the invasion of Baghdad and the fall of the Saddam regime, IPT disbanded, though some of its members stayed on to work in Iraq. CPTers in Iraq decided to continue as a CPT team in Iraq.

On a drive through a residential neighborhood in central Baghdad in late April 2003, members of our team stopped at a site and documented hundreds of pieces of unexploded ordnance, including mortars, rockets, cluster bomblets, mines, and missiles, piled up and unguarded. An American reporter for MSNBC did a piece about the site. He saw about twenty children a day maimed and dead in hospitals because of unexploded munitions. We went to a hospital and saw four-year-old Ali who had picked up a bright yellow cluster bomblet near his house, blinding him and causing brain damage.

Over the next month, our team documented unexploded weapons at over twenty-five sites and talked to Iraqi residents and U.S. military personnel about the problem. Team members took their report, which included a map and photos, to a U.S. sergeant. He told them military personnel had removed the ordinance that was stable enough to transport and that the ordinance left behind was unstable and could explode at any time.

Another staff sergeant, who came to see a particular site, told CPTers the unexploded ordnance units didn't have the resources to work faster. "Perhaps you could put tape and danger signs around it," CPTers told the sergeant. He answered, "It's up to the individuals to keep their children from walking around sites like these." CPTers pointed out, "The oil ministry buildings are extremely well-guarded. We're wondering why there aren't resources to clean up the weapons or at least to guard them until they can be cleaned up."

After this, team members called on people around the world to send brightly colored tape to U.S. and British legislators and embassy staff, asking them to see that they were sent to Iraq for protecting Iraqi civilians.

We often looked for opportunities to talk to and listen to the frustrations and fears of U.S. soldiers, whom we saw as victims of the war. Many believed they were bringing freedom and democracy to Iraqis, but others thought their presence did more harm than good. They were usually surprised to see us. "You mean you're going around Iraq without any weapons or armed guards?" some asked in amazement. I usually responded, "Without weapons, we are safer than you are. We can go into places that you can't and not be seen as a threat."

Throughout the coming month, our team spent time listening to the voices of Iraqi people in Baghdad, Fallujah, and Basra. We carried out a survey of opinions of seven hundred Iraqis regarding security, the availability of jobs, medical care, food, and education since the U.S. invasion. On June 18, 2003, team members and members of a delegation held a public vigil in central Baghdad with posters and fliers that described the conditions of life for Iraqis, based on the statistics from the survey. Our flier stated, "In the aftermath of a conflict that consumed thousands of lives and billions of dollars, with massive ongoing costs to the Iraqi people, all based on a fragile promise of freedom, WE ASK THE QUESTION, *this* is freedom?"

Our team met and began to collaborate with many Iraqi organizations and individuals working nonviolently to deal with the myriad problems of their devastated society. Women's groups advocating for safety and legal rights for women and organizations advocating for the unemployed were among the groups we accompanied as they protested peacefully in the streets.

In June and July of 2003, we made several visits to the city of Fallujah, where we listened to Iraqis and U.S. military talk about the violent clashes between them. A public school teacher told us about a nonviolent gathering of residents in May protesting U.S. military takeover of a school building. According to the teacher, someone in the crowd threw a stone at the U.S. soldiers. The soldiers overreacted and shot into the crowd, killing eighteen and wounding about seventy-five people. This led to other clashes.

In a series of contacts, our team met with Iraqi city officials and religious and tribal sheikhs, hearing their frustrations about the presence of U.S. military in their city. We also talked with the U.S. commanders working out of the municipal building. We encouraged both sides to meet and talk about these problems, and we attempted to bring them together.

The team tried to visit the U.S. detention center at the Baghdad airport to speak with soldiers and observe how Iraqi prisoners were treated, but we were denied access. While waiting, we met Iraqis searching for family members who had disappeared or been arrested by U.S. soldiers.

After that, word got around about our team, and Iraqis started coming to us asking for help finding their fathers, sons, or husbands. We started going with Iraqis to American offices, prisons, and military bases to help find family members. If they were in prison, we tried to learn what they were charged with. We began to collaborate closely with several Iraqi human rights organizations also working on detainee issues. A lieutenant colonial told our team that whereas the military was coordinating with the Red Cross for dealing with prisoners of war, no system existed for locating prisoners arrested after the invasion or for granting them a fair trial.

On October 27, 2003, the International Committee of the Red Cross (ICRC) headquarters in Baghdad was bombed. Most of its staff was evacuated. The few that remained in a nonpublic office were not able to offer adequate services to families of prisoners. That fall, the Coalition Provisional Authority established the Iraqi Assistance Center (IAC) in the Green Zone—a highly fortified area in central Baghdad that became the headquarters for the coalition offices, the new U.S. embassy, and the new Iraq government offices—where we could get information from a computer database about only a minority of the prisoners we were inquiring about.

The pain on the faces of two brothers was visible as they spoke of the death of their seventy-year-old father by suffocation while hooded during his arrest by U.S. soldiers. Many other families told us about violent, middle-of-the-night house raids, which sometimes started with soldiers shooting at their houses, followed by soldiers kicking or knocking men of the household to the floor to subdue them, then ransacking the home and destroying or taking personal property. Soldiers later told us that it was standard practice for them to go into homes and unleash forty seconds of "absolute fury."

As prisoners in the detention system were released, we heard stories of physical and mental abuse during their arrest, interrogation, and imprisonment. It was common for them to be held for months without charges or a hearing. Family members had no access to information about the detainees' whereabouts and well-being. Along with other international organizations, we estimated that at least 80 percent of security detainees had no involvement with acts of violence but were rounded up in neighborhood sweeps.

We were disturbed by what we found and decided to direct major energy to a Campaign for Justice for Iraqi Detainees, which would include writing a report on the treatment of prisoners in the U.S. detention system. In December 2003, the team completed the report on seventy-two prisoners in the U.S. detention system in Iraq, describing the violations of human rights of prisoners and their families and making suggestions for change. Whether these detainees were guilty or innocent, we believed they should be treated humanely and given a fair legal process for resolving their cases.

We sent our report to government officials in the United States. We also sent it to Lieutenant General Ricardo Sanchez, the top American military officer in Iraq, and to Paul Bremer, head of the Coalition Provisional Authority. In partnership with Iraqi human rights leaders and organizations, we took part in local actions that increased the Iraqi people's awareness of these problems.

Organizations and individuals around the world took part in our Adopt-a-Detainee Campaign, which included circulating stories of prisoners and their families, leading public actions in their communities, involving the media in educating people worldwide, and putting pressure on government officials in the United States and Iraq to change the system.

During our 2004 Lenten campaign, Break Every Yoke: Iraq Fast for Justice and Healing, the team prayed, fasted, and held poster-size pictures of Iraqi detainees in our public vigils in Baghdad, Kerbala, and two villages near Balad. Families of detainees often joined us, bringing with them pictures of their detained family members as we stood in busy Tahrir Square in central Baghdad, calling for a change. Together we advocated for fair trials, family visits, legal representations, release of those found innocent, establishment of a transparent and accountable judicial process for security detainees, and for investigation into the mistreatment of prisoners. CPT was among several international organizations whose investigations and reports made it difficult to keep the abuse of detainees hidden and led to worldwide exposure of the abuses.

Many of the estimated six thousand Iraqis passing by us each day stopped to express their appreciation for what we were doing or challenged us with "Where were you when Saddam was imprisoning and torturing us" or "They're all terrorists and should be in prison." Listening to their anger or pain often led to deeper dialogue.

One of the Iraqi organizations with which we worked closely was the Iraqi Human Rights Watch of Kerbala (IHRW-K). When we met members of this group in August 2003, they had already been defusing live hand grenades left from the war and been out on the streets of Kerbala

21

facilitating peace agreements between groups engaged in physical combat. In March 2004, they invited us to Kerbala to participate in a joint vigil for justice for detainees.

Over time, the members of IHRW-K expressed interest in being trained in the theory and practice of nonviolence. In January 2005, over thirty men and women of this mostly Shi'a Muslim group participated in a five-day training organized by our team. We used a hands-on teaching approach preparing Iraqi participants to facilitate the various learning activities. "We feel compelled to use our suffering for peacemaking instead of avenging wrongs done to us," several participants told us. At the end of the training, the group decided to call themselves the Muslim Peacemaker Team (MPT) and voiced their desire to train other groups and spread a network of nonviolent organizations around Iraq and the world.

When making decisions about their first projects as a new organization, MPT discussed the possibility of going together with CPT into the city of Fallujah, which had been attacked two months earlier by coalition forces. But this brought up many realistic fears and reservations. "We are Shi'a. They are Sunni. What if the people of Fallujah don't accept our coming?" one asked. "What if we are attacked or killed?" The group was open and sincere. After about a half-hour of discussion, one in the group said, "But this is what peacemaking is all about. Nonviolence asks us to deal with the divisions in our own society." And so it was decided. We just needed to figure out how and when to go.

On March 14, 2005, we met with city officials on the outskirts of Fallujah. They told our group of five CPTers, two MPTers, and four Iraqi human rights workers and friends that we had a one percent chance of being granted entry by soldiers guarding the many entry checkpoints around the city. At that time, international media and representatives of human rights organizations and the UN had not yet been allowed into Fallujah to see the damage caused by the November 2004 attacks. It may have been the medical equipment that one of the Iraqi human rights workers in our three-car convoy brought with her for the hospital in Fallujah that allowed them to make exceptions to their orders.

It was a sobering experience to drive and walk through that devastated city, seeing 60 percent of the buildings destroyed. In a large area of southern Fallujah, a mass of rubble, we saw large, extended families living in ten-by-fourteen-foot tents next to the ruins of their homes.

One family invited us in, and soon we were sitting around the floor of the tent, drinking tea and listening to their story. They were among the two hundred thousand refugees who left before the attack and lived for two months in a school building in a nearby village. Then in February, they were forced by the U.S. and Iraqi military to move back into Fallujah, even though they no longer had a house. We expressed our sorrow for the pain and destruction our military caused them. When we started to leave, the family thanked us profusely, and the women hugged and kissed the women in our group. We all had tears in our eyes. We had done nothing to change their situation, but had merely listened and cared. We would let others know about their pain.

Following this visit, CPT and MPT visited Fallujah six more times in 2005 for work projects and to build relationships between Shi'a and Sunni Muslims. Full-time CPTer Tom Fox took part in four of these visits. He participated in the May visit, when Shi'a Muslims from Kerbala and Najaf, Sunni Muslims from Fallujah, and American and Canadian Christians from CPT worked together to clean up rubble in a street in Fallujah. His last visit was in October 2005, when CPTers and MPTers went to support Fallujans in plans to commemorate the first anniversary of the 2004 attack.

In the year leading up to CPT's kidnapping crisis, violence increased in Iraq, and a number of foreign aid workers were kidnapped, prompting the team to reduce its size and visibility. Iraqi partners acknowledged the potential dangers of working with CPT, yet they encouraged CPT to remain and continue its work. The team's work priorities were (1) nurture Muslim Peacemaker Teams, (2) tell the truth and share stories not covered by western media, (3) network with and support Iraqi nonviolent movements, and (4) support people in the United States, Canada, and the United kingdom calling for an end to the occupation of Iraq.

Throughout the year, we had been hearing reports of torture and brutality at the hands of Iraqi special police forces, also called the brigades. In September 2005, we had ended our Adopt-a-Detainee Campaign. Now we shifted our "truth-telling" work to reporting abuses experienced by Iraqis within the new Iraqi detention system. UN human rights workers, who were unable to freely leave the Green Zone to investigate abuses, encouraged us and provided instructions for interviewing and writing testimonies of Iraqis who had survived torture while in the custody of Iraqi forces. Our team began fact-finding work regarding how the Iraqi detention system operated, with the intention of compiling the results into a report. We did this carefully, knowing the work might draw negative attention to the team. But we believed that continuing to tell the truth was an important part of our violence-reduction work.

While documenting testimonies of torture, we discovered that many of the Iraqi victims were of Palestinian origin; their families had been forced to leave the Palestinian territories in 1948 or 1967 when the Israeli military won major offensives. Their families emigrated to and settled in Iraq, though international agreements did not allow them to become full citizens of their new homelands, to be given passports, or to be allowed the freedom to travel or own property. Many of the twenty-three thousand

Palestinians in Iraq still live in crowded neighborhoods or ghettos—commonly called the Palestinian camps—in the cities of Baghdad and Mosul. Many Iraqis resent the Palestinians in their society because Saddam forced landlords to rent properties outside these camps to Palestinians at a subsidized rate, and it was believed he gave them other subsidies. During 2005, violence against the Palestinian Iraqis increased substantially.

One of the many testimonies the team took during the summer of 2005 was of a Palestinian family and their lawyer about a raid and the arrest of three adult sons by Iraqi security forces. The three were detained in the custody of Iraq's militia in the Ministry of Interior (MOI). According to their lawyer, they were tortured and then forced to confess to a terrorist act on a nightly television show, *Terror in the Grip of Justice*, directed by MOI General Adnan Thabit. Two-and-a-half weeks later, they were formally charged with a May car bombing in Baghdad. Before a judge, the brothers recanted their confessions, explaining that they had been tortured and forced to sign confessions. Due to visible marks of torture, the judge threw out their confessions and ordered a new investigation. Shortly before CPT left Iraq (April 2006), the team learned that the brothers continued to be held.

On October 1, Tom Fox accompanied two Palestinian brothers to a meeting with a UN human rights worker in the Green Zone to discuss the ongoing issues of night raids, arbitrary arrests, and torture-induced confessions that residents of the Palestinian camp had experienced in recent months. That same day, the brothers asked our team to accompany a group of Palestinians to the Syrian border.

Three days later, a busload of Palestinian refugees from Baghdad, accompanied by three members of CPT, a member of MPT in Najaf, and a team translator, departed for the Syrian border (for this story, see chapter by Sheila Provencher.)

Our team took other testimonies of Iraqis who had been tortured by Iraqi security forces. Much of the violence was connected to sectarian violence between Sunni and Shi'a. We learned from these torture victims as well as from Iraqis working in the Ministry of Interior that U.S. officials were aware of torture taking place in Iraqi prisons. In one instance, at a facility where men were being tortured, an American official, "Mr. Brown," accompanied by three U.S. soldiers, came to the holding cell and took photographs of each inmate. In another case, after Iraqi police tortured three prisoners at a prison in the Ministry of Interior, American personnel interrogated the men further.

In the midst of this work, our team hosted the second fall delegation to Iraq in November 2005. This one was small, with only three participants. Jim Loney, Norman Kember, and Harmeet Sooden.

This delegation arrived in Baghdad on November 22. In the next few days they visited the largest power plant in Baghdad, met with Muslim and Christian religious leaders, spoke with the director of a nongovernmental organization teaching youth conflict resolution and tolerance, and visited the Baghdad Radiotherapy Center, the only center of its kind in Iraq.

The delegation's plans crumbled and their traumatic ordeal began when they were kidnapped, along with Tom Fox, the full-time CPT Iraq team member who was accompanying them, on November 26. Suddenly our team was thrust into a tornado of emotions and activities. For many weeks, responding to this crisis became our central work (for this story, see chapter by Greg Rollins.)

As our Iraq team worked for the captives' release, we were also confronted by the continuing needs of the Iraqis around us. We agonized that our focus was so consumed by our own crisis, limiting our ability to respond to their needs. But as the team on the ground, we had a unique responsibility and sense of urgency to do all we could to open doors for the release of our kidnapped friends. As additional team members entered Iraq to join our team, we were able to continue our vigilance and work for our colleagues' release, yet free each other to return to the work we were doing before the crisis.

In mid-January 2006, an Iraqi human rights worker asked us to join her in accompanying a seventy-year-old man to an Iraqi military base prison. A week earlier, in the second of three raids on his village, U.S. and Iraqi forces had arrested two of his sons, his wife, and the eighteen-year-old new bride of the eldest arrested son.

When we got to the base, the guard refused to let us in, telling us there were no women prisoners. Pushed on this issue, the guard told us to come back the following morning to speak with a commander. The next morning we were taken to the commander's office, where he sat with five members of his staff. He described his anti-terrorism work in Baghdad and the surrounding area and then described the case against the family members. The eldest son was accused of murder, the younger of being a witness, and both of being members of the resistance. He said the women were being held for their protection.

We saw no signs of mistreatment on the women when they were brought into the room. They answered the commander's questions carefully, saying they had not been mistreated. We asked to speak with them alone but were not permitted. Then the two brothers were brought in and stood before the commander. Although the elder son was wearing a loose, hooded jacket that obscured parts of his body, we saw signs of torture on his face, hands, and feet. The commander questioned them, and they seemed compelled, in this setting, to deny any abuse. During this time, an

American officer, who identified his work as training Iraqi police, entered the room. He remained for a short time, observing the proceedings, and then left. The commander promised to release the women in two days. When he started to use our presence to further intimidate and shame the sons, we ended the meeting and left. Three days later, only the women were released.

In early February 2006, one of the leaders of the MPT in Najaf brought to the team's attention the case of a man from Kerbala whose brother had been imprisoned for eighteen months in a British prison on the edge of Basra. He and two of his friends were arrested in July 2004 while visiting Basra. When they were first arrested, they were asked if they were members of Muktada al-Sadr's Mehdi army, which they denied. They were detained as "imperative risks to security" and never learned of charges of wrongdoing. Under Multi-National Force-Iraq regulations, people held under this classification are not entitled to know what evidence or security information the arresting body has against them.

Two weeks later, two CPTers and a human rights worker from MPT in Kerbala accompanied the brother to the Shaiba Temporary Logistical Facility. After some persistence, we were able to talk with a British Command Legal who was on the Divisional Internment Review Committee for the prison, the committee that makes recommendations to the Joint Detention Committee about the release of prisoners incarcerated for more than eighteen months. The committee was jointly chaired by the Iraqi prime minister and the U.S. commander of the Multi-National Force-Iraq.

We outlined several concerns about the prisoner's situation:
- There were no specific written charges.
- The prisoner seemed at serious risk of dying in prison because of his mental state, which began to deteriorate while imprisoned.
- The prisoner's lawyer had been able to visit his client only at the times set for family visits and could advocate for his client only through written submissions, which he believed were never taken seriously. His seventy-five attempts to arrange a face-to-face meeting with British officials were unsuccessful.

The legal adviser explained the laws in effect in the prisoner's case and outlined next steps in the process. He listened to these issues and expressed concern that the prisoner had been detained so long. He promised to pass these concerns on to the committee making the decision about release or continued imprisonment. He thought a decision would come soon. He promised to provide the lawyer appropriate access to his client but said that regulations deny lawyers personal access to the committees determining the fate of the prisoner.

Two weeks later, we made a follow-up call to the British military legal adviser in Basra. The representative from his office told us that the only means to information about the status of the prisoner's case would be a letter requesting it, written by the prisoner and his lawyer. We contacted the brother. We found that he had not heard of any decision about the prisoner's fate. Two months later, before leaving Iraq, we checked again. We learned that the prisoner had still not been released.

Throughout the time of the CPT hostage crisis, we maintained contact with the leaders of the Palestinian camps in Baghdad. The violence and attacks on Palestinian men continued to increase and came in the form of house raids and detentions, pressure to admit to crimes while under torture, and brutal killings. We recorded their testimonies and accompanied family members to offices in the Iraqi prison system to seek information about men who had been detained or had disappeared. In a week's time, Palestinian leaders reported that of three men who had been kidnapped, one was found dead in a sewer in Najaf, one was still missing, and the other had been released, only to be shot and killed the next day. Another man was forced out of the camp one night and found hanged the next morning.

"It costs a lot to leave, but the risks of staying are greater, so I am willing to give up my house and job to try to allow my children to have a future," said one of the leaders when he came to ask our team to accompany two busloads of Palestinian families, this time to the Jordanian border to try to gain entry as refugees.

On March 19, 2006, two team members left Baghdad with a group of eighty-eight refugees that included thirty-six children. They arrived at the border that evening. With the help of the Iraqi and Jordanian offices of the United Nations High Commission for Refugees (UNHCR), they were allowed to leave the Iraqi side. Jordanian border officials, however, stopped the Palestinian convoy and refused to let it drive toward the Jordanian border. The buses drove back to the area just outside the gates into the Iraqi side, where the families unloaded the buses and set up camp.

Just as they were setting up the one large tent they had brought along, a dust storm blew in. That night they accepted the offer of border guards to stay in the buildings of the guard posts. The next day the Iraqi Red Crescent Society brought four tents and other supplies for the sixteen families. Within days the UNHCR in Amman authorized the shipment of material goods, and the Iraqi border officials allowed them all to stay in two buildings in a small compound.

After we left the border, we contacted international media, which began to report the plight of the Palestinians in Iraq. International refugee agencies began working on resettlement plans. Within the next two weeks, two more groups of Palestinians left Baghdad and were allowed to join the group we had accompanied. There were then 129 refugees in the small encampment. For seven weeks they had a meager existence on the border until they were accepted into the refugee camp in Syria, where the earlier group of Palestinians from Baghdad had been settled in November.

During this period, we returned to our work of collecting torture testimonies. When we began this work six months earlier, it had been the team's intention to write its own report. Because of the kidnapping of our teammates, we were not able to proceed with the number of interviews we had planned. We gave the completed interviews to the United Nations so they could use them to call for further investigation by international organizations.

"Telling the truth" also meant reporting about the lack of water and the slowness of progress and inadequacies of reconstruction efforts in rebuilding the sewage system and water treatment plants in Sadr City, where the U.S. government had agreed during the previous summer to build twenty small water treatment plants.

According to officials in the Sadr City governor's office, only one has been built, providing less than two thousand liters per day. Leaders told our team about large neighborhoods of Baghdad where no water was available and where the water being trucked in daily was inadequate. Where water *was* available, it was polluted, causing an epidemic of water-borne diseases. The director of a major hospital in Sadr City told us that 60 percent of the population of that neighborhood of about three million people has hepatitis A or E.

In Najaf we visited the only major hospital that provides medical care for the mid-Euphrates region. It was still undergoing reconstruction and had very little medical equipment and supplies. Medical staff worked without MRI or CAT scan machines or rehabilitation equipment, and the one X-ray machine was working poorly.

In the morning of February 22, 2006, an Iraqi friend was at the CPT apartment, interviewing team members for her weekly radio program. A sheik from Sadr City called the team to cancel a meeting that afternoon because of the bombing and total destruction that morning of the Al Askari Shrine, one of the Shi'a Muslims' holiest sites. The bombing set off a wave of violence against Sunni religious sites and leaders, as well as gun battles on the streets of Sadr City and all around Iraq. Police began to close streets and bridges. Our visitors left quickly so they could get home before it became too difficult or dangerous. Prime Minister Jaffery called for three days of mourning for the shrine bombing and imposed a curfew.

The next day Iraqi news services reported 165 Sunni mosques attacked, ten Sunni imams killed and fifteen abducted, eighty bodies found in Baghdad, and forty-seven pulled off a bus in Baqubah. But there were also reports of Shi'a and Sunni marching together through Baghdad neighborhoods, calling for the violence to stop, and Shi'a citizens guarding

Sunni mosques during times of prayers. Shi'a friends told the team that the attack on the Al Askari Shrine was, for them, comparable to 9/11 for the United States. Grand Ayatollah Sistani designated the day of the bombing as Black Wednesday. He and Muktada al-Sadr and other Shi'a clerics urged the Shi'a not to retaliate against Sunni Muslims but to work for peaceful relations.

As the days went on, the three-day curfew order was extended to five. There were many public displays of sectarian unity, but the shrine's destruction also turned the violence between Shi'a and Sunni into an escalating spiral of retaliation.

When the travel restrictions between Iraqi cities lessened, members of MPT-Najaf and MPT-Kerbala, along with a leader of a Sunni human rights organization met with us at the CPT apartment in Baghdad. The question we discussed was how to respond to the increase in sectarian violence. We decided to develop an umbrella organization to build bridges between religious and ethnic groups. Those present would invite individuals and organizations from Shi'a, Sunni, Christian, Kurd, and other groups to join a network to work together for unity. Activities would include building bridges between groups in places of tension, training teachers in nonviolence techniques and human rights, offering workshops for youth and adults, and working together on issues such as prison monitoring and creating centers for women and youth.

This project was barely launched when the curfews and travel bans between cities made it increasingly hard for those involved to travel, meet together, and carry out joint projects. With the increase of violence and security measures, participating groups faced mounting difficulties even in continuing work in their local communities. They had not been able to make much progress with networking beyond. The very problem they had set out to deal with was making it difficult for them to do so.

In the midst of these activities, Tom Fox's body was found in western Baghdad. Not only did our team carry each other in our grief, but our Iraqi friends also surrounded us with their love. Neighbors came to our apartment and stopped us on the street, speaking of their memories of Tom.

Especially touching were the comments of two close Iraqi friends of the team. One, a Christian leader, told us, "When they bombed my church, it didn't weaken us, it made us strong. When we lost our friend Tom, the suffering is hard, but it gave us courage." The other, a member of the MPT, told us, "I told my Muslim friends that Tom would go to God, because he was working for peace. Some of them said, 'But he's a Christian.' I answered, 'But he gave his life for us.'"

With Tom's death and then the release of Jim Loney, Norman Kember, and Harmeet Sooden two weeks later, our team's focus and energy were drawn toward dealing with these highly emotional events and taking care of many practical concerns.

The plan had been for members of the team who had been in Iraq throughout the crisis to leave Iraq and for other team members to rotate in so there would be a continual presence while the debriefing and evaluations took place. But this did not work out when three persons ready to rotate onto the team in Baghdad in March and April were not granted visas.

Before leaving in mid-April, we tried to complete as many of the tasks or projects we had started as we could. One task was consulting the team's Iraqi partners. These were people and representatives of organizations we had worked with who understood the work and goals of the team. We asked them for their current assessment of CPT's work in Iraq, we asked about the additional danger or problems to Iraqis working with us, and we asked for advice for the future of CPT in Iraq.

"We believe you are very useful here, but you must leave Baghdad at least for a time," one said, voicing the concern of most of those consulted. "We don't want another of you to die." Some suggested we leave Baghdad until the situation stabilized and work could continue, and relocate now to another area of the country where our presence would not greatly increase the danger of Iraqis working with us.

We took this advice seriously. In the wider team discussions in the United States, the team wrestled with admonitions from friends to be more cautious and not risk another tragedy. But we also reaffirmed our commitment to following Jesus' way of nonviolent suffering love, which meant taking risks, and to "devote the same discipline and self-sacrifice to nonviolent peacemaking that armies devote to war," as stated in CPT's Statement of Conviction. We looked at the situation in Iraq and felt called to continue our peacemaking presence there.

During the summer of 2006, a small team returned to Iraq, but made its base in the northern part of the country. We explored possibilities for work in this region, as well as for reaching out to other areas of the country. After broad consultation, our team concluded that there was work to do there. It would include accompanying individuals and working with local peace and human rights movements, assisting MPT in training and nonviolence networking, and reporting what Iraqis from around the country are experiencing as the violence escalates.

It has been a difficult year for the team and for all the members and friends of CPT. While we regretted that during the crisis we were less able to respond to the overwhelming needs of the Iraqi people, the team was able to return to some of its work and did not lose its deep connection with Iraqis and their struggles.

As we look ahead, we feel a keen responsibility to be wisely careful, yet to not let fear and suspicion dominate us or keep us from taking bold initiatives. We walk forward into our future work with hope that comes from knowing that God can enter seemingly impossible situations and transform them. We are continually encouraged by strong and creative Iraqis who continue to risk their lives for their people and who continue to keep alive a vision of peaceful alternatives to the escalating violence that rips their society apart.

Peggy Gish is a mother, grandmother, farmer, community mediator, and long-time peace activist from southern Ohio. Since 1995 she has been involved with Christian Peacemaker Teams in the West Bank and Iraq. She first went to Iraq in October 2002 and has continued as a full-time member of the Iraq team. She is the author of *Iraq: A Journey of Hope and Peace* (Herald Press, 2004).

3

The Response from Baghdad

Greg Rollins

*Names in this chapter marked with * have been changed.*

Maxine Nash and I were teasing each other when the call came. I picked up the phone and our translator *Abed said, "Greg, I have some bad news, man. The delegation has been kidnapped."

Knowing Abed liked to joke around, I said, "Very funny, Abed. When are you guys coming home?"

"No, I'm serious, man, the guys have been kidnapped." His tone of voice was calm and somber, almost frightened, yet I still thought he was joking.

"No, seriously, when are you guys coming home?"

"I am serious, Greg, the guys have been kidnapped."

Dread spread through my body, leaving me numb. I told Maxine that the guys had been kidnapped then grabbed a pen and paper and asked Abed to explain what had happened.

Abed said that the six of them—our four colleagues, himself, and the driver *Ali—had just left the office of the Association of Muslim Scholars (AMS)[2] in western Baghdad when they were stopped by two cars; one pulled in front and one behind. Three men with handguns got out of the forward car. One asked Abed why he was in the van. Knowing that kidnappers almost always kill foreigners' translators, he said he was working with the driver. The gunmen told Abed and Ali to get out of the van and took their cell phones. Two of the gunmen climbed into the van and drove away with the four hostages (the third returned to the forward car). Abed and the driver watched them go. Abed and Ali then walked back to the AMS to call us. Abed told me he had also given the AMS a statement of what had happened.

---

[2] In April 2003 the AMS was formed by Sunni clerics with Dr. Harith al-Dhari, a noted religious scholar, as its leader. Among other endeavors, the organization expresses the goals and political aspirations of Iraq's Sunni population. They are staunchly nationalist and anti-occupation.

It was four-thirty in the afternoon; Abed said that the guys were kidnapped only fifteen minutes earlier. I told Abed to come to the apartment so he could tell us in greater detail about the kidnapping. He said he would see us soon.

Although we were worried and knew how serious the abduction of our colleagues was, our reaction to the kidnapping was not one of panic or fear, but of practicality. When the phone call ended, Maxine informed Anita David and our landlord while I called Doug Pritchard in Toronto. I told him what Abed had told us but asked him not to inform anyone about what had happened until we had spoken to Abed more thoroughly.

We said a quick prayer, and went to work. First, we made a brief list of people we should call: Iraqi friends and acquaintances who might give us advice or know the identity of the kidnappers. As grace would have it, *Mr. Sa'ad, a friend of the team and an Iraqi human rights worker, dropped by for a visit just a few minutes later. We told him what had happened and he offered to do whatever he could to help.

For the rest of the evening, we phoned people on our list. Several were from the AMS. Because they are an anti-occupation group with ties to insurgents, we initially wondered if they had played a part in the abduction or if they had contact with the kidnappers. We soon dismissed this idea, knowing they had nothing to do with the kidnapping.[3] At the time, however, our calls to them left us frustrated. We assumed everyone at the AMS would know about the kidnapping, yet several of the members were shocked. They had no idea it had happened.

There were other people to call in Baghdad as well as in the city of Fallujah, another place well known for its ties to insurgents. CPT has a number of friends in Fallujah, but they were likewise unable to help. One of them, an imam who was a friend of Tom, would have loved to help but couldn't. Militants had assassinated one of his elder imams just that day.

After two long hours, Abed finally arrived at our apartment. He provided a detailed account of what had happened, saying he felt guilty for telling the gunmen he was with the driver. Perhaps if the kidnappers had known he was the translator, they would have taken him with the other hostages. But our landlord and Mr. Sa'ad assured Abed he had done the right thing. If he hadn't lied, the gunmen would have killed him on the spot.

With a more detailed account of what had happened, we called Doug. We then called a friend at the United Nations, hoping he might know Iraqis we could contact. Our friend advised us to call the British, Canadian, and U.S. embassies and even offered to call for us if we sent him the information. We sent it to him but asked that he not send it on for

---

[3] During the course of the CPTers' captivity, the AMS issued two very supportive statements on our behalf.

several hours. We wanted to allow space for private negotiations to take place before governments—and eventually the press—became involved.

We were playing for time. Because we wanted to make direct contact with the people holding our colleagues and to enter into dialogue with them if possible, we called Iraqi friends. We wanted to allow enough time to hear back from these Iraqi friends before approaching officials. If our friends could make contact with the kidnappers and privately negotiate for release, the outcome could be positive.

But that did not happen. The team was thus faced with a difficult dilemma, our options reduced to two: either contact the embassies or contact the Iraqi police. We were averse to both options because the involvement of governments and/or police meant the use of force, which we wanted to avoid. Moreover we feared that if the kidnappers believed we contacted officials they might harm our friends. We didn't know which of the many sides in the conflict had kidnapped our colleagues or what their reaction might be if governments became involved.

The first day of the kidnapping finally came to an end. It had been only a few hours—no more than ten—but felt like a week. We asked Abed to spend the night with us in case the kidnappers called and we needed an Arabic speaker. He stayed with us for the next five days. (We expected a call because Tom, at the time of the kidnapping, had a CPT cell phone, CPT business cards in Arabic and English, and an introductory sheet to CPT, also in Arabic and English.)

During the following two weeks, the team was overwhelmed with activity. In the first couple of days I came down with the flu, Anita had daily tension headaches, and Maxine didn't sleep. We neglected the simple things in life like house-cleaning and cooking—some days we barely had time to eat; we worked late each night and woke up early every morning; we took phone calls from the family members of our kidnapped colleagues; we held team meetings every couple of hours to make decisions—every decision needing to be made in thirty seconds while new problems arose every fifteen; we conducted numerous press interviews each day; we received constant advice from numerous people; we spoke with Doug or another staff member in the Toronto office every few hours; we wrote dozens of statements for the press or aimed at the kidnappers in case they followed our website; and every day we brainstormed people who could make statements of support on our behalf.

During this time we worked as best we could with the media in Iraq. Part of our strategy was to air as many different statements as we could. We hoped the kidnappers would see or hear these statements and understand the work we were doing. This, however, was not as easy as it sounded.[4] Often we had to run around the city looking for a news station to televise our statements. This could take hours, and in some cases, after doing the hard work of locating a station, we learned the media never aired the footage.

At the end of each day the three of us were exhausted. We would sit and talk about our difficulties. Sometimes this talk would turn to laughter as we made fun of the kidnappers or ourselves and what we had done that day. It helped us relax. We also wondered where our four friends were and how they were doing. We talked about how much we longed to see them and what we would say to them if they walked through the door at that very moment. Usually we agreed we would say nothing; we would just hug them.

In all this chaos, I never got used to sleeping in an empty room. As Tom's roommate I missed the comfort of his presence. The day Tom was kidnapped he left his computer plugged in. The light on his computer faded in and out with its own rhythm. It made me think of Tom's heart. Each night I would lie in bed and watch the room as it briefly lit up, then returned to darkness. Some nights it was too surreal to watch. Once, while Maxine and I sat and talked in my room, she commented that the light also reminded her of Tom's heartbeat. I asked her if we should unplug the computer, which was not being used. Neither of us had the courage.

The outpouring of the Muslim community throughout this time was an amazing gift. They took risks in speaking across sectarian and political lines for Christians, two of whom were citizens of the powers occupying Iraq. Their call for the release of our teammates was a great act of friendship. In the Middle East, groups like Al-Quds International Foundation, the Mufti Muhammad Saleem Jalaledde, and Hamas and Fatah in Palestine called for the release of our colleagues—as did the Middle East Council of Churches. In Europe, groups like the Muslim Council of Britain made similar statements.

Other people around us stepped up in different ways, as was Iraqi custom. On two separate occasions a young man told Anita, then Peggy (who arrived in Baghdad later) that when a kidnapping happens in Iraq,

---

[4] Our attempts to get media coverage over the next several weeks led to a spokesman for a Sunni organization writing a statement for TV that never aired, the taping by a news crew of an initial plea from the team to the kidnappers that ended up lost (it reappeared a few days later and about ten seconds of the plea were eventually aired), the issuing of a statement on our behalf by a friend from a Shi'a organization that was taped at the TV station and aired the same night, an attempt at taping a second plea to kidnappers by the team that proved so difficult to arrange we opted for print, and finally a successful press conference by the team after the release of Jim, Harmeet, and Norman.

neighbors of the family even contribute to the ransom. Our landlord, his wife, and his family were our greatest supporters, often cooking dinner for us where we were too busy to do so ourselves.

On November 30 at midnight, we received a call from a reporter saying a video of the guys had aired on TV. In it the kidnappers called themselves the Swords of Righteousness Brigade and claimed the hostages were spies. Maxine and I watched the footage on our landlord's TV. The video worried us. Still we were glad to see our friends alive and in good condition.

One of the most difficult parts of the kidnapping was the delay in learning new information. Though our team was on the front lines of the situation we were usually the last to hear. Each time the kidnappers released a video we found out about it when a journalist called to ask our opinion. Getting information in this manner was frustrating. It made us feel helpless and foolish in the face of the press. Yet there was nothing we could do about it. We couldn't appoint someone to sit in front of the TV day and night waiting to see if the kidnappers released a video. None of us had the energy or time to do that. Even if we had, there wasn't enough electricity, since we received only five hours each day. We couldn't pick and choose how information came to us, especially in Iraq where gathering information is nebulous at best.

Immediately after the airing of the first video, Mr. Sa'ad called to say he had information. The next day he came to our apartment. Someone claiming to bring news from the kidnappers had approached one of his friends. This "link" told Mr. Sa'ad's friend to tell us our colleagues were fine, but that the kidnappers wanted proof our friends and CPT were not spies. We had suspicions about whether the link was real. It is not uncommon in Iraq for people to exploit situations like ours for money or self-interest. We asked Mr. Sa'ad if there was a mention of money. According to Mr. Sa'ad, the link wanted one thousand U.S. dollars for his efforts but the kidnappers had not asked for money. Mr. Sa'ad informed the link that any talk of money would come after the release of our friends. The link agreed. This gave us hope in the midst of an overwhelming situation, one we had never encountered before.

Without a second thought, we produced a CD including photos of our four friends at demonstrations or doing violence-reduction work. We included writings and photos by Tom and Jim about things they had seen in Iraq and other troubled places like Palestine. We also included materials about Jim's advocacy on behalf of Canadian Muslim prisoners. We didn't know if the kidnappers read English but we took a chance that the kidnappers could find a translator. Mr. Sa'ad took the CD and gave it to the link.

On December 3, a second tape aired. This one demanded that all prisoners in Iraq be released within the next forty-eight hours or the kidnappers would kill our friends. We were worried; however, some time later Mr. Sa'ad called with a word from the link. The link explained that the message was intended to distract the governments. Our friends would not be executed. This calmed us, but we still had serious doubts about the reliability of the link. The link also said that the kidnappers thought Jim, Norman, and Tom were not spies, but weren't sure about Harmeet. Thus, we spent all night making a second CD to highlight Harmeet's activism and work for oppressed people, especially in Palestine with the International Solidarity Movement. When the deadline came forty-eight hours later, we sensed our friends were okay.

Over the next few weeks Mr. Sa'ad continued to call or visit and pass on messages from the link. Sometimes the messages were vague; for example, "You will get good news soon." Other times the message stated that the kidnappers would release the guys within a few days. But after a few days our friends were still in captivity. After several weeks of this we grew increasingly frustrated. Our suspicions about the link grew stronger with every broken promise. Whenever we asked for proof that these people actually had our colleagues, our requests went unanswered.

While we communicated with the link, we also wrote letters in Arabic that we posted on our website. For me writing these letters was surreal. Our Iraqi friends had advised us to address the kidnappers as "Our Brothers holding our colleagues." Our friends told us that this was the way it is done in Iraq. It is respectful, indicating a connection among the people. As I wrote these words I found myself amazed. I was writing to kidnappers, calling them my brothers. Never in my life had I imagined such a thing.

It was also interesting to hear statements made in the videos released by the kidnappers. In one video aired on TV, Tom and Norman talked about the need to end the occupation of Iraq. While many believed the words were forced on them, we thought otherwise. We felt our friends were speaking from their convictions.

By the end of the first two weeks the pace of our lives changed and we found ourselves waiting. The statements of support kept coming, but we saw fewer of them. The videos from the kidnappers were also few and far between (the December 3 video was not followed by another until January 28). We grew tired of waiting. For the first time since the kidnapping we had time to think about ourselves. We realized that if we did not look after ourselves we would burn out. So we did what we could to keep ourselves sane.

At the end of each day I began to read and to watch the sun set from our rooftop. Maxine listened to music and went to sleep early. Anita played games on the computer all night. Some mornings we gave ourselves time to sleep in. Some afternoons we took time to nap. We created routines again, such as a cooking schedule and daily worship, which included lighting four candles each morning.

With these routines in place, life felt slightly more normal. We were a bit more centered. Anita and I took time to write thank-you e-mails to the many organizations who had spoken on our behalf. As we made our way through the list of names we were overcome by the participation of groups like the al Aqsa Martyrs Brigade and al-Qaida speaking on behalf of Christians. Anita took a look at me, smiled, and said, "We might not be able to enter the U.S. again." I replied, "That's okay, I live in Canada."

On December 2, we had received a call from *Paul, a friend of CPT working in Iraq. He had a trusted Iraqi friend with a track record of locating and negotiating the release of hostages. Paul's friend also knew Tom and was anxious to help. Because he no longer lived in Iraq, he recommended that CPT hire an experienced team of Iraqi private investigators who would search for the kidnappers and find out what they were after. According to Paul, the investigators would go to various contacts in an attempt to learn where the kidnappers were holding our friends. Once they had learned this they would approach the head sheikh or leader of the area and ask them to mediate a release.

Paul asked if we wanted to hire the investigators. We were unsure of what to do. There were many considerations in hiring them. Could we trust them? What if the investigators found the kidnappers and the kidnappers wanted a ransom? CPT has a policy never to pay ransoms. Other considerations included the team's Statement of Conviction that said we would try to enter into dialogue with the kidnappers, try to learn their motives, and articulate them to others.

In the end we delayed in answering Paul for several days. With the approach of the second deadline, Paul became increasingly worried about the safety of our friends. His Iraqi friend advised him that it was critical to contact the kidnappers soon. Paul was unaware of any other attempts to contact the kidnappers, so he decided to hire the investigators himself.

As the kidnapping dragged on Maxine, Anita, and I realized that we could not do the work in Iraq alone. We would need more CPTers to enter the country to help work for the freedom of our colleagues. Peggy Gish was the first additional team member to enter Iraq in mid-December. With her, Peggy brought new energy. Our work became a bit lighter, though it was still difficult. We were tense and tired. Tempers sometimes flared, and relationships between teammates became strained. Major fights or battles between us never ensued but we did need to talk to each other and adjust our ways of working.

Meanwhile, the link had informed Mr. Sa'ad that our translator Abed was in on the kidnapping. This was a shock to us. We were not sure what to believe. We had known Abed for years and trusted him completely, but at the same time were learning what Iraqis had known for years: people aren't always what they appear and loyalties can shift during difficult times. We decided to confront Abed. He denied being part of the kidnapping and without further need to think about it, we knew he was telling the truth.

December came to a close. Christmas was quiet. We exchanged a few gifts and thought about the guys. A few days before Christmas, Maxine bought the team a tree. It ended up serving two purposes: first as an actual Christmas tree and second as a way to tell when the electricity was on. In Iraq there are constant power outages due to neglected infrastructure. When the lights on the tree began to blink off and on, we knew power had returned. It was reassuring when this happened, especially at night when we often worked by candlelight.

During this time we kept in contact with Paul about what his investigators were up to. After a couple of false leads the investigators believed they had located our friends in a house in the west of Baghdad and established indirect contact with the kidnappers through a local sheikh. They said that the kidnappers had been intending to kill the Canadians but decided against this because of what they heard about CPT's work. They said the kidnappers had agreed to provide letters from our friends to give to their families for Christmas (which would constitute a proof of life). Paul was hopeful but the day after Christmas the investigators said that they had lost contact with the kidnappers. The kidnappers were said to have relocated our friends after receiving a warning that the Iraqi interior ministry knew of the house and planned on raiding it.

By this time the work around freeing our friends changed from looking for statements of support and soliciting media coverage to preparing ourselves for if and when the guys were released. We also made plans for the future of the team in Iraq after the kidnapping crisis was over. We were not sure if the team should stay or leave. We drafted a list of Iraqis we could contact for advice and evaluated the reasons to stay or go.

As the New Year entered Iraq so did more team members. Beth Pyles and Michele Naar-Obed came first. A few weeks later Allan Slater arrived. We still had no idea how long the kidnapping would carry on. It could end at any minute or drag on for a year. If the latter turned out to be the case, we would need many people to become familiar with the ins and outs of the kidnapping. We also wanted to return to other CPT work.

It was hard to go back to work. As the violence in Baghdad grew worse many of our translators and drivers did not want to leave their homes, much less go out in public with foreigners. Others didn't mind leaving their homes but were not comfortable being seen with CPTers because we had become too well known in Iraq.

As January continued, Maxine, Anita and I found ourselves facing a new struggle: when should we leave? The three of us had been in Baghdad since the kidnapping began—Maxine had actually been in Iraq since August, while Anita and I had only been in country since the end of October. None of us wanted to leave. In a war zone a bond develops with those you live and work with. The idea of leaving while kidnappers still held our friends felt like a breaking of that bond. Our decisions about staying or leaving varied from day to day. Sometimes all three of us were staying indefinitely. Other times we were leaving when the proper time arrived. In the end I was the only one who decided to leave. The team was large enough at that point and if I had stayed it would have been for reasons of self-interest and the hope that the guys would be released while I was there. As a team we recognized that if the kidnapping went on for several more months, CPT would need me to return rested and re-energized as soon as possible. For the sake of continuity we felt that at least one of the team members present at the time of the kidnapping should be on team at all times.

When the day came for me to leave, I had no idea if or when I would return to Iraq or what the fate of our friends would be. It was hard for me to say goodbye to my teammates, our translators, and our drivers who all came to see me off. As I climbed in the taxi that took me to the airport, one of our drivers stood on the steps of our building and cried.

The team tried to get back to its work. Meanwhile, Paul's investigators said they were pursuing new leads to identify where our friends had been moved. In the second week of January they said they had found a person in the underworld who claimed to be a middleman. He was someone who had provided them with accurate information in the past and said that the kidnappers wanted one million dollars for each of our friends; otherwise they would kill them. He even told the investigators the location where he said our friends were being held, explaining that the gang holding them controlled that area with hundreds of fighters and had no fear of the Iraqi security forces. The investigators asked for proof of life and the middleman said he could get them photos and letters in return for fifty thousand dollars (which they suspected was a fee for him, not for the kidnappers).

This demand made us skeptical. It is unusual for someone to ask for money in return for proof of life. Given a choice between this lead and Mr. Sa'ad's link, we preferred to pay closer attention to Mr. Sa'ad's link. Neither group had provided us with proof of life, but Mr. Sa'ad's connections were easier to listen to. They didn't threaten to kill our friends.

When I left Iraq and went to Jordan in mid-January, Paul and I met with one of the investigators who happened to be there. The investigator said he had met a masked man in Baghdad who claimed to be the leader of the kidnappers. He made a phone call in the investigator's presence telling someone to "not kill the American." He repeated his story that the group who claimed to hold the guys wanted a ransom—one million dollars for each person. If we didn't pay it they would kill our friends. He did not think the kidnappers would wait much longer. When I asked the investigator what he thought about this demand, he was perplexed. He said that one should never give a ransom without first receiving proof of life. Yet in this case he believed none was needed. He had dealt with these people before. He believed they held our friends.

I left the meeting confused. Part of me was worried, but part of me could not believe these people were telling the truth. I relayed the information from the meeting back to the team. They decided that without proof of life they wouldn't deal with the alleged kidnappers. If they actually held our colleagues they would give us proof of life without issuing a demand for payment.

Paul was also unsure. He could not afford to pay the money demanded by the middleman, and he was skeptical about the validity of the middleman's claim. Moreover, now that someone from the team had met with the investigator directly, Paul felt he should completely step back and let CPT decide how to proceed. In the meantime he asked the investigators to try to persuade the middleman to provide proof of life without payment or to find another contact who could provide proof.

As the weeks passed without any movement the investigators became concerned. The alleged kidnappers might soon realize there was no chance of ransom and might kill our friends. They wanted to give the location to the authorities but they agreed not to do so in case that would result in a raid, thus endangering our friends, the rescuers, and the kidnappers.

For the team, time stretched on. When they could they continued the work they had done prior to the kidnapping. More video footage aired on the Al Jazeera television network. It showed all four men, though only Tom spoke. The footage was designed to get the United States to release detainees. When Mr. Sa'ad talked with the link, the link continued to say that our friends were fine, though the team had developed serious doubts about the validity of the link.

Tragically the team did have to face the death of one of our kidnapped colleagues. On March 10, Doug called the team at 8:45 p.m. saying that Iraqi police had the body of a foreigner killed in Baghdad. The body had been found on March 9, in the morning, by some children playing in a desolate, garbage-strewn area of western Baghdad, by the railroad tracks of a residential neighborhood. The police believed the body was that of Tom Fox. The U.S. embassy told the team they were trying to make a positive identification and that they could not confirm it was Tom. They said the tests would take several days. The team made numerous calls to various sources inside and outside of Iraqi, but could get no further information. Several hours later, Doug called back to say the body had been identified as Tom.

Although the team was aware that the kidnappers might kill our colleagues, nothing could prepare the team for Tom's death.

To honor Tom they decided that someone should escort his body back to the United States. Beth was scheduled to leave in a few days, so she was chosen (for more on this story, see chapter by Elizabeth Pyles.) While Beth was saying her goodbye to Tom in Balad, the team organized its own goodbye in the form of a public memorial at the church they attended regularly. Many Iraqi friends—both Christian and Muslim—came to pay their respects.

In the days that followed the team spent time gathering the details of Tom's death. They spoke with a man who had seen the body. They learned that despite media reports, nothing indicated Tom had been tortured before he died. The team also had customary black mourning banners made in Arabic, one of which said, "To those who held [Tom], we declare, 'God has forgiven you.'" The team hung the banners in the neighborhood where Tom's body was found. The banners gave notice of Tom's death—as is their usual purpose in Iraqi culture—and sent a message to the kidnappers. Although the team was not ready to forgive the kidnappers, God had forgiven. The team's hope was that God's forgiveness would change the hearts of the kidnappers as well as the fate of the three men still held.

At this time Mr. Sa'ad called to offer his condolences, saying he felt responsible for Tom's death. The team expressed to him that Tom's death was not his fault. Still the news of Tom's death had given Mr. Sa'ad heart problems and he had spent the previous day in the hospital. He told the team that he no longer believed the link was real. There had been too many broken promises, too much misinformation. After the news of Tom's death was released, the link called Mr. Sa'ad and said the death was a mistake; the other three men were still alive. "Be patient," the link said. "Just a little longer and the others will be released." The team ignored the link's words, having accepted long before that he was not real. The team again assured Mr. Sa'ad that Tom's death was not his fault. The only people at fault were Tom's captors.

With Tom's death on their minds, the team continued to work on issues unrelated to the kidnapping as they believed Tom would have wanted them to do. A couple of weeks after Tom's death, the team began to thin out once more. Michele Naar-Obed and Allen Slater returned to the United States and Canada. Peggy Gish and Beth Pyles left to escort Palestinian refugees to the Jordanian border, from which Beth would return home. Until Peggy returned, Anita and Maxine were the only team members left in Baghdad. Once the Palestinians were safely at the border, Beth continued on to the United States and Peggy continued on to Jordan for a few days before returning to Baghdad.

On March 23, the day after Peggy had returned to Iraq, Doug once more called the team in the morning with news about the guys. This time, however, the news was good: Multi-National Force-Iraq soldiers had released Harmeet, Norman, and Jim. Jim's partner Dan Hunt had informed Doug earlier in the day. The crisis was over. The guys were free.

Later that day the three women on the team were able to enter the Green Zone and visit with Jim, Harmeet, and Norman. Although the embassy staffers allowed them to visit only for an hour that day, the team made the most of it. The guys seemed strong, though thin. They were alert and in good spirits. Jim shared that they had not seen Tom for forty days, since February 12. Their captors continuously told them Tom was fine. They didn't learn that Tom was dead until their release.

The three had already thanked the soldiers who freed them, then thanked the diplomatic staff they met at the embassy. In a brief statement read by the team at a news conference the guys wrote, "We are deeply grateful to all those who worked and prayed for our release. We have no words to describe our feelings of gratitude and joy at being free again." The team added its own thanks with the words, "We are grateful for all who participated in this operation, and that no one was hurt."

The rest of the day—and in the days that followed—the team was inundated with phone calls from the press and from friends. When the team turned the phones off, people showed up at the door.

Once more the team visited the guys in the Green Zone the day after their release, where they celebrated Harmeet's recent birthday with cake and gifts. During the short two-hour visit they also gave the guys the details about Tom's death. Jim, Norman, and Harmeet listened in silence.

The team was profoundly relieved and grateful that no one was wounded or killed in the release of Jim, Harmeet, and Norman. They celebrated by taking a deserved day off: Peggy volunteered at the Sisters of Charity, an orphanage around the corner from the apartment; Maxine went shopping with a friend; Anita read a novel. The phones continued to ring, but the team rarely answered.

As for the link, it turned out that Mr. Sa'ad and the team were right about him. He had not been in contact with the kidnappers. A few weeks after the guys were released Mr. Sa'ad reported that the Iraqi police arrested the link, though the arrest was said to concern a different matter.

After the guys had safely returned to their countries, the team turned to looking at the future of CPT in Iraq. Almost all our Iraqi advisors and friends advised the team to leave, at least for a few months or until the violence had subsided. Others suggested the team relocate to safer areas like Kurdistan in the north or Amman, Jordan, or even lobby in the United States. When all the information was gathered the three women left the country in early April 2006.

As they left they were torn. The team's Iraqi friends were still in danger every day. The team's friends were also torn. They were happy to see the guys freed and the team safe outside the country but they would miss CPT. The bond they had forged with CPT was strong. It was the reason so many Iraqis had stepped forward to help when the guys were kidnapped. The bonds formed in Iraq and other places where CPT works encouraged Muslims around the world to come forward when CPT needed them most. They helped CPT despite the fact that many had never met Tom, Norman, Harmeet, and Jim, and probably never will.

Greg Rollins volunteered full time for CPT from 2001 until 2006. He spent three years working on the Hebron team in the West Bank before being denied entry into Israel. The following two years he spent on the team in Iraq.

4

One Family:
From Syria to Jordan, Stories of Compassion

Sheila Provencher

The children started crying when they heard the news. Little Mohammed, nine years old and usually so naughty I'd dubbed him "the Menace," did not say a word. Mouth stretched in the strained smile of a child trying not to sob, he hid his head and rubbed a dirty hand across his eyes. Twelve-year-old Aiya held my hand. Thirteen-year-old Yousra sat round-eyed and silent. Baby Houda, too young to understand what had happened, looked at his tearful siblings with a worried expression.

We sat together in a clay hut on once-blue, dirt-streaked mats donated by the United Nations High Commission for Refugees (UNHCR). Tea boiled forgotten on a squat one-burner gas tank in a corner of the earthen floor. No running water, no furniture, just a single naked light bulb to illuminate the room. There was no civilization, it seemed, for miles around—only the small village of Al Hol, tucked far away in the northern desert of Syria, and this refugee camp perched on the hill above its eastern edge.

Who were these children? Why did they weep when they heard that Tom Fox and three of his friends had been kidnapped in Iraq?

They wept because Tom was family.

It all started in Baghdad back in the summer of 2005, when members of CPT met Iraq's Palestinian refugee community. Iraq's Palestinians are people without a homeland, increasingly threatened with violence in Iraq.

In the fall of 2005, some Palestinian human rights workers and families decided to seek refuge in Syria. The activists who planned the flight asked CPT to accompany them to the border. They feared that an Iraqi security checkpoint could halt the bus and detain all of the men. They also hoped CPT could "help raise our voices to the world" so that the international community would come to the aid of all Palestinians trapped in Iraq.

Tom Fox, Beth Pyles, me, our translator Omar, and Sami Rasouli from Muslim Peacemaker Teams traveled with the five Palestinian women, seven children, and seven men who risked the journey. "We will be responsible for each other," said Thaer, the activist and main architect of the flight. "You can help us get through the Iraqi army checkpoints. After that, if there is trouble on the road, don't be afraid. We will protect you with our bodies; we will be human shields for you."

Along that dangerous road between Baghdad and Syria, we became one family. When Syria would not let us in, we lived together for two weeks in UN tents in the desert no-man's-land.

My journal reads:

October 4, 2005
We made it through the desert to the Syrian border, but the authorities will not let us through. Desert in all directions, by 8:15 a.m. we are beginning to bake in the sun.

October 10, 2005
Tom practices yoga every evening as the sun starts to fade. Tonight little Mohammed joins him, his skinny figure a contrast to Tom's tall frame. The little one hops and teeters dangerously as he attempts the same one-legged stance that Tom performs with ease.

October 12, 2005
Omar and I started a "tent school" for the five older children. I fumble through English lessons, while Omar teaches art. Tom takes baby Houda by the arms and swings him back and forth. "You'll dislocate his shoulders!" I protest.

"Nah," Tom laughs. "I've raised two kids. I've had lots of practice with this." Sure enough, Houda giggles with delight.

October 15, 2005
Most of the children are sick with the flu. Some adults are coughing too. There's not enough food; it's always just vegetables and rice, no protein. The days blend together. When will it change? When will we get the glorious news that some country in the world will welcome these people?

October 17, 2005
Tom and I have to return to our team in Baghdad. The refugees express fear about what might happen to them. Thaer reassures them and us, "We will rely on ourselves now."

One month later, the Syrian government finally allowed the refugees into the country. But they were not "home free." Officials chose to confine them, with meager supplies, in a UNHCR camp in the far north. On Thanksgiving Day 2005, I left Baghdad and traveled to Syria to visit the people whom Tom, Beth, and I called "our refugee family." I intended to spend two weeks with them before returning home to the United States.

I had been with them for two wonderful days. What a joyful reunion! But soon everything felt like a bad dream from which we could not wake.

I was outside, sitting at nightfall on a scraggy desert hill, when Thaer's cell phone rang. From where we sat, I could almost see the border of Iraq. Yet Greg Rollins' voice in Baghdad seemed to come from far away.

"I'm sorry I have to tell you this," he said. "Tom Fox and the whole delegation have been kidnapped."

"What?!" He had to say it twice, then again over my sobs. We had tried to prepare for this. But when it finally did happen, daily events took on the liquid unreality of nightmare. The adult refugees, already reeling from the stress of life with little food and no clear future, blanched when I told them. "No!" "Haram! (forbidden)," they cried. The children wept. Their Amu Tom (Uncle Tom), so strong, so tall, was now helpless somewhere, just like them.

The adults, having survived three wars, were sadly accustomed to such tragedy. So we all got up the next day and continued on, trying to manage the simple challenges of daily life in harsh surroundings: hand-washing clothes, cooking over a single burner, calling embassies to try to find a permanent refuge.

And yet in the midst of their own fears and anguish, each member of the extended refugee family reached out in some way to help me and to help CPT.

"I will go back to Baghdad," Thaer declared seconds after we received the news. "I know Baghdad better than CPT, and I can help them." This was unthinkable. He had received a death threat before we left. The CPTers still in Iraq told me they did not want anyone to return at the time, and I knew they would not want the refugees to risk their lives. Instead Thaer called everyone he knew in Iraq who might have the ability to help.

A Syrian Orthodox bishop and colleague of the camp director invited me to his residence so I could use the Internet. "I have contacted anyone I can think of who might be able to help," he said. "And I am praying for your colleagues."

Mohammed's mother pulled me aside and whispered, "Last night I did a special do'a (supplication to God) for Tom and his friends." She and I started praying together regularly after that: all five daily Muslim prayers, from dawn to dusk.

The children talked about Tom incessantly, recounting games they had played weeks ago at the border camp. "Haram," Aiya whispered once again, gazing sadly at the stars. How could anyone take away the amu they loved?

My own feelings veered between numbness and anguish. Even in the midst of such wonderful friends, I felt very isolated as the only English-speaker in a place far away from Internet, TV, even radio. I was countries removed from my CPT teammates, my family, my church community, and other CPT connections.

And yet in a deeper way, I felt closer than ever to my captive friends, their families, my CPT teammates, and in fact to all who were suffering. The physical discomfort and psychological hardships of the camp—dirt floors, meager food, lice, not enough water, a foreign language I could barely understand, the isolation of the desert, and worst of all, uncertainty about the future—all reminded me that with every breath I shared the discomfort, pain, and uncertainty of my captive friends and their families. I also wondered about the people who had done the kidnapping. What had happened in their lives to bring them to the point of violence? What were they suffering now?

The difficulties united us. I tried to express this feeling of unity in an e-mail home:

December 9, 2005
For the past week, I feel that we are all breathing together, breathing the same breath, the same Spirit—Tom and Jim and Harmeet and Norman, the men who took them, their families, all of you and all those around the world—in some deep way, all One.

Please God, help us all to see this reality and be free, even in the midst of pain.

Journey to Amman

Early in the second week of the kidnapping, Thaer's cell phone rang again. It was Doug Pritchard, CPT co-director, calling from Canada. "Can you go to Amman?" he asked. "Jenny and Peggy are there now, and they need help with media and support work related to the kidnapping." Amman was about two days away by road. While I felt sad to leave my refugee family, I was grateful for a chance to join other CPTers in the response to our friends' captivity. I spent the next day visiting each individual family in the refugee camp, saying goodbye to these people whom Tom, Beth, and I had grown to love. "Tom will visit here someday soon, I know it," Abu Mohammed said to me.

At dawn the next day, I boarded a bus that bounced through eight hours to Damascus, then took a taxi another four hours to the Jordanian border. At each stage of the journey, whenever a security guard, border officer, or bus driver asked for my identification, I displayed my CPT card and explained that I was a friend of the four peace activists who had been kidnapped in Iraq. My passport has never been processed so quickly, before or since. Everyone knew the story. "Oh, I am so sorry," a young officer at the border said. "You know, this is not the way of Islam." He stamped my passport and thanked CPT for the work we do in the Middle East.

At long last, I walked into the lobby of the Al Munzir Hotel in Amman. It felt like coming home. CPTers have been staying in this small, homey hotel for years, and all the staff know us by name. Jameel, the irrepressible young man always behind the front desk, ran around to give me a hug. "I can't believe it," he said as tears filled his eyes. Haji Ali, a survivor of Abu Ghraib detainee abuse and usually rather stern, burst into tears. He tried to express what CPT meant to him. Jameel nurtured us with tea and the daily lunches he cooked in the kitchen. CPTers Jenny Elliot, Peggy Gish, and Justin Alexander brought me up to speed on their efforts to organize press conferences, media packets, and action networks. Mazen, the hotel owner, constantly asked what he could do, and surrendered his office countless times so we could use the fax machine, printer, and telephone.

We met new friends as well: Ehab Lotayef, a Canadian-Egyptian Muslim who journeyed alone to Baghdad to meet Muslim leaders and media to appeal for our friends' release, and Anas Altikriti from the Muslim Association of Britain, who traveled to Iraq and collected statements of support from more than sixty individuals and organizations. The generosity of those in the Muslim community who risked their own safety and comfort for our sakes made me weep with more gratitude than sorrow.

The members of our emergency CPT-Amman team changed nearly every week, but we passed on the work like a baton. Peggy, Jenny, Justin, Kim Lamberty (who sacrificed a trip to At-Tuwani, a village where CPT works in the West Bank of the Palestinian Territories), Beth Pyles (who got on the first plane she could when we asked her to come), and Michele Naar-Obed all pitched in with the often tedious but crucial work.

Keep moving, keep the story alive. Prepare press releases and photo packets, walk over hills to the journalists' offices, edit e-mail lists. Write articles, organize petitions, coordinate with CPTers in Hebron, At-Tuwani, Iraq, the United States, Great Britain, and Canada. Visit embassies, meet with Canadian and U.S. officials, prepare plans for any outcome. Try to obtain visas for the CPT members hoping to reenter Baghdad. Get up in the wee hours of the night to listen to George Bush's speech on Iraq, and write a response for the press by six a.m.

One day we went to the offices of Al Jazeera television. "I am so glad you came, I was thinking it is time for us to broadcast another appeal," the young woman in charge said as Peggy, Kim, and I walked in. "Could we tape a statement right now?" she asked. Yikes! We frantically wrote a piece, and I practiced the first and last sentences in Arabic, hoping to communicate in a more personal way. "Our hearts are with all Iraqi detainees and with their families," I practiced over and over.

"Wait, you need makeup," the station leader said. She dug into her handbag and produced lipstick, mascara, foundation, and powder, which she slathered onto my face in liberal amounts. "Only for you guys would I do this," I said silently to my captive colleagues... a joke I hoped to share with them someday.

Together

Every Friday at the Al Abdali bus station in Amman, a vast market sprawls through the football-field-sized parking lot. Racks of used clothing stand next to tables of vegetables, used books, and cheap electronics. "One dinar! One dinar!" holler the vendors, as smoke from barbecued lamb kebabs and heaps of roasted nuts fills the air. The fragrance of slightly burnt onions mingles with the scent of spices, tomatoes, and deep-fried falafel. Children laugh as they sprint between the stalls, and head-scarved women sift through piles of blue jeans marked at three dinars a pair.

All that bustle of life. Did anyone else feel as if they were sleepwalking through unseeing crowds? "Yes," I realized. In Canada, in the United States, Great Britain, and New Zealand, my captive friends' families also wandered through crowds of Christmas shoppers and bright tinsel that could not ease the ache of Jim's, Norman's, Harmeet's, and Tom's absence.

Who else knew such pain? Well, what about Iraqi mothers, U.S. soldiers, and Palestinian refugees? What about the men who pointed guns and thought about becoming suicide bombers?

Pain need not leave us all alone. We were all together, even if we forgot that deep reality most of the time.

A few nights before I left Amman, Jameel called our room. "You all have to come down now, okay?" he said. We thought that maybe there was a news update on TV, so Peggy, Jenny, and I hustled down to the lobby. But the TV was off, the lobby empty. Jameel ushered us into the tiny kitchen. Hamdi, a seventeen-year-old employee who worked around the clock, was waiting for us there. So was Abdu, an Al Munzir fixture for the last six years, now recently engaged to marry. They stood in dim light around the single kitchen table. Four lit candles were stuck to the table with wax. Their flickering lights illumined four handmade paper boats, each inscribed with a name: one for Harmeet, one for Norman, one for Jim, and one for Tom. "We Love CPT" said another piece of paper, stuck into the side of one of the boats.

Jameel conducted the group. "Okay, now we have to hold hands and pray." We held hands, and everyone prayed silently. "We love them, we pray that God sets them free and they come back here soon," said Hamdi.

"When they get released, give them each their boat, okay?" Jameel entrusted the paper boats to us, and in typical fashion insisted on making hot tea with sage for everyone before we went up to bed. Jameel dreamed of the day when all four of our friends would return to the Al Munzir hotel, for a joyful feast to celebrate their release.

Afterword

Jameel's dream never came true, and Abu Mohammed's hope that Tom would visit the refugee camp in Syria will not come to pass.

What was it all for? CPT's years of work in Iraq, Tom's life, all of our efforts to reach out and secure our friends' release, their own presence in Iraq to begin with—did any of it make a difference? Iraq is still in torment. The violence spins out of control, ethnic tensions explode, torture and suicide bombs happen every day, lines for gasoline stretch for miles, reconstruction has stalled, there's no electricity and not enough fuel.

What good did you do? What difference does it make? You could do more good by working in the United States. You should have brought medicine or supplies. You should have carried weapons, you should have used guards, you should, you should...

The chorus of doubts can be powerful. But throughout my two years in Iraq and throughout the experience of my friends' captivity, I have seen the fruits of nonviolent presence blossom, often in unexpected and humbling ways.

When our friends disappeared, Muslim leaders all over the world spoke out on behalf of CPT. As a result, millions of Christians now know that their Muslim brothers and sisters took huge risks to help CPT in our time of greatest need. Millions of Muslims now know that some Christians risk their lives, without using guns, for peace in the Middle East.

When Tom died, Sunni, Shiite, Kurdish, and Christian Iraqis gathered for a memorial service in Baghdad. They read from the Bible and the Qur'an, listened to Tom's own writings, and remembered the man whom they loved as their own. Tom brought people together, even in death.

The Palestinian refugees sent a message to Tom's family from their camp in Syria. "We all loved Amu Tom—children, men, and women," it read. "Tom was like a tree planted in the ground, and its fruit went to the sky, to Heaven." Those refugee children will never forget the gentle giant who gave piggyback rides to the babies.

I once heard Archbishop Desmond Tutu say, "True peace and real security will never come from the barrel of a gun. They will come when we act from the perspective that people matter." Tom, Jim, Harmeet, and Norman's work in CPT was about living as if people matter—even those people who, forgetting their own humanity, commit heinous acts of violence.

And how can we act as if people matter? By listening to them. After two weeks with Tom, our Palestinian friends said, "We love Tom. He does not talk much, but he is always listening." His daughter Kassie said in an interview that the most important thing Tom did in Iraq was to listen to people who had no one else to hear their stories. The same is true of Jim. Most memories I have of him in Iraq are of him standing, notebook in hand, and listening, writing down the stories. In the village of Abu Sifa, where tanks destroyed two homes. Outside Abu Ghraib prison, where families desperate for news of their loved ones swarmed around him. In the streets of Baghdad, where children still asked for him two years after his last visit. I don't know Harmeet and Norman well, but I suspect that they too share this gift of listening.

It is worth risking everything to come close enough to listen, to experience the other's pain and joy as our own. CPT was and is in Iraq to work. But above all, we are there to listen. To just "be with." By being with, by listening and feeling, we touch the heart of nonviolent love. And if all people come close enough to listen, wake up to the reality that we are brothers and sisters, how can we hurt one another again?

Sheila Provencher is a Catholic member of Christian Peacemaker Teams who served full time in Iraq from December 2003 to December 2005. Sheila is a lay minister, writer, and student currently studying premedical sciences in preparation for medical school. She hopes to work in the field of global medicine and human rights, while continuing to respond to a passion for inter-religious dialogue and peace education.

5

Excerpts from Letters to Tom, Norman, Harmeet, and Jim: Written from the Village of At-Tuwani, West Bank, Palestine

Kristin G. Anderson-Rosetti

At-Tuwani is an ancient Palestinian village twenty kilometers south of Hebron. The village consists of five main families, totaling approximately a hundred and fifty residents. The people are subsistence farmers; they raise sheep and goats (some of which are kept and eaten and/or used to produce dairy by-products for family consumption, while others are sold at the markets), and harvest wheat, lentils, olives, and garden vegetables. The village has one main well for drinking water, a diesel generator that provides electricity five hours each day, a primary school, a mosque, a women's cooperative, and a clinic.

According to the Oslo agreements, the village and all its lands are in Area C, thus under complete Israeli military control. The Israeli military maintains a continuous presence in the area, asserting control over basic resources (such as land and water) and the flow of goods and people. Moreover, since the establishment of an Israeli settlement in the 1980s and an outpost in 1999 (both on land annexed from the village), the villagers have been victims of violence perpetuated by extremist settlers residing in the outpost. Israeli settlers regularly poison, damage, steal, and kill their crops, animals, and wells. Settlers physically assault young and old Palestinians of the area and are rarely held accountable by the Israeli authorities for criminal actions.

Since the fall of 2004, CPT and an Italian nonviolent organization, Operation Dove, have shared an accompaniment project in At-Tuwani.

1. We see you
November 29, 2005
Dear Tom, Harmeet, Norman, and Jim,

We're not supposed to speak of you, but not speaking feels like strangulation.

The heart doesn't understand secrecy. So, I write.

We heard the news yesterday while drinking tea with a shepherd's family in their cave. We received the call and left the cave. We left our tea glasses full and didn't say goodbye. We hid our faces and fear in the folds of our arms.

Back at our house in At-Tuwani we still couldn't show our faces. Our Italian teammates led the children wanting English lessons to the building next door, telling them we felt ill.

The next day, in the fields of At-Tuwani, we didn't speak of you. We focused on the fields, the farmers, and their families. We focused on the soldiers that were coming, the soldiers that were screaming, the soldiers that were grabbing and pushing us on the hill. Hours later the sun had moved, the soldiers had moved, and the tractors had not restarted since the soldiers' aggression. Still, we did not speak of you.

When the night passed and the day came, we traveled to the police station in Hebron to file complaints against the aggressive soldiers. We watched men with guns usher in other men with blindfolds and bound wrists.

We see you.

We speak of you only behind closed doors, only among ourselves. In these hours, every breath trips, slightly, on unfolding and unknown realities.

2. First testimony
November 30, 2005
Dear Tom, Harmeet, Norman, and Jim,

Yesterday the people of At-Tuwani heard the news about your captivity. Today the village released a video to the Arab media.

Our CPT translator and friend, Hafez, borrowed our video camera to take testimonies on your behalf. Six people from At-Tuwani and the Msafer Yatta area, including the mayor, several farmers, and two women, spoke for more than thirty minutes. They spoke with one audience in mind: their Iraqi brothers and sisters. They told their brothers and sisters in Iraq details of the Israeli occupation in their lives, how the Israeli military and settlers engage in violence against them and their land on a daily basis.

The people told their stories in two parts: life in the village before CPT and life in the village with CPT. They explained how CPTers live with them, how CPTers help protect their children and accompany them on their land. They spoke about how soldiers' behavior changed when CPTers came to the village. They said their lives are better now.

The village hopes that their testimonies will be shown on major Arab TV stations. Hafez said they must be shown. He said that people holding you must hear the voices of their Palestinian brothers and sisters.

He said that when they hear the words of the people of At-Tuwani, they will know you.

When they know you, he said, they will set you free.

3. Little big stuff
November 30, 2005 (later in the day)
Dear Tom, Harmeet, Norman, and Jim,

Ignoring a pain in my chest takes me through the day, but not into the day. This day, a ten-minute phone call captured me, finally drawing me into the day.

Because I am in Hebron now, my contact with At-Tuwani is through Hafez. In the last day, he has called frequently to see how we are doing. He has called to see if we have any new news. He has called to report what he saw on the news. In our last conversation, he spoke about the urgency of your release. He told us the village had a meeting and decided to organize a demonstration for your release.

The village is organizing a demonstration, for you.

Hafez has taken a leadership role in the organizing and is working around the clock to make it happen (it will happen less than two days from now) and to make it right.

He is calling every family in the entire Msafer Yatta area, urging all to come. He is also arranging transportation for those without.

A man in Yatta has begun making demonstration banners and will work through the night to complete them in time. Hafez says this is the only man in the city who can make the banners, because he is the best. Others in At-Tuwani are preparing speeches and contacting Arab media outlets to cover the demonstration. The village is in motion.

Listening to the details of preparation, I was overwhelmed. I'm not sure if I was more overwhelmed by Hafez's act of taking time to share the details or by the logistics of what this village, in the middle of the desert, in the middle of an occupation, is doing.

But the village's advocacy is providential. Since we heard about your captivity, we have been significantly restricted in what we can do and say. We have been instructed by CPT not to speak publicly about you, but to allow our Arab friends and partners to speak for you (and us).

This night, with the knowledge that an entire village is organizing on your behalf, our frenzy and agony are interrupted. In this space, I hear Hafez reiterate that the village of At-Tuwani is not asking for our help. The village is organizing on their own terms, out of their own convictions. They are organizing for us.

4. Everything I am doing
December 1, 2005

Dear Tom, Harmeet, Norman, and Jim,

Upon returning to At-Tuwani this afternoon, we discovered that Hafez has not gone to work since he heard you were taken. Hafez is the lead organizer of the demonstration, his first demonstration as lead organizer. Although Hafez did not want to talk about his absence from work, my teammate and I asked if this absence would be problematic.

"*This* is what I must do," was all Hafez said.

Reeling, I silently considered Hafez's absence from work. I know Fatima, Aisha, and five children depend on the income he earns to provide everything they cannot produce in and around the house. I know Fatma (the mother of Hafez) needs expensive eye surgery and Hafez's brother needs help paying for hospital bills. I know that Hafez does not always receive the wages he dutifully earns and that his relationship—and thus job—with the Palestinian Authority is tenuous. I know...

Hafez's voice interrupted my thoughts.

"This is what I must do."

Pausing, I juggled these words in my head, but my northern European decent, U.S. citizenship, white middle class, female, colonized mind was simply too small to comprehend. In an attempt to circumvent this head-heavy dissonance, I shifted the conversation, asking a question about an Israeli high court case regarding the village's land (because I assumed I did comprehend the gravity of the legal proceedings poised to deny land rights to the village).

Hafez stopped me mid-question.

"Really, Kristin, I cannot think about anything else right now. Right now everything I am doing is for them."

5. It takes a village
December 2, 2005

Dear Tom, Harmeet, Norman, and Jim,

They did it for you today. Nearly the entire village of At-Tuwani, and dozens of others from Yatta and Msafer Yatta, gathered after morning prayers to call for your release.

Before the demonstration began, kids came running into our house in search of pictures of each of you. When one would leave, another would appear a minute later, wide-eyed and arms stretched out for a picture of their own. A young woman came with the picture of you, Tom, playing the recorder. She said it was beautiful and asked for another.

When we joined the village at the school (the gathering place of the demonstration), the first thing I saw was the children, and you. More than twenty children had eight-by-ten photos of each of you. Some of the kids were holding the photos and some had the photos taped to their chests.

The children assisted each other with the precariously taped photos, shifting them and straightening them, while others toyed with the edges and wandered about looking to be photographed.

The mothers and grandmothers held signs of their own making, while the young men held the four banners made in Yatta. One of the banners read, "CPTers sacrifice their blood to help us and to help the world know about our struggles. The people, women, and children of At-Tuwani ask for the captors to let the CPT free."

The people processed from the school to the clinic, where a press conference was held.

Several men and women spoke while children sat at their feet. Other children ran to the second floor of the clinic and hung banners, photos, and a Palestinian flag.

Each statement given by the people closed in a similar fashion:

"With all the injustices we face as Palestinians and Iraqis we do not want to be unjust, especially towards those who are helping us in these difficult times. So I plead with the kidnappers to release CPT members in gratitude for their humane services."

"I plead with the Islamic resistance in Iraq to help in freeing these people and I would like to thank all those exerting the efforts to secure such a release."

"We demand that they are to be set free as a reward for their good deeds here in Tuwani and in the rest of Palestine."

"As such, we plead with the kidnappers to grant clemency for our friends in Iraq CPT. God willing our message will reach them as we hope all the best for the Iraqi resistance movement from the marginalized people of Palestine."

Only two photographers, one Spanish TV crew, and CPTers documented the event (other journalists cancelled, saying they did not want to be far from the cities because of Palestinian primary elections being held the same day). However, over a hundred people were present. A shepherd from the nearby village of Jinba came to the demonstration though this was the day lawyers and Israeli authorities were to meet at his house to discuss land confiscation orders and plans for construction of the Separation Wall on his village's property.

Hafez said the people came because it was their duty.

I don't know why they came. I only know that they came.

6. They don't know you
Early December 2005
Dear Tom, Harmeet, Norman, and Jim,

If I had to choose, I would name anger as the village's prominent initial reaction to your kidnapping. Before the people even knew your names, they declared anger and disbelief. They were outraged that anyone would do this to CPTers. When your names were first announced, they didn't recognize your names. However, not long after, they realized that you, Tom Fox, are one of the kidnapped.

The people remember you. They remember you with them in their fields and homes. Even if your visit totaled only a number of days, the village remembers you.

The people of At-Tuwani have never met you Norman, Harmeet, or Jim. They know your faces only from photos. They listen to what is said about you on the news and what we tell them of you. The people do not demand information. Nor do they require long-term relationships as prerequisites for connection. The people simply understand that there is a connection between you and them. They honor this connection by reaching out to each of you.

The people of At-Tuwani confront violence daily. Just in the last days, soldiers have harassed and kicked farmers off their land, preventing them from necessary plowing. Soldiers have erected temporary checkpoints near the village and stopped people, cars, and tractors, detaining people for indiscriminate periods. Soldiers have failed to protect the children who walk to the At-Tuwani school from the village of Tuba, resulting in several incidents of harassment and physical attack on the children by settlers.

Violence and the anticipation of violence mark each and every day.

Still, the people choose to reach out to you. You four.

Even more, every day the people learn of the violent deaths of their brothers and sisters elsewhere in the Occupied Palestinian Territories. They also hear of their Iraqi brothers and sisters being killed by the dozens and even hundreds each day, each week.

Still, the people choose to reach out to you. You four.

7. To Be Present
December 6, 2005
Dear Tom, Harmeet, Norman, and Jim,

I love it.

I can still see the grandmothers, removed from the thistles of the countryside, parading down the streets of Hebron in their black, rubber *hills of At-Tuwani* shoes, marching for you.

The grandmothers joined nearly a hundred residents of At-Tuwani, Yatta, and the Msafer Yatta area for a demonstration calling for the freedom of prisoners in Palestine and Iraq. The people, most of whom rarely come to Hebron, traveled to the city at risk. They risked facing problems with Israeli soldiers at checkpoints along the way (a risk made greater today by an increased military presence at the checkpoints, a result of a suicide bombing in Israel yesterday). The people also risked being absent from their villages in the case of settler or soldier attacks against their families, lands, or homes. Nevertheless, almost half the village of At-Tuwani, from the grandmothers and grandfathers to the youngest grandchildren, came to Hebron.

The people carried their banners, and some new banners too. The new banners were huge color pictures of each of your faces. Written below the faces were the words "Our friend: Tom; our friend: Norman; our friend: Harmeet; our friend: Jim."

Although significant media outlets did not attend (this time because of the suicide bombing the previous day), the demonstrators did what they came to do. One man told us that the village of At-Tuwani had to be present at the demonstration. He said it wasn't enough that Palestinians in Hebron marched and spoke for CPT.

The people of At-Tuwani had to be present.

8. She'll come get you
Mid-December 2005
Dear Tom, Harmeet, Norman, and Jim,

Conversing after a shared meal with the Hereni family, our attention turned to the four of you. We spoke about the lack of tangible progress in your release and bits of information we wish we knew. It seemed like we'd been delving into these uncertainties for months, not weeks. Pauses dotted the conversation, which spiraled into several different conversations in Arabic and English. Moments later, half the room burst into laughter. The staccato voice of seventy-five-year-old Fatima was audible over the laughter, "Yes, yes. Too long. Okay, let's go. I am ready. I will go and I will get them. Let's go."

She actually stood up and left the room (with a smile).

Everyone continued to laugh, and Hafez translated to ensure we understood: "My mother says she will go to Iraq to get our friends. Really, she says she'll go." We joined the laughter, knowing that if anyone could march into Iraq to get the four of you, it would be Fatima.

That night, tucked in the moonlit hills of At-Tuwani, I considered the distances between us. I considered the distance between me and you, Tom, Jim, Norman, and Harmeet. I considered the distance between me and the village of At-Tuwani. I considered the distance between me and the village, and you and your captors. I considered the distance between the village and your captors.

In these distances, I found unexpected solace. I saw the beginnings and endings of each distance dissolve into likeness. I saw through the lies of our separation.

I found us all so very close.

9. As her own
March 11, 2006
Dear Tom, Harmeet, Norman, and Jim,

Alone, I cried.

Alone at a small retreat center in Kentucky, I cried. I wept. I sobbed. Pounding at the floor, my lifeless fists failed to numb any of the pain.

Over and over again, through my tears and through my silence the same words spilled from my lips. "It's not okay, it's not okay."

"It's not okay, it's not okay, it's not okay."

Meanwhile in At-Tuwani, residents of the village entered our tiny house and sat on the floor. In turn, each spoke to the CPTers and members of Operation Dove. Heads down and heads raised, they said they were sorry and they said they were sad for what happened to you, Tom.

One man sat in silence. "I can't believe it is true," he'd said earlier that day when he heard the news. "We will pray to God that it's not true."

Hafez said that the person who killed you was not a real Muslim because according to Islam, believers are called to save, not to kill. He quoted the Qur'an saying, "When you kill one person, you kill all the world and when you save one life, you save all the world."

Fatima, the grandmother who had never before visited inside the CPT house, spoke last. She told the CPTers that she was going to plant an olive tree for you, Tom. She vowed to care for the tree as if it was one of her own children. She said she would plant the tree in forty days, the end of the Muslim mourning period.

Meanwhile, alone, I sobbed. Crossing the distances, I called my colleagues in Palestine. They told me of Fatima's tree for Tom, and my tears raged on.

10. In stride and celebration
March 26, 2006
Dear Tom, Harmeet, Norman, and Jim,

In between settlers killing two goats, settlers assaulting a young boy with spray resulting in temporary vision loss, settlers beating that boy's father, police arresting two shepherds, the death of this year's bee crop, other lost crops, and a worsening water shortage, the village celebrated your freedom.

Though I wasn't there, others told me our neighbor family cooked a big meal the night they heard you were freed. Kiefa prepared the meal, and Nasser encouraged overindulgence, saying, "Eat, eat, this is a celebration!" Others offered thanks and, through wide smiles, conveyed their happiness. One man told a CPTer that he hoped the three of you would someday visit At-Tuwani.

Days later, at a specially convened village meeting, the people again expressed their joy at your freedom, and their sadness over Tom's death. They spoke of the deepening trust between the village and CPT and saturated the room with "*Ilhumdulla*" (thanks be to Allah).

Back in the United States, I clenched my fists, tightened my jaw, and smiled past the point of pain. I jumped up and down, emitting embarrassing squeals. Under the infant branches of a small tree, I unfolded my body. Looking to the roots of my companion, I dug each of my fingertips into the earth. Smiling, I cried.

11. As *our* own
Mid-June 2006
Dear Tom, Harmeet, Norman, and Jim,

Fatima holds the hands of her youngest grandson as he grasps at the bucket of water. Fatima, her son Hafez, and three of her grandchildren are pouring buckets of water on Tom's olive tree. Although several of us CPTers carried buckets of water up the hill, the Hereni family assumes all tree-tending responsibility.

I find myself staring at Fatima, clothed in her traditional embroidered dress, white scarf over her head. I wonder what she would have said thirty years ago if someone had told her that decades later she would be planting and caring for an olive tree in honor of an American man she once met who was killed in Iraq.

What or who is Tom Fox to Fatima Hereni? Is he a foreigner, an American? A man, a Christian, a non-Muslim? A peacemaker, a resistance fighter?

Is he a father, a musician, a mentor, a friend? What does she even know about Tom?

"What is the connection, Fatima?" I shriek in my mind.

Fatima pauses. She drives her hoe into the ground, digging out fist-sized rocks. Hamoudi, the youngest grandson, grabs at a full bucket of water. He grunts and whines at the container that is bigger than his two-year-old body. Fatima turns to the boy when she is ready.

In the late afternoon sun, the shadows of the Hereni family and the olive tree of Tom Fox extend toward village land occupied by a settler outpost. With intention, I move to the small shadow of Tom Fox's tree. Before me, the hands of the Hereni family move in and through the earth.

I watch closely, because in these hands, I see what has taken root.

Kristin G. Anderson-Rosetti served as a full-time CPTer from August 2002 to December 2005, primarily in Palestine (in both Hebron and At-Tuwani), also joining the CPT teams in Kenora, Ontario, and Douglas, Arizona. At present, she is a CPT reservist and a consultant for Operazione Colomba. When not practicing her Italian, Kristin creates art, cello music, and satirical musings.

6

With a Lot of Help from Our Friends:
The Call from Palestine for Release of the Peacemakers

Rich Meyer

Bad news, but keep it secret

After ten years, our Palestinian and Israeli friends know that at CPT-Hebron we do not have TV. Thus we often get calls when they think we should know breaking news. On Sunday, November 27, 2005, before the media got hold of the story, our team received a short phone call about the kidnapping from the CPT office in Toronto. We were given strict instructions to keep this information to ourselves. Though we were told how many were taken, we were not given names.

A CPT delegation that was in Jerusalem when we received the call came to Hebron the next day. We decided not to keep them in the dark about the biggest concern on our minds right then, our friends in Iraq, and told them the situation. We asked them not to mention this in messages home. They and their leader, CPTer Elizabeth Garcia, continued with their activities, gave us room for our work, and supported us in every way they could.

For two days, difficult as it was, we maintained the confidentiality of this news. During that time, we did get a few calls about reports of foreigners kidnapped in Iraq—were they ours? Then a British paper broke the news that Norman Kember had been kidnapped and Al Jazeera television ran a video showing all four. Palestinian friends called us with the news when they saw it on TV, and team members began to receive calls from hometown press. Finally CPT issued a press release with bios of Tom, Norman, Jim, and Harmeet.

The videotape of our friends gave us an assignment. For the next ten days, the focus of the Palestine CPT teams was on how we might help win the release of our friends. The note from the captors to Al Jazeera accused them of being spies. Our first task was to counter that.

The call goes out

Our phones rang throughout the day Tuesday with offers of sympathy and support. Our lawyer and supporter Jonathan Kuttab said that he would be able to submit positive stories about the good work of CPT to Arabic media. Our team's longtime friend, journalist, and human rights activist Hisham Sharabati took immediate initiative. After quick consultation with us, he, and Hamed Qawasmeh began contacting Hebron representatives of Palestinian political parties. By late that night, they had signatures from eight groups identified as The Islamic and National Forces in the Governorate of Hebron on a statement appealing for the release of the four.

This statement, released at a press conference at the Ali Al-Baqa'a mosque the next morning, became the model and the testimony relied on for many more appeals over the next weeks. The statement was based on their "long experience confronting Israeli crimes and violations with CPT since 1995, and wish to confirm that the members of this group have had and still have a major role... in the protection of the property and the lives of Palestinian citizens." The statement opened with a verse from the Qur'an and closed, "Freedom for the Iraqi and Palestinian people, shame and disgrace on the Zionist and American occupation." Signatories represented the spectrum of Palestinian politics: the Islamic Resistance Movement (Hamas), Palestine People's Party (PPP), Democratic Front for the Liberation of Palestine (DFLP), Democratic Union of Palestine (FIDA), Fatah, Popular Front for the Liberation of Palestine (PFLP), Palestine Liberation Front, and the Palestine Popular Struggle Front.

Our media guidelines from the CPT Crisis Team emphasized that we should try to stay off-camera at the press conference the next morning; western faces speaking English was not the appeal we wanted to present. The media did not exactly agree with our wishes (one wide-angle camera shot did show a CPTer), but we had no shortage of Palestinians to send the message.

The press conference was opened by Sheikh Najib Al Ja'abri, a leader in the mosque in the Haret e-Sheikh neighborhood of Hebron. The second speaker represented the PFLP; the third represented the PPP. All spoke about their warm feelings toward CPT, based on years of working together. The fourth speaker was Naim Daour, from Hebron University. He talked about the repeated closures of the university and about CPT's efforts to help reopen it. "Sometimes it is hard to tell who is working for us and who is against us, but really Christian Peacemaker Teams helps us. Whoever is holding CPTers has made a mistake."

Fariel Abu Haikal, headmistress of Qurtuba Girls' School, emphasized the difference between CPTers and the American government. "Saif al-Haq ('Sword of Right') I don't know, but these problems in Iraq, they come from George Bush. He is the problem, not CPT." She described the accompaniment CPTers provide for teachers and students at her school, who are often assaulted by Israeli settlers from the nearby settlement of Beit Hadassah.

The last Palestinian to speak was Jamal Miqbal of Beit Ummar. Jamal and his family live in the shadow of the Israeli settlement of Karme Tzur, and the Israeli military issued a demolition order on their home. Many CPTers have stayed at their home, both in tense times when the Miqbals feared the bulldozer would come and in more relaxed seasons.

Time and again, we were astonished and humbled at the lengths to which Palestinians would go to help CPT. After the press conference, one Hebron political leader approached us and offered to go talk to someone in Baghdad if we thought he could help. Hamed Qawasmeh, we learned, lost his post with the governorate for helping with our press conference, or more specifically, for complying with our request to hold the press conference in a location of Islamic religious significance. When we tried to thank people for their support, their uniform response was, "No, don't thank us. We have to do this; it is our duty."

Later that day, a Palestinian National Authority official from Ramallah issued "A Plea to the Iraqi People" that read in part: "This is an organization that has helped and continues to help our people living under Israeli occupation in the city of Hebron and in other regions throughout our occupied homeland. They expose themselves to danger in order to provide protection to our women and children in front of Israeli military checkpoints."

Also on Wednesday, the International Solidarity Movement (ISM) called to offer their help. Harmeet Singh Sooden had been a volunteer with ISM less than a year earlier and was planning to join them again after his CPT delegation to Iraq. The ISM media office in Ramallah obtained statements from one of the top Muslim clerics in Palestine, Mufti Ikrema Sabri, calling for release of the four peacemakers. He also spoke directly against the kidnapping of civilians, on the basis of Islamic teaching. ISM also directed journalists to the Palestinian mayor of Jayyus, who said he remembered Tom Fox, and a villager from Salfit, who recalled when Harmeet stood with him through tear-gas at a demonstration against the Separation Wall.

ISM planned a demonstration for the release of the four peace activists that would take place the next day, a press conference for the following Monday, and another press conference in Nablus with Palestinian religious leaders the following Wednesday. ISM produced large, high-quality, color photo-banners of each of the four captives that showed up well at these events. Two CPTers attended the Thursday demonstration, where the Al Aqsa Martyrs Brigades released a statement: "Therefore, we ask the kidnappers to release those hostages in order for them to go back and stand by the side of justice and peace, and by the side of the persecuted

65

nations, notwithstanding the actions of their governments who are directly responsible for all the violence in the region." The CPTers did what they could to ensure that the signs and banners in Arabic were prominent.

Several of the members of the CPT At-Tuwani team came to Hebron, where we developed our own crisis team. It was composed of the team members most skilled at organizing mass-media contacts and at computer and Internet production and distribution. This was intense work. A number of us on the Palestine teams knew members of the Iraq team through close personal connections and through relationships built with them in CPT.

Stresses on team members mounted quickly. When one takes on a task that other lives depend on, one wants to do it as well as possible. On completion of the task, one thinks hard: is there anything more I could have done? Is there more a teammate could have done? Most of the time in CPT, we learn and improve skills as we work. We are often conscious of mentoring people as they try new tasks. But this felt like the wrong time to let people learn "on the job." We needed to assign people with the best skills for each task.

As we focused more of our attention on Arabic satellite television and Arabic media, the role of Palestinian friends of CPT grew. More and more Islamic leaders and Muslim groups around the world followed the lead of CPT's Palestinian supporters and issued statements, and Palestinian friends called us every time they saw something about CPT in the Arabic media. This was how we heard about each video communication from the captors via Al Jazeera. Palestinians helped both by monitoring Arab television to tell us what was being said and by translating our releases so that we could send Arabic copy to Arabic media. CPT's website started to carry our own statements in Arabic.

The fact that Tom, Jim, and Harmeet had all worked in Palestine was very important, and it meant that we were able to locate photos of them in a Palestinian context and testimonials from Palestinians who knew them. In the case of both Jim and Harmeet, we were able to say that their captivity was actually preventing them from coming to work for Palestinians. (Jim had been due to join the Hebron team immediately after the delegation in Iraq.) The large photo-banner of Tom showed him in Palestine, holding a sign that said, "Stop the Wall."

The media picked up on the connection made in the first statement from the National and Islamic Forces: these people are working against occupation here and in Iraq. Palestinian journalists went out of their way to publicize the press conferences, demonstrations, and calls for release of the peacemakers. The early advice that CPTers should try to stay off-camera was relaxed, and for a few days CPT tried to get one piece by a spokesperson onto Arabic satellite television each day. We soon learned that in Palestine we had better access to Arabic media than CPTers in any other area of the world. This was in part from our long history of work and relationships, but also, we learned, because most Iraqi media were by now based in Amman, Jordan, due to difficulty working in Iraq. By the end of December, the Palestine project had added more than three hundred contacts to our e-mail list of Arabic-language media.

On Friday, December 2, the villagers of At-Tuwani organized a demonstration calling for the release of the four peacemakers (for this story, see chapter by Kristen Anderson-Rosetti.)

Fourteen thousand detainees

The connection with the Palestinian Prisoners' Society brought another point of appeal to the fore: the kidnappers were calling for a release of detainees—the very work the captives and other CPTers in Iraq, Palestine, and Canada had been addressing! In fact, the large photo-banner of Jim Loney showed him at a demonstration for the release of Arab detainees in Canada. The call from the Prisoners' Society was "release the peacemakers so that they can continue to work for prisoners and detainees."

And so we decided that whenever we talked about our four friends (though in fact none of us on the team knew Norman or Harmeet), we would use the opportunity to highlight the situation of Iraqis held by U.S. and British military forces in Iraq. Like our four friends, fourteen thousand Iraqis are being held without charges. Like us, many families and friends had no contact with their loved ones and did not know what would happen to them.

On December 3, I was the guest interviewed live on Al Jazeera satellite television network in the afternoon news program. I spoke from a studio in Jerusalem, while my interviewer was in Qatar. I doubt I will ever address a larger audience in my life or speak my piece with a heavier sense of what is riding on my performance. I was asked what CPT was doing to win the freedom of the four peacemakers; I said that we were trying to explain who we are and what we do, and that we trusted in the power of truth. Christian Peacemaker Teams here and in Iraq are working against occupation, I said, and we are working for detainees. Just once (as instructed by media guidelines) I said that the four are not spies. Throughout I felt that the Al Jazeera journalists in both Jerusalem and Qatar were supportive. They were doing what they could to help. There were no trick questions, no ambushes, and on the air they expressed their hope for the safe return of our friends.

On December 5, Mufti Ikrema Sabri spoke again at a press conference in Ramallah. He said, "There is a duty for all Palestinian people, institutions, and factions to commit to sending a call to release these people who have been kidnapped. They are very important for helping us continue our struggle, whether here in Palestine or in Iraq, to gain our countries' freedom. We repeat our call to release all the civilian people who have been kidnapped all over the world, not only these four." A representative of the National and Islamic Forces in Palestine also spoke, as did CPTer Kristin Anderson-Rosetti. She thanked the "hundreds of Palestinians who have issued statements and supported us. …We miss our friends and desire them to return to us. …While remembering them, let us remember the thousands of peaceful people being detained by occupying forces throughout the world, and while we ask for a release of our friends, we will continue to work to end the occupations in Palestine and Iraq."

Our Palestinian friends had a much better sense than we did of what voices carried weight in Iraq. They often used connections to Palestinian religious leaders, asking them to speak out. We discovered that on some occasions Palestinians in Hebron were called to confirm that in fact CPT did deserve the support of these luminaries. For example, when ISM friends in Nablus arranged for the Qadi, the Mufti, and a Greek Orthodox priest to speak for freedom for the four, these speakers did not have direct acquaintance with CPTers. They did, however, trust their advisers.

As December 8 approached with no further communication from the kidnappers, we decided to keep doing what we could to present the work of CPT in the media. A camera crew from Canadian Broadcasting Corporation (CBC) came to shadow two CPTers that day. I think they were hoping to film our reactions if there was another video or an announcement of tragedy. But the next video showed all of our friends alive and together. No new deadline was issued.

O ye who believe!

Many of the statements of Islamic leaders for release of the CPTers in Iraq included a Qur'anic reference to ground their appeal. It is useful for non-Muslims who have contact with the Muslim world to note these verses and their arguments. Here is a summary of several:

"O ye who believe! If a wicked person comes to you with any news, ascertain the truth, lest ye harm people unwittingly, and afterwards become full of repentance for what ye have done," The Holy Qur'an 49:6. (National and Islamic Forces of Palestine, Hebron, November 30, 2005.)

"Our god tells us that if any person comes to us as a volunteer in peace, with no weapons, we must protect him." (A poster at the press conference in Nablus, December 7, 2005, as reported by ISM. The source for the statement may be Qur'an 8:61, "But if the enemy incline towards peace, do thou [also] incline towards peace, and trust in Allah: for He is One that heareth and knoweth [all things].")

"Since our Islamic religion rejects injustice and exhorts for safety and justice and that there should be no soul killed wrongfully... 'and no bearer of burdens shall bear the burden of another'(Qur'an 17:15). Thus, every soul that has committed a crime or sin should hold its own burden, and not someone else's, and this is the principle of individual or personal responsibility. Therefore, no one should be punished for a sin committed by someone else, and this is part of the fairness of our Shari'a." (Mufti Jalaleddine, Sheikh of Saida and the South, December 5, 2005.)

"I am your brother Abu Qatada, Omar bin Mahmud Abu Omar, who is imprisoned in Full Sutton jail in Britain. I urge my brothers in the Brigades of the Swords of Right in Iraq, who are imprisoning the four Christian peace activists, to release them in line with the principle of mercy of our religion. Our prophet said mercy should be shown unless there is a reason in Sharia that prevents it" (message delivered via videotape).

"Then shall anyone who has done an atom's weight of good see it! And anyone who has done an atom's weight of evil shall see it" (Qur'an 99:7, 8). God says, 'Every soul draws the burden of its acts on none but itself,' this establishes that the responsibility is a personal responsibility, there is no son responsible for his father and no brother is responsible for his brother. Therefore, how can a person be responsible for their government's action? This is the injustice in this case." (Sheikh Dr. Abed Al-Latif Al-Humaum, general director for the Popular Islamic conference.)

Waiting for resolution

CPT decided that it would be useful to have two CPTers in Amman to be in contact with Iraqi media and to plan for "resolution." Jenny Elliott and later Kim Lamberty left the At-Tuwani team to help in Amman. When they left, Jerry Levin from Hebron was on stand-by, ready to go to Amman at a moment's notice. "Resolution" in our vocabulary came to mean an end to the crisis, whether through freedom or death. It was difficult, however, to ponder the possibility of our friends being killed, and I think that in order to do our work, we had to imagine them being freed. When we asked Hisham to translate two draft press releases, one for the event of the release of our friends and one for the eventuality of their death, he translated the "good news" quickly, but delayed for weeks translating the death notice.

We received many messages of support from Jewish Israeli friends. They and we both realized that there was very little they could do publicly on our behalf; any public support from them might be counterproductive.

As the crisis wore on, we needed to continue our other work in Palestine at the same time as we continued to work for the CPTers held in Iraq. In fact, after all the wonderful things Palestinian friends had said about CPT, we felt an even stronger obligation to do our work and do it well. In late January and early February, the team again considered ways to highlight the situation of the thousands of detainees held without trial in Israeli jails. Lack of progress on this problem, which touches nearly every Palestinian family, continues to be a critical factor in the conflict here, as evidenced by the events that touched off the war in Lebanon in July 2006.

Death and freedom

Hisham Sharabati organized a candlelight vigil in Hebron on the one-hundredth day of captivity. A few days later, March 10, at three a.m., the CPT teams in Palestine got word that Tom Fox had been killed. The team waited until four a.m. to call Hisham to ask him to translate a press release into Arabic. He said, "You should have called me immediately!" After doing the translation, Hisham also arranged for the press conference, which was held in conjunction with a demonstration of the Palestine Prisoners' Society; this both called attention to the plight of Palestinian prisoners and helped us associate CPT with this concern as we made our statement on the death of Tom. Tracy Hughes represented CPT on the podium and had her picture taken along with several mothers of prisoners. Later George Rishmawi, a friend from Beit Sahour, organized a candlelight memorial service for Tom in Manger Square in Bethlehem. Rachel Corrie and her sacrifice were likewise remembered.

When Jim, Harmeet, and Norman were released later in the month, the Hebron team phones rang nonstop with Palestinian friends expressing their delight. "We must have a *big* party," many said. There were also calls from the local media, and within an hour a long-time friend and journalist, Sa'ed Shiyoukhi, was in the Hebron apartment, filming an interview with team members. In a Palestinian tradition for celebrating the release of prisoners, the team brought out chocolates, a stash they had been saving in hope. There were many calls from the British press to Scottish CPTer Maureen Jack, who was on the Hebron team at the time. And fortunately Donna Hicks, one of the few CPTers who had met Norman Kember, was also present.

There was euphoria at the good news, but it did not last long. Tom's death was fresh in our minds. At the time of Tom's death, instead of doing the work of grieving, CPTers needed to keep working toward the release of the other three. His death increased our anxiety while the others were still captive. Their release freed us of a responsibility and allowed us to mourn. Thus, in a sense, it was a sad time. Three—not four—were free.

When Tom Fox was killed, an old woman in At-Tuwani planted an olive tree in his memory. I hope that someday Jim, Norman, and Harmeet can meet her on their "Thank you, Palestine" tour.

As CPT's Palestine project support coordinator, Rich Meyer spent several months each year with the teams in Hebron and At-Tuwani. A CPTer since 1997, Rich also farms forty acres in northern Indiana, fixes cars, and calls square dances.

7

The Road Traveled in Colombia

Sandra Rincon
Translation by Joel Klassen

Colombia is my country of birth. All my roots, dreams, and hopes are based on the expectation that one day the conflict that has—for sixty years—destroyed the most beautiful things about my people will end. These six decades of war have uprooted more than three million Colombians from their land, have enriched only five percent of the total population, have benefited an economy of war represented by more than three illegal armed groups and one legal one, and have delivered all the natural riches of Colombia to the country's large monopolies and transnational corporations. Without a doubt, they are the winners in the bloodletting in Colombia.

In this context of a long-lasting war and a high level of human rights violations, organizations like Christian Peacemaker Teams arrive to support the initiatives for peace of communities that valiantly resist displacement as they strive to live an alternative to the conflict and construct from their pro-peace positions the basis for a new Colombia, a Colombia at peace.

For six years, CPT has been present in one of the regions most affected by the conflict in Colombia, the Magdalena Medio, location of the largest oil refinery in the country and of the biggest gold cache in Latin America. From our home base in Barrancabermeja, we accompany several rural communities, bear witness to the actions of the armed groups against the civilian population, prepare and participate in nonviolent public actions created by social and human rights organizations in the region, and pray that the gospel of peace will spread throughout Colombia.

The impact of our work on our own lives is profound. We can see the pain in each person who has been a victim of the violence of war, and we exert ourselves to make these stories known and to support every Colombian who rises from this suffering each day to resist and to dream anew. From them, we learn what life, joy, and faith mean, especially when we feel sadness, skepticism, or near-hopelessness that things can change.

And it is, perhaps, that profound connection with our partners that makes CPTers feel linked to something bigger than our own understanding and our own reasoning. This connection makes all in CPT a living body, one that suffers and experiences joy, and one that is nourished by the support, prayers, and unconditional love of our families, friends, and even of strangers.

"Normal" life on the Colombia team takes place amid visits to communities, routine office tasks, meetings with partner organizations and friends, and work to make known the situation we witness in the region and in the country. In the course of this normal life, at the end of November 2005, team members were participating in a workshop for young conscientious objectors to war in Bogotá. They had just returned from a visit to the Nasa indigenous nation in the south of Colombia, which has lived their resistance to colonial violence for five hundred years. We had also visited the rural community of the Opon, with which we have been working for five years. In Barrancabermeja, we participated in a powerful public action organized by the Popular Women's Organization on the International Day Against Violence to Women. Finally, we were completing office work, articles, records, and the like. We had plenty to do.

Because of all this, the news of the kidnapping of two members and two delegates of CPT in Iraq fell on us like a bucket of ice-cold water. As CPTers, we recognize that our work carries risks. But to pass from a theoretical preparation for crisis to the reality of an actual crisis is something no one can fully anticipate.

During a telephone call to the CPT office in Chicago, team member Joel Klassen learned the news. He told me, "Sandra, let's pray. Some people are kidnapped in Iraq—and we know two of them."

"Okay," I replied, utterly frozen, yet at the same time suffering from the extreme heat of the region, which made the event all the more surreal. Suzanna Collerd and Noah Dillard were notified about the news at the workshop in Bogotá. John Giraldo, one of the leaders of the conscientious objectors, offered strong support to both.

A few hours after talking with the Chicago office, the team received a call from Toronto, from Team Support Coordinator Robin Buyers, who had been named to the Crisis Team. She relayed, "Officials have advised the Crisis Team that, in the hope of an early release, no one from the organization should know about the kidnapping at this point unless necessary. Please don't tell any team members." So Joel and I, still confused as to what was going on in the CPT offices, called the CPTers to whom we had told the story so that the "snowball" of news would not get rolling.

How frustrated I felt, so far from any real news. Truth was what my being most demanded. By evening, frustration was compounded as we waited for more instruction. All we could think of was informing the rest of our teammates about the kidnapping.

As it turned out, the kidnapping was accompanied by other tragic news that Saturday afternoon in November. The team learned that Gloria Lizcano, the mother of John from the workshop and a member of the Mennonite church, had died in an accident caused by a motorcycle security convoy of the Colombian president. Many CPTers knew Gloria; they had stayed in her house or met her when she visited the project in Barrancabermeja on a national delegation. Tears fell as we shared laments, as well as memories of Gloria. All the while, some of us did not know what had happened to our friends.

All was difficult and sad. Suzanna and Noah, together in Bogotá, were deeply affected by the news of the kidnapping. Everyone was, in some way, overcome by so many terrible events.

Many questions swirled about my head: When would we be able to tell the news to Pierre Shantz and Jim Fitz, who had just arrived from the countryside? When would they be able to know the names of the kidnapped? When could we sit down and pray? When would we learn it was all an error and our friends were free? What had happened in Baghdad? Why?

The next day, an e-mail was sent to the entire organization of CPT. We who read it searched every word for clues, but the message and many more would be guidelines for public actions and clear suggestions about what should be said about the situation. It was not enough.

Then a full day after the first call, Joel and I were able to inform our teammates of the news. It was a difficult job, as we could not say the names of the kidnapped, which had not yet been publicly released. "Tell me who they are," Pierre pleaded, full of anxiety. "One of them could be my friend."

That afternoon our team prayed for the liberation of the four in Iraq. We could not imagine that four months would pass before the crisis ended. That afternoon we looked at one another. We remembered our human condition, our fragility.

After that Sunday, our team resumed our work and planning. Joel recalls of those days, "The initial shock of hearing about the kidnapping passed, and I began to recognize that something long expected had happened: the lives of CPTers were being threatened in a way more direct, more immediate—in a way that felt more threatening—than ever before."

A group from our team went to visit Micoahumado, eight hours from Barrancabermeja. Others attended Gloria's funeral in Bogotá and later returned to the project. Those who remained at the office prepared a press conference with the aim of sending a message to the captors about CPT's work in the world.

Deeper in our hearts beat the constant yearning for news of the hostages' release. Almost every one of us had a direct connection with two of the detained, with Tom and Jim. Suzanna trained for CPT with Tom; Pierre and Joel were close friends of Jim; Noah knew both men from training; and Scott Albrecht who had arrived two days later, had worked alongside Jim in CPT's Toronto office; team member Stewart Vriesinga, on break in Canada in those days, was Jim's longtime friend. He worked side by side with Robin in the Toronto office, answering media questions about Iraq and the kidnapped CPTers. To me, Jim and Tom were acquaintances. Like all of those close to the hostages, our team entered a spiritual and emotional captivity.

When the news of the kidnapping went public globally, the solidarity and support expressed by the community of the Opon, our partner organizations, friends, and church were a gratifying sign that we CPTers were not alone. The activities we organized to promote the liberation of detained and kidnapped people in Iraq, including the four from CPT, received widespread support from the people who value our work in the Magdalena Medio.

At the press conference we organized, gigantic banners were hung. They displayed photographs and personal descriptions of Jim, Tom, Norman, and Harmeet, as well as an image of a candle, John 1:5 written below: "The light shines in the darkness, and the darkness did not overcome it." These banners accompanied our team for the length of the hostages' captivity.

On December 8, 2005, the first announcement of a death threat against the four men brought a torrent of emotions. As a team, we had to accept what was actually happening. We had to rely on faith and had to help create actions that would lead to an early liberation. The first video was a grueling test for our organization and for every CPTer as an individual. It signified the beginning of a hard pilgrimage that would include announcements and later extensions of death threats, as well as periods with no news of the condition of our friends.

As the first execution deadline arrived, Colombia celebrated the Festival of Lights. Our team took advantage of the occasion to invite our supporters to undertake a simple vigil of song, prayer, and personal reflection. This was the first of many emotional gatherings we would organize during this time. It was also an experience of invaluable support, affection, and solidarity that energized our team as we awaited resolution.

In the middle of December, the team attended a regional meeting of the Assembly of Victims of Crimes Against Humanity by the State. There we shared our news and listened to the stories of others. We heard from mothers who had watched their children "be disappeared" or kidnapped and killed. These mothers stood in solidarity with us and we with them.

We tried to continue the normal work of CPT-Colombia, but bit by bit our concern for our four friends diminished our ability to focus. During the whole ordeal, we spent thousands of hours searching for recent news on the Internet. Each call we made from the countryside to the office began with the same question: anything new? Always the same answer: no. The videos seen hundreds of times on the news and the Internet struck us with fear and at the same time gave us incentive to speak, to struggle, to learn. They made us move from the sea of confusion and fear that something terrible would happen into the space of hope.

Team members rotated, some departing for breaks, some returning to the project. In the middle of February, Robin Buyers joined us. Her role as support coordinator had been filled by Erin Kindy in December and January, but Robin was now returning to this role. Robin's arrival had a profound impact on the team, as she was part of the CPT Crisis Team and a friend of Jim. It was not possible for Robin to disconnect from her role in the Crisis Team, nor was it possible for her to neglect the work in Colombia at a time when so much needed to be done. The accumulated exhaustion of nearly two months of the crisis was evident in her and the Colombia team. Tensions and misunderstandings within the team surfaced more frequently than usual during this time. The burden was, at times, overwhelming. But after two months, the team slowly began to reincorporate itself into the life of the Colombia project.

In early March 2006, Suzanna experienced an acute sadness with no apparent cause. It was the kind of foreboding she sometimes felt before difficult occurrences. Shortly thereafter, on March 10, CPT and the world learned of Tom Fox's assassination.

Our common response was one of speechlessness, tears, mourning, confusion, and pain. For the first time, one of the candles we had lit for the hostages had to be extinguished. The same candle would be relit in the name of detained Iraqis.

Condolences from our Colombian partners arrived swiftly. We received messages, expressions of sorrow and consolation, and we knew that thousands of prayers were whispered in Colombia in memory of Tom and in supplication for the liberation of all Iraqis. To keep working meant for many CPTers to recognize anew our fragility—that we are as fragile as those we are attempting to accompany, and that we mustn't forget this. Ten days later the team prepared a public action to mark the third year of the invasion of Iraq and to demand that it end.

"We are living what so many of you already are familiar with," said Stewart Vriesinga in a reading from that day, "to wait without knowing. ...A wait that seems interminable. To feel rage, without knowing where to direct it. To feel impotent, unable to do anything. To feel incapable of holding this vigil one day more, but at the same time preferring to know nothing if the truth is the worst. ...Last week we received news that our dear friend, Tom Fox, had been killed. Now we must learn to continue the struggle despite the anguish, despite the fear, despite being vulnerable. Many of you are doing this already. We ask for your help and your support."

The effect of the vigil was healing. Although we were anxious beforehand, each member of the team was able to contribute her or his grain of sand to the vigil, and through that, to express feelings and thoughts that begged expression.

Five days later, the team was awakened by shouts of joy. "They are free!" Robin exclaimed. What peace, liberty, and happiness we felt in that moment! What a time to give thanks to the Spirit of Life, to friends, family, and others! Jim, Norman, and Harmeet were all free. Now our souls, bodies, and spirits were also free ...ready to return from Iraq, where they had been held for 118 days.

Nonetheless our joy was far from complete. The memory of Tom passed through the minds of every one of us. Many tears fell again and will continue to fall for years, to water seeds sown by the men and women who gave their lives for peace.

As accompaniers, we were able to understand, perhaps for the first time, what the disappearance or kidnapping of a loved one means. We would listen now in a new way to the stories of communities, families, and individuals whose loved ones had disappeared—stories full of questions, stories that help them to preserve the memory of these beloved for days, months, and years.

I remember many conversations about our kidnapped friends in which we imagined them—especially Jim and Tom, whom we knew—having discussions about nonviolence with their captors. We imagined them as a group creating strategies to survive the hardship of captivity, strategies that revitalized their commitment to love even their enemies. And we imagined them celebrating Christmas, the New Year, and other special days seeing their captors in all of their humanity, fragility, and goodness.

We needed to imagine our friends' well-being, because it was too difficult and frightening to imagine otherwise. So we imagine that Tom died at peace. We imagine that the testimony of Tom's life left his captors with a new way of imagining their own lives and their world—imagining it at peace.

We imagined these things in order to believe that everything would turn out well for the fourteen thousand detainees in Iraq. We imagined these things for three thousand two hundred kidnapped people, and the thirty thousand forcibly disappeared, in my country, Colombia.

Sandra Rincon is a Colombian who trained as a psychologist at the National University of Colombia. She did counseling at the university before joining CPT full time in 2003. Sandra has worked in Colombia and Kenora, Canada, and was part of CPT's Women's Delegation to the Democratic Republic of Congo in 2006.

8

The Baghdad Morgue

Michele Naar-Obed

I arrived in Amman, Jordan, on New Year's Day 2006. Beth Pyles and Kim Lamberty, two CPT reservists, had been in Amman doing media work and arranging for visa applications to get into Iraq. I finally settled into my hotel room around four a.m. and after a few hours of sleep was greeted by Beth, Kim, and the hotel staff with hugs, hot coffee, and a bag of trail mix. It wasn't long before I was brought up to speed and incorporated into the work of the Amman team.

The Iraq team in Baghdad was hearing rumors that the release of our four colleagues might be imminent. These rumors had been circulated before, so the team was cautiously optimistic. Nonetheless, the three of us in Amman began to look into transportation, housing, and a place where the team might retreat after the release to debrief. It wasn't long before the rumors proved false, and so I'd stepped onto the emotional roller coaster that would characterize the next several weeks.

The CPT Crisis Team in North America asked us to brainstorm ideas on how to reach the hearts and minds of the captors. Since we didn't know who the real captors were, we tried to leave no stone unturned. We put ourselves in the mind-set of each of the different possible groups. What could we say or do to reach the hearts of a criminal gang, of insurgents, of Iraqi nationals, of a militia group, of a militia group backed by an element of the coalition forces? Then the thought that neither Beth nor I wanted to articulate was given voice. What if our colleagues were dead? Had anyone considered checking the morgue? Although we briefly discussed the idea with our team coordinator, who called in daily, we didn't raise this possibility with the Iraq team until joining them in Baghdad.

On January 10, 2006, I left Amman for Baghdad. Beth followed two days later while Kim went on to South America. The day I arrived in Baghdad, we received a call from a trusted contact telling us that Jim, Harmeet, Tom, and Norman were all in good health and that release would come soon. Once again I let my hopes soar—enough so that the idea of checking the morgue was put out of mind. Three weeks and several similar phone calls later, Beth and I were finally able to raise the subject of the morgue at a team meeting.

The idea that our colleagues might be dead had been haunting the recesses of every person's mind. The team agreed fairly quickly that checking the morgue was a necessity. With that part of the decision made, we talked about how and when—and who. We talked about the emotional toll such a trip would take. We reflected on each team member's background and past experiences, and on what would help us get through the ordeal. We shared our strengths and weaknesses, concerns and fears, and we prayed.

We decided to pair up and make multiple trips. Anita David and I would be the first team to go. Finding a willing translator and driver would be necessary. Due to the instability in Baghdad, it took weeks to make arrangements. The frequency of car bombs in our neighborhood was increasing, translators were afraid to work with us, and requests from Iraqis to help with other projects delayed our trip. More than we cared to admit, the fear of what we would find at the morgue likely fed our procrastination.

On February 22, the Al-Askariya Shrine in Samarra was blown up. Chaos and violence escalated exponentially, and strict curfews were placed on Baghdad and surrounding provinces. There were days when travel by car was prohibited. Sometimes the travel ban would be lifted at four p.m. only to be reinstated at six a.m. the following day.

On February 28, after many aborted attempts, a translator and driver accompanied Anita and me to the Baghdad morgue in Medical City to look for the bodies of Tom, Harmeet, Jim, and Norman. Dressed in our black jubas (a full-length robe-like dress) and full headscarves, Anita and I were able to blend in pretty well with Muslim women—though once we spoke, we would be easily identifiable as foreigners. Our translator pleaded with us, for his safety as well as ours, to let him do the talking. We agreed that to the best of our ability, we would keep our mouths shut.

Our driver pulled into a crowded parking area and our translator gave us last minute suggestions before we exited the car. We began our trek toward the morgue by walking down a pedestrian-only street. The curb was lined with women huddled in groups, most dressed in their traditional black robes and head coverings. All of them appeared anguished. Many were sobbing, some pounding on their chests and throwing hands and cries up to Allah. We assumed their men were at the morgue searching for family members, and we walked past them briskly, our faces down-turned.

After entering an alley, we saw the rear doors to the morgue. Water mixed with body fluids streamed into gutters along the side of the alley. To the left of the morgue entrance, we saw dozens of men and one woman pressed against a Plexiglas window. Most had their mouths and noses covered with handkerchiefs to dampen the stench of death. Backed up to the morgue door was a battered Iraqi police Nissan pickup truck.

Our translator asked some of the men about the protocol for viewing the dead while Anita and I tried to get our bearings in the surreal environment. Pulling us away from the crowd so nobody would hear our English, he explained that since bodies were appearing daily in large numbers, they were immediately photographed and given an ID number. The photos were available for viewing on a computer screen. If the body could be identified, a more detailed report could be obtained from the medical examiner. Then he pointed Anita and me in the direction of the Plexiglas window.

Making our way through the crowd, we were funneled into the narrow space between the pickup and the window. As we approached the back of the truck, we saw the body of a young man lying on a burlap bag in the pickup bed. His face was partially covered with the bag and his body covered with flies. He was wearing a black jogging suit with a bright green, five-petaled flower on one leg. His hands and feet were exposed and appeared withered, as if they had been in water for a long time. He looked to be in his twenties.

Anita was able to look inside the morgue. She saw bodies on the floor atop black plastic body bags and clear plastic sheets. Most were pressed against the wall. Some were dressed and others were naked. One showed evidence of being badly beaten.

I tried to make my way toward the window. One could get a fairly clear view when standing with small groups of four or five at a time. While I was waiting my turn, my eyes locked with the one other woman who was, at that time, wedged into a corner. She tried to speak to me in Arabic. I looked around for our translator who was milling about among the larger crowd. Conscious of my promise not to speak, I was unable to call for his assistance.

The woman continued to speak and it seemed like she was pleading with me. I felt helpless and stupid and wished I were one of the flies and could fly away. I broke eye contact and looked down, choking back my tears. I tried to focus on our mission of looking for Tom, Jim, Norman, and Harmeet. I was acutely aware that I was not an observer, but a participant in this deathwatch. These were our colleagues, our family members we were looking for. I was no longer the CPT human rights worker observing and documenting abusive policies against Iraqis. I was another distraught human being caught in the ugly, bizarre, and inhuman consequences of war.

Finally, a spot opened for me at the window. Behind it, a man sat at a desk next to a computer screen that cycled the photos of bodies and body parts at three-second intervals. Each photo had a number written in Arabic in the corner. Many of the corpses were hideously distorted, and I had no idea how they were categorized or dated. All I could do was look for someone or something familiar. Tom, Jim, and Norman would be somewhat easy to identify since they were Caucasian. Harmeet, who is of East Indian descent, would be more difficult.

After a hundred or more photos had been viewed, they all began to look the same. Photos of whole bodies, photos of faces, and photos of mangled body parts all looked alike. I looked at the men standing next to me. Everyone seemed to have a similar glazed look in their eyes. Every now and then someone would suck on their teeth and shake their head in disgust. While I was there, no one made a positive identification.

I gave up my spot at the window and turned to look for Anita. The Iraqi woman was still wedged in the corner but I would not allow myself to make eye contact. I covered my face with the sleeve of my black robe, which had absorbed the putrid smell of death, and walked toward the crowd where Anita was waiting. Young men were carrying empty pine caskets into the morgue while others marched out with filled caskets hoisted on their shoulders. They sang a death chant as they walked down the alley.

I looked at Anita and shook my head to indicate that I didn't see anything of Jim, Harmeet, Tom, or Norman. As we began to walk away from the crowd, our cell phone rang. Anita and I were a bit panicked as we realized one of us would have to speak. Anita, almost whispering, said hello with a slight Iraqi accent. She squinted her eyes as she listened and answered, *"Nam"* ("Yes" in Arabic). After more listening she said, *"Moshe, moshe"* ("Okay, okay") and hung up.

Finding our translator, we walked down the alley, turned past the women huddled in groups along the curb of the pedestrian street, walked toward the parking lot, and got into our car. Once all the doors were closed and the engine started, Anita told us a car bomb had exploded in our neighborhood. Our team members were safe, but teammate Allen Slater had been at the site just five minutes prior to the explosion. As we drove home, we saw ambulances and emergency vehicles heading frantically toward Medical City. More bodies on their way to the morgue.

Michele Naar-Obed lives in Duluth, Minnesota, with her husband, Greg, and daughter, Rachel. They are members of the Loaves and Fishes Catholic Worker community providing temporary housing to homeless families and individuals. She is a reservist with CPT and has served in Iraq on four different occasions, returning from her last trip March 2006. Michele has participated in numerous acts of nonviolent civil disobedience against U.S. militarism and has spent over three years in prisons and jails.

9

Where It's Easier for People to Be Good

Alayna Munce

Picture this: a slightly decrepit, semi-detached, three-story Victorian brick house sitting on a side street in an economically marginal urban neighbourhood, a stone's throw from an expressway. Those who have lived in the neighborhood awhile might remember that there used to be a wide and cozy covered wooden porch on the front of the house. A few years ago, someone finally admitted that the wood had rotted irreparably, and the bulk of the porch, with the exception of the part needed to access the door, was torn down. Now there are pale patches on the brick where the porch used to be. The house looks like it lost half a mouthful of teeth in a fight and can't come up with the money to replace them.

The front room of this house—what would normally be a living room—is empty of furniture but for a layer of threadbare blankets and rugs covering the battered hardwood floor and, in the middle of the room, a low coffee table bearing scores of tea lights and small, framed photographs of four men.

If you were to observe this room over a period of days—days that bled into weeks that hemorrhaged into months—you'd see the arrangement of tea lights and photos shift and change. Watch. The little candles burn to nothing and are replaced. Pools of wax accumulate, are scraped up, and accumulate again. At one point, a clay dove in a tray of sand appears. At another point, a photo of the Sacred Heart etched into a stone wall of a prison camp is added to the improvised altar. Sometimes the tea lights are lit, sometimes not.

Against one wall of the room there is an unlit fireplace, and on the mantel there is a tall votive candle. Day and night, day in day out, this votive candle is always lit.

Over the course of any given day, people come and go from this house. Singly or in small groups. Often they let themselves in and disappear into other parts of the house. The door is never locked. There are smells of cooking. Arguments. Laughter. This side of an overseas telephone conversation in a language you can't place.

Often the front room is empty. As life goes on around it, this room seems to be holding its breath.

Every once in a while someone slips in through the front door, takes his shoes off in the cramped and dark foyer, and places them on the heating grate under the hand-lettered sign requesting that shoes be removed and placed there. He then enters the front room sock-footed and sits for a while on the blankets with his back against the wall.

Every evening a little before nine, someone shows up, takes her shoes off as requested, kneels before the low table, and begins to light the scores of tea lights. As she works, others begin to show up. Some slip in silently and choose a wall to sit against, hugging their knees. Some hug and speak in low voices in the foyer before entering the front room. There are often tears. Eventually the people stop arriving and the quiet in the room deepens. Then one of the assembled stirs. Maybe she opens a book and begins to read. Maybe he speaks.

They stay about an hour. There seems to be an understanding between them about what comes next. Whatever else happens during the hour, near the end there's always a period of silence—sometimes longer than others—a period that every night resolves into a song. Always the same song. One or two voices begin it, and the others join in, and as the song is repeated some voices break off from the whole and sing it against the grain in rounds. The result is a simple but disarming harmony. The words of the song go like this:

> I can make all things well.
> I may make all things well.
> I will make all things well.
> And all shall be well.

At first the room fills every night so full with people that they're sitting three deep against the walls and on each other's laps and it's hard to breathe and still there are people spilling out into the foyer and sitting on the staircase in the hall, listening through the banisters to the voices in the front room. Chairs appear for the elderly. Babies are passed from arm to arm. Then, as the days and weeks pass, the numbers dwindle until some nights there are only a handful of people, some nights only two or three. Periodically the numbers surge again, as if by some mysterious call or migration instinct.

Whatever the case, the candles are lit; the silence comes near the end and resolves itself into the song.

The moon waxes and wanes. The stars, largely obscured by city lights, shine unobserved.

Around the house, the night seems somehow deeper than it has other winters; there's a sense of the sky stretching high and far and dark around a troubled globe.

The house in the picture is a house of hospitality attached to Zacchaeus House, the two houses together forming the core of the Toronto Catholic Worker community. The room in the picture is the makeshift chapel of that community, site of a four-month vigil. The dark months in the picture are the ones between November 26, 2005, and March 23, 2006, the time of captivity of the four Christian peacemakers kidnapped in Iraq. The men in the framed photographs are Harmeet Sooden, Norman Kember, Tom Fox, and Jim Loney, the kidnapped four.

The people coming and going from the picture are the core and extended community of Jim Loney.

It used to be a tricky thing when people asked me the what-do-you-do question. Now it's more straightforward—I'm a writer and a waitress, and though each of these roles has its own complex story, at least the cultural templates of the stories are recognizable. But when I was living in the Toronto Catholic Worker community, I used to have to take a deep breath, quickly suss out my interlocutor, and depending on my sense of the person's patience and genuine interest, decide whether to sidestep the question or launch into The Spiel.

So, for those readers who don't know about the Catholic Worker movement, here's a short-ish version of The Spiel:

The Catholic Worker Movement was begun in 1930s New York by a woman named Dorothy Day. She was a radical journalist who, after converting to Catholicism, needed to find a way to live her faith and her politics together. She eventually met a wandering French worker-philosopher named Peter Maurin, who espoused ideas about personalism. Together they began a newspaper in the tradition of other popular radical papers at the time—the *Socialist Worker* and the *Communist Worker*. They called theirs the *Catholic Worker*. In addition to covering strikes and workers' struggles, they wrote about ideas; ideas like pacifism and green revolution and voluntary poverty and the need to be personally responsible for the people around us through the works of mercy, not through the mediation of the state; ideas like every Catholic home should have a "Christ room" where they could welcome a person in their midst who needed a home. Eventually people started showing up at their doorstep (it was the Depression, after all), and the phenomenon of the Catholic Worker "house of hospitality" was born.

Today, there are Catholic Worker communities all over North America. Some focus on resistance to militarism, some on green revolution, some on hospitality. All are effectively anarchist (that is, anti-hierarchical) in structure: there is no central body to apply to when you want to start a Catholic Worker community; you just do it. And you don't ask the government for help or permission either. You get a house and welcome the poor into it, and in doing so you inevitably encounter your own poverty. You make it work. That's what Jim Loney and his friends Dan Hunt and William Payne did when they began Zacchaeus House in the early 1990s and it became the home of the Toronto Catholic Worker movement.

Peter Maurin used to say that we need to create a society where it's easier for people to be good. It was the attempt to live out this statement that made me fall in love—complicated love, but love nevertheless—with the Catholic Worker.

When I came to it, the Toronto Catholic Worker community centered on first one then two houses of hospitality and over the years included several households in a row on a side street, an extended network of neighborhood supporters and activist friends, a farm, a worker co-op bakery, a worker co-op sawmill, much activism, some civil disobedience, a newspaper, and the sharing of everything from worship to childcare, from meals to vehicles. There were (and continue to be) shifting and overlapping circles and layers to the community; people come and go through the layers, all the while collaborating with and spawning other groups. I stumbled into acquaintance with it all in the early nineties through the man who was to become my husband, and through the community I got to know Jim and myriad others—refugees, addicts, do-gooders, lost souls, idealists, con artists, kids, crazy people. Most were several of these things at once.

I lived a couple of doors down from Zacchaeus House for many years and learned that the kind of bond one develops in community is different from the bonds of family or friendship. It's a little of both and at the same time it's neither. Choice is involved as it is in friendship (though, depending on levels of privilege, there's more choice in the matter for some than there is for others). But there are also givens the way there are in family; the way you don't get to choose who your brother is, you don't always get to choose who happens to be your neighbor or your housemate, who happens to show up on your doorstep. And I learned that there are, if you stick around for it, gifts in givens.

I told my friend Jo Roberts (a long-time member of the Toronto Catholic Worker and a close friend of Jim's) that I had agreed to write a chapter about the community's experience of the time of captivity. "Good luck," she snorted. "I've given up on that story ever being told."

Jo is not generally a flippant or negative person, so the response was uncharacteristic. It made me think, and I came to believe that the reasons for her moment of discouragement were twofold. Part of it was the simple despair we all feel when we can't find words for a powerful spiritual experience. But part of it also had to do with being unseen, with a cultural lack, with the frustration of living a vivid experience that falls through the gaps between people's reference points. The story of the pain and beauty we lived as a community during those four months can't be told, not only because it doesn't fit into a media sound bite—that's true too, but it's also more than that. For the most part our culture can't imagine what it's like to live in an extended community that has bonds as intense in their own way as family.

The four months of Jim's captivity were, for his community, a remarkably vivid time. Much of that intensity, of course, had to do with the acute agony and uncertainty of having a loved one in prolonged danger and being largely helpless in the face of that danger. But the vividness also had to do with how effortlessly the community pulled together during the crisis. How we all rose to the occasion, rose into our best selves. I hesitate to say it, but it's true: though it was an excruciating time of waiting and unknowing, it was also strangely ecstatic.

People saw roles they could fulfill, and they stepped into them. Some did tireless direct-action work. Others cooked. Some organized worship and vigils. Some simply prayed. People answered phones, gave interviews, gave massages, donated money, hosted visitors, did translations, or just listened. There was an uncanny abundance in the midst of the crisis: food appeared when needed, rides appeared, volunteers appeared. It's odd, but alongside the terrible uncertainty of the time, there was a kind of peace.

And of course the sense of peace was intensified by the feeling that all over the world, people were also rising to the occasion—Islamic leaders eschewing sectarian concerns and speaking out for the hostages, Palestinian children holding pictures of the four, Muslim detainees in a Canadian jail making statements that the safety and freedom of the CPTers was more important to them than their own freedom and safety. My friend Michael Armstrong called it an "explosion of goodness."

The community's nightly vigil was for me the most expressive emblem of this peace. It fell together with barely any discussion and continued nightly for the entire four months, accommodating an astounding variety of needs and circumstances. And through that prolonged prayer, an intimacy occurred, an attentiveness took root, an openness began to work in us. It was an openness to each other, to God, and to the captives, to be sure—but it was also an openness to all captives in Iraq and to their loved ones. And even to the captors trapped in their terrible role.

For me the nature of prayer itself changed during the vigils. Something in me began to balk at petitionary prayer. Instead of calling to God for a certain outcome, I began to feel us called to simply pay attention, to feel us honoured to be called. It was like being in an altered state. Our love for Jim became a gateway to a wider love. When we sang Julian of Norwich's words at the end of each night—and all shall be well—they did not fall on my ears as a Pollyanna assurance that Jim would indeed come home, that everything would turn out all right. Even if Jim did come home, everything would not be all right in the world. I began to hear the song as a call to trust that even if events were heartbreaking, we could, with attentiveness, live a gift out of them.

In Flannery O'Connor's short story *A Good Man Is Hard to Find*, a dysfunctional family on vacation gets lost on a back road and encounters a madman on a killing spree. The madman calls himself the Misfit. The story's point of view rests largely with the grandmother of the family who is, in many ways, a typical human: manipulative, self-absorbed, bigoted, delusional, trying her best. Near the end of the story, with the rest of her family already shot, the grandmother experiences a moment of grace in which her head clears and she sees the pain and alienation of the Misfit. She reaches out and touches his shoulder saying, "Why, you're one of my babies. You're one of my own children!" The Misfit then shoots her, and in the last line of the story he says to his sidekick, "She would of been a good woman if it had been somebody there to shoot her every minute of her life."

It's a dark story, obviously. I've thought of it often in the time since Jim's captivity. I suppose the reason it keeps coming to mind is that the struggle we've been left with in the wake of the hostage crisis is how to be good without that gun to our head. How to move the grace and epiphanies of the crisis into the day-to-day. How to live with that urgency, but without the violence urging it.

Over the years I was a member of the Toronto Catholic Worker, we struggled long and hard over how to work and worship together given the variety of needs, backgrounds, limits, and energies in the community. What I think we learned most of all—through much chafing and discord— was this: trust that each will give what they can, trust that what needs to happen will happen. And if it doesn't happen, things go better if you let it go. We'd done much groundwork, so the effortlessness of our coming together during the kidnapping was not a miracle without foundation. And I don't mean to suggest that we didn't snap at each other and encounter our worst selves and push ourselves unhealthily and drop the ball and lose heart during that time. Just that we also experienced a grace.

One hopes to be converted by experiences like ours during Jim's captivity. But conversions have both a past and a future—they need foundations and have to be renewed daily. We were lucky enough to have the foundation (the work of community is the work of nonviolence). The question for me remains: can we keep building?

It comes down, I think, to attention. To finding ways to foster attentiveness, both personally and communally. Jim did come home. Tom Fox didn't. Who knows what has become of the captors. There are still tens of thousands of people being detained without charge or trial in Iraq. In the wake of the crisis, I notice that those detainees and their families are further and further from my mind. I've decided, as the anniversary of the kidnapping approaches, to take some time each night before sleep to light a vigil candle and ask myself this question: without the gun to my head, how can I help to build a society where it's easier for people to be good; where it's easier for all of us (captors and captives, misfits and mothers) to widen the scope of our attention, to see our enemy as our very own child?

Alayna Munce is a long-time friend of James Loney and of the Toronto Catholic Worker. She now lives a few short blocks away from the community. Her first novel, *When I Was Young & In My Prime*, was published by Nightwood Editions in October 2005. She is currently at work on a book of poetry.

10

Taken Twice

Dan Hunt

One summer in our youth, Jim and I hiked the top ninety kilometers of the Bruce Trail. I forgot my good hiking boots and had to wear a pair of paper-thin running shoes I bought at the Salvation Army, but it didn't matter. It was late August and we feasted on wild apples and blackberries we found along the trail, followed sheer limestone cliffs, and swam in the freezing, Caribbean-blue waters of Georgian Bay.

Official campsites along the trail were few in number and far apart, and it became clear one day we would not make it to the next campsite. This delighted Jim for a couple of reasons. He could break a rule he didn't agree with, and he figured he could select a much finer campsite than the designated ones. He chose a boulder beach we were traversing as our accommodation for the night. We swam, cooked, and went to sleep in the open, under a full moon, next to waves lapping upon the shore.

Jim fell asleep instantly, and I lay awake under the bright night sky for a long time. Jim's sleeping bag was open to his navel, and I lay there looking at him, imagining what it would be like to slip my arm around him. I was full of conflict having been taught by my faith—and my entire culture—to loathe the fact that I loved a man whose beauty overpowered all my senses and kept me awake at night.

This was my first love. I remember being so surprised that a man could fall in love with another man. I knew I was sexually attracted to men, but it had been easy to keep this attraction in the box labeled "sinful." That is, until I experienced being in love, an experience that slowly incinerated the cultural and religious prohibitions that imprisoned me.

That night I believed, naïvely, that if I could only put my arms around Jim I would be happy forever. With heart pounding and adrenaline surging, I inched toward freedom. Pretending to be asleep, I moved my arm so that it lay beside Jim's, just touching him. I moved a few millimeters out of the closet. That was all. Still, on that night, I was happy.

So began our glacial courtship. Jim and I were frozen by our conceptions. We had, after all, met as young men who wanted to join the Roman Catholic Church as priests. We were in love with our tradition and wanted to give our lives in service to it. It took a long time to understand that on a subconscious level we were attracted to the priesthood in part because of the requirement of celibacy—a convenient, accepted, even laudable way to avoid our sexuality.

Many people, when they begin to burn their way out of the closet, allow the fire to consume their religious tradition. I understand why. While claiming to grant freedom and life to queers,[5] many religious traditions in fact destroy the sacred capacity to love that God has placed in our hearts. I still smolder within my religious tradition, and always will so long as it refuses to recognize the holiness of my love. It may be that in the end, like so many others, I will have nothing left but the ashes of my tradition.

Our thawing happened degree by degree. A year later, it was Jim's turn to act. We found ourselves sharing a bed in a hotel room packed with friends who had gathered for a friend's wedding. Once again I was awake throughout the night, Jim's proximity banishing all hope of sleep. In the early morning, Jim slipped his arm around me and pulled me close. For a few furtive minutes we lay like that, smiling, and then it was over. The experience was enough to sustain me in our long courtship and coming out, the long stumbling path to freedom and claiming our love for each other.

Things really began to thaw when I discovered beautiful images of our experience in poetry. I made Jim cards with the words of Walt Whitman, "Love buds put within you and before you whoever you are...," and the words of Rumi, "I drank water from your spring, and felt the current take me." We discovered and warmed ourselves in a poetry of love written for us. We could see ourselves as beautiful, and good, and so we slowly released ourselves from the bonds of shame our religious tradition held us in.

Fourteen years later we lay in bed together as partners on the eve of Jim's departure for Iraq. We had spent the evening with good friends. Jim asked me, "How would we spend this night if we knew it was going to be our last one together?" On his first trip to Iraq, Jim had been in the vehicle that rolled on a highway and killed CPT member George Weber. It was Jim who stayed with George's body and accompanied him home. On his second trip to Iraq, Jim and four other team members were robbed at gunpoint and threatened with death.

I told Jim how I supported his work, how I thought his sudden or violent death would impact me. With unknown prescience, I told him my worst nightmare: that he would be kidnapped, his image flashed across the

---

[5] The word *queer*, once used pejoratively, is the self-identifier of choice for many people for several reasons. The term *homosexual* originated as a medical term denoting an illness, causing many people to reject it as a self-identifier. The term *gay* is non-inclusive, as if refers solely to men. Acronyms that are inclusive of all sexual minorities are cumbersome. For these reasons, the word *queer* is favoured.

Internet in an orange jumpsuit and me powerless, because of being gay, to act to protect him from a videotaped execution. Jim responded that kidnappings of internationals had been on the wane for the past few months. Kidnapping seemed unlikely.

I put my arm around Jim and held him tight while he slept. I continued to think about his question. If this were our last night together, I would want to hold him close just as I was doing. I would want to experience what I had read about in Buddhism, being entirely in the present moment without fear, without regrets, without clasping. Just right in this moment. Right here. Right now. No past or future.

I didn't succeed at all, but I held Jim. I held him and imagined that it was the last time I would ever do so. I marveled at his beauty. I soaked up his warmth. I took in his smell and absorbed his breathing, his heartbeat. I tried to be right there, and to be grateful. In the end tears came as I imagined what it would be like to lose him. And then I fell asleep too.

Five days later, the call came.

It was my mom who answered the phone. "It's a Rebecca Johnson," she said, frowning. I knew this was not good. Rebecca had tracked me down at my mom's on a weekend. I stumbled toward the phone.

"Dan," she said, "I need to tell you that Jim has been kidnapped. It happened while they were leaving a mosque four hours ago. The driver and translator called the team to let them know."

Blood rushed to my head; I could hear my heart pounding. "I'll let Jim's parents know," I said. I sat down on the arm of a couch, struggled for breath, tried to make sense of what I had just heard. My mom waited apprehensively. "Mom, Jim's been kidnapped," I told her. I took a deep breath and called Pat and Claudette Loney.

That evening friends of my brother dropped by the house. According to the initial strategy developed, no one was to be told about the kidnapping. My brother's friends were invited in and I carried on as if nothing were happening. I had begun to live as someone other than I was.

I am not certain when I first realized how thoroughly I would need to disappear in order to protect Jim. I do remember William Payne emphasizing this, probably in our first conversation after he learned of the kidnapping. "The risk to Jim's life will increase exponentially if it's known he is gay," he said. It was good that he said it. It was a reality I still hadn't fully absorbed.[6]

---

[6] Since the fall of the Saddam regime, gay Iraqi men have been targeted by a systemic program of social cleansing.

Neighbors were warned not to mention me to the press. Staff at my workplace were told to keep my identity secret. Both William and Robin Buyers made fervent appeals to the media to keep me out of the public eye. When our street swarmed with cameras, I crept into prayer vigils through the back door.

Initially my public disappearance seemed like an inconsequential strategic decision, one that would be easy to bear. I was responding to homophobia that was far away, in Iraq. It wasn't real. How quickly that changed. When Jim's picture was first published on the front page of the national newspapers, the headline right next to it was about the promise of Stephen Harper, Conservative Opposition Leader at the time, to re-open the debate on same-sex marriage in Parliament if he was elected. At that moment the reason for hiding stopped being an abstraction and became painful. Harper's position on marriage was just one point on the spectrum of homophobia, a spectrum that ranges from schoolyard taunts to Sunday sermons condemning our "unnatural lifestyle" to religious edicts that say gay men should be killed in the worst possible way. As I walked through the snowy streets of my neighbourhood, seeing Jim's face in every newspaper box, I had no idea that the myth we were creating would almost crush me.

Publicly, Jim became known as an upstanding Christian boy and community-worker from a typical, small-town, all-Canadian nuclear family. It was the only picture of him that was safe to portray. I, and everyone connected to me, including the community Jim and I began with William in 1990, had to be erased if Jim was to have any chance of surviving.

That community, the Toronto Catholic Worker, swung into action immediately and laboured relentlessly. William, who was living in Buenos Aires doing graduate work for two years, happened to be in Toronto when Jim was taken. William put his thesis on hold and did whatever was needed to work for Jim's release. He spent long hours in the CPT office, enduring precarious housing with no dependable income, moving his possessions and his life back to Toronto. My dear friend Jo gave up her income and travel plans, and went to work in the CPT office while keeping a constant eye on me. Michael, another housemate, kept our house running by doing the dishes, laundry, and cleaning. More than that, he kept his heart open to my suffering and gave voice to prayers and rants that I could not. Madeline and Luke coordinated nightly Catholic Worker vigils. Helyn brought groceries and Alayna coordinated food for the CPT office. Richard and Madeline invited me to spend time with them and their three boys, who so loved Jim. Sarah worked nights in the CPT office before heading off to her job.

Countless others helped too. Joseph and David, who live outside the city, made Toronto their home base and did anything and everything asked of them. Len and Anna gave up their income while Len organized countless public vigils. My former boyfriend, Andre, lent computer support and photographed public events. Rory and Mark helped with the Shine the Light campaign. Diego came from Washington. Miguel dropped by to cheer us up. The Stocking clan was ever-present at vigils. Together these friends supported Rebecca, Robin, Hobo (Bob Holmes), and Doug at the CPT office in the constant work required of them. A different community of friends organized in Kitchener while people came from hundreds of miles to join public demonstrations. It is impossible to enumerate everyone's contributions.

Each night of the captivity, when I was most alone, I took to our bedroom one of the four vigil candles I kept alight for each of the captives. It was my ritual, a symbol of bringing Jim into the room with me at night. I would read that old familiar poetry to him, and to myself. I always read a passage from Daniel Berrigan's "The Whale to Jonah":

Be still, Jonah, sleep at last. ...In the belly of your savior, in the perilous, fathomless sea, where salvation is a miracle and death is most likely—sleep. ...Until then I bear you through the pathless sea. Another than you plans for you, another than you breathes for you, another than you loves you, another than you sees before and after, yesterday and tomorrow. While you lie there, ignorant of where you come from, where you might be going, indeed of who you are.

These words I read to Jim each night became my way of holding him. They reminded me of our communion and helped me to bear my anguish.

Anguish is the word I have adopted to describe how I felt throughout the kidnapping. No single word is adequate. To begin to understand my experience, one must grasp two distinct but inseparable sources of anguish. Each magnified the other.

The first source of my anguish arose from the fear and helplessness surrounding Jim's captivity, the not-knowing, the grim imaginings of what was happening to him. I wondered if he would ever come home, and if he did come home, how he would be changed. It was an anguish of grief, torment, and powerlessness; enervating uncertainty stretched between two extremes—safe homecoming and violent death.

Two days after learning of Tom Fox's murder, I awoke in the middle of the night. I lay there for hours, rocked by a wild storm of grief. In a strange way it was a relief. Finally I could feel something. For two days I had moved only in slow motion, as if immersed in molasses, my body and mind disconnected from me, belonging to someone else. At least grief meant I was awake and aware.

I began to plan Jim's funeral, what I would say in his eulogy. I thought of how to explain who Jim was and what I thought his life meant; how I would tell of his passion for the Catholic Worker, for social justice, for Catholicism itself and how it shaped his interior life; his embrace of nonviolence and his trips to Iraq; how kids in his life would greatly miss him; his energy-and-joy gifts to the world. I would tell how he loved camping and the wilderness; how mischievous he was; how I loved him; how my final words to him would echo the final words to Kassie Temple of the New York Catholic Worker in her eulogy: "Well done, good and faithful servant!"

Being a hostage myself in a desert of endless waiting, trying to squarely face and allow the possibility of Jim's death and torture, was the first anguish.

The second anguish was the fear of being removed from Jim's life entirely, not knowing—if it came to that—whether I would be permitted to plan and speak at his funeral. When Jim was kidnapped, there was some unfinished business in his family. It fell to us, Jim's family and me, to work through that business even as we contended with the kidnapping. We did a good job of it, but it was not easy.

I believe the unfinished business was the consequence of the Catholic Church's homophobic teaching that queerness is objectively disordered, sinful beyond conception, threatens the stability of family and society, and ranks so high in the hierarchy of sins that it's the only issue on which bishops take real political action. Though they love him dearly, Jim's family had not fully accepted the reality of his gayness. When someone's essential way of loving is not fully acknowledged or seen, then the full picture of who that person is—even if it is one's own child—cannot be known. This is the violence the Catholic Church bestows on families under the façade of compassion toward its queer sons and daughters.

It took some time for me to figure out the extent of the unfinished business. Jim's family lived far from us, and I had not visited them often. I once attended a family wedding with Jim and over the years had some brief interactions with his parents, usually when they were mailing something Jim had left at their house, such as keys or a wallet. I assumed they knew who I was in Jim's life.

Early on, the Royal Canadian Mounted Police (RCMP) asked his parents and me to each complete a hostage profile to assist them with media work and negotiation strategies. Developing the proof of life questions fell to me. These would be used to verify that anyone demanding a ransom was actually holding Jim—questions that he could easily answer, and that only he could answer. I assumed this meant Jim's parents and the authorities knew and recognized my status as Jim's partner.

When Jim's family was called upon to make their first public family appeal for his release, a CPTer named Jerry Stein reviewed the appeal over the phone with me. Jerry stayed with Jim's family for the first three weeks of the crisis. He said that they wanted me to know I was included in the statement. They included a line about Jim's friends that was intended to acknowledge my place in his life. I felt fully recognized, included, and grateful. When I hung up the phone after that call, I sobbed with relief.

By December 5, 2005, Jim's entire family had gathered in their hometown of Sault Ste. Marie. Donna, Jim's sister-in-law, invited me to come be with them, and I flew up the next day. It was an intense time. In forty-eight hours a second family appeal was made, a second video of the captives was released over the Internet, and a death threat with an impossible demand came and went. I set up a prayer space in the room Jim lived in as a child. I was welcomed into his family's home. Some members of his family were explicit in acknowledging my relationship to Jim. I left after only a few days, needing to be with my own friends and family. Before leaving, I gave Jim's parents a notarized copy of my power of attorney for his personal care. After the visit I concluded there was no longer an elephant sitting in the middle of the living room, or if there was, it was a small one.

I was mistaken. In a conversation with Jim's brother Matt just before Christmas, he mentioned a family conference call with Foreign Affairs Canada (FAC)—a call I hadn't known about or been included in. Transportation arrangements for Jim in the event of his release had been discussed and included the possibility of sending a family member to accompany him home. I was stunned that Foreign Affairs had not discussed these arrangements with me. Thus far, my only contact with government officials had been through the RCMP who assured me they recognized me as Jim's spouse. I contacted the RCMP right away, re-faxed them my power of attorney, reiterated that I was Jim's next of kin, and asked to be put in touch with the appropriate person at FAC.

On the Friday afternoon before Christmas Eve, the RCMP responded with an office number in Ottawa. They neglected to tell me about a twenty-four-hour emergency number that had been given to other members of his family. It was four agonizing days before I could reach someone. My Christmas without Jim was spent with a new fear that he had been taken from me in yet another way.

Meanwhile, the Loney family had become frustrated dealing with so many different parties independently—CPT, RCMP, FAC, and me. They resolved to get the parties together for a conference call in early January as a way to improve communication and coordinate strategies, thereby improving the likelihood of Jim's and the other captives' release. That first call took place in early January, with a second call scheduled for later that week. Weekly calls continued for the duration of the crisis.

During that first call, two things were said that sliced into my consciousness. I asked about accompanying Jim home and I stated that I wanted FAC to include me in those arrangements. The response from the FAC official: "I'll take a note of that." Translation: No. You are not family. Someone in Jim's family said, "We have already chosen who will go on our behalf." Translation: We don't recognize who you are in Jim's life.

While driving home from work the next day, I managed to get the same FAC officials on the phone. I pulled into a dark parking lot in an industrial nowhereland. Rain poured down on my car as I explained who I was in Jim's life. They quizzed me. Do you own property together? Do you have a joint bank account? Are you married? I offered all the evidence I had that we were spouses. That wasn't enough. I said I live in a house with three lawyers and offered to get an affidavit that Jim and I shared the same bed. "I don't want to go there," was the reply. At the end of the conversation I asked, "If Jim were on his way home tonight, would you send me to meet him, along with someone from his family?"

"Based on what we know right now, no, we would not send you."

The fear of being displaced, not just "symbolically" in the media world but in the real day-to-day unfolding of the crisis, began to take over. Mental-health warning signs appeared. I parked in a parking garage and couldn't find my way out of it. When I had finished my errand, I couldn't find the car again. Then I found myself driving and not knowing what street I was on. It was the only time in the crisis that my coping ability began to erode.

I retained a lawyer. The lawyer called FAC. I sent them documents proving that Jim and I were partners. I e-mailed Jim's family to explain what I was doing and why I felt I had to do it. The next day, FAC called and said they were prepared to acknowledge that I was in a long-term common-law relationship with Jim, and as his spouse, was his next-of-kin. I wanted a written statement that in the event of a critical decision they would take direction from me. FAC refused, said it would be a "family" decision. I boiled over and shouted thermonuclear invectives into the phone. FAC eventually relented and gave a verbal assurance that my wishes would be followed. I said that was no longer satisfactory; I wanted it in writing. They held their position. Then I remembered the advice of the lawyer I had seen: if at all possible, work it out with Jim's family. I said I was going to call them to see if we could work it out. FAC encouraged this.[7]

---

[7] While this experience with FAC was particularly difficult, I don't want it to overshadow the fact that the staff at FAC and the RCMP laboured intensively on Jim's behalf and demonstrated exceptional commitment to getting him home. They

We did work it out. An especially astute intervention from Ambassador Donna, Jim's sister-in-law, paved the way. She asked whether FAC could get both Jim's parents and myself on the line to make a decision if a critical situation arose. It was easy to agree to this. I believed the three of us could make a better decision than I could alone. But I did ask to prevail in the awful event we could not reach agreement, and this was granted.

All was not fairy-tale happiness at that point. Coming to understand the reality of what it means to be queer so that a full acceptance can take root, is a long process. Jim's family had to come to a new understanding of who Jim was, to learn to see me and to know who I was, all in the midst of a very public ordeal. Jim's family had made a space for me, but it wasn't always easy for them to keep me in it. There were times when the public story became the de facto truth, and I ceased to exist at all.

I remember one conference call when the new Minister of Foreign Affairs, Peter McKay,[8] repeatedly referred to Jim as "your son." No one on the call spoke up for me. Corroding with self-doubt and self-reproach, I agonized: do I speak up, or do I let this ride? Why make a fuss in the midst of a life-or-death situation? Because this was "behind the scenes," it was a place where I should be acknowledged. But if I did speak up, would I run the risk of alienating myself from Jim's family and the government? I chose not to speak, fearing I would be viewed as shrill and demanding, pumping my selfish "gay agenda" when Jim's life was on the line.

While Jim's parents were taping their first appeal for Jim, then Prime Minister Paul Martin called them. He said the government was doing everything it could. He never called me, reinforcing to Jim's parents, and to me, that I did not exist.

Why was it so difficult to be seen? When Jim filled out his passport application, he listed me as his next of kin, but then he wrote "friend" instead of "spouse" on the emergency contact line (though he was always very public about our relationship). Maybe Peter McKay and Paul Martin had never been told about me? Maybe FAC didn't know who I was because the RCMP didn't tell them, or maybe they decided they could overlook what was on the passport application without making an inquiry. Or maybe they couldn't see me because of the powerful public story being told. Maybe someone somewhere didn't want me to be who I was.

---

worked constantly, more than I can ever know, to bring him home safely. I was and am amazed at the level of commitment and support provided by the Canadian government and by the goodness of the staff who supported us.

[8] Stephen Harper was elected Prime Minister during the kidnapping and subsequently introduced a motion to reopen the debate on same-sex marriage. Minister McKay voted against the motion.

Or maybe it was none of these. This is exactly how discrimination works: you receive the impact of it without knowing the real cause. You burn inside, wonder why your partner didn't fill out the form the way you would have liked him to, yet understanding, at the same time, why he didn't. You remember what it was like the first time you indicated that a man was your spouse on a form with no category for him and were asked about it in front of everyone in the crowded reception room. You understand how deeply rooted homophobia is within yourself.

I still find it difficult to dissect the various levels of homophobia that I experienced during the kidnapping. The impact of being erased in the national media is difficult to explain. All the significant family members of the hostages were able to speak of their love and concern, and to receive the immense public outpouring of support that was generated. I could not, and neither could Jim's closest friends at the Catholic Worker in Toronto, even as they radically altered their lives to respond to the kidnapping. Homophobia rendered us invisible.

The media is very powerful. It shapes the way we view the world and the way we experience ourselves in it. Though I knew a myth was being created, it was difficult not to let the myth have the power of truth. Media coverage of the kidnapping was so intense that not being included in it began to annihilate me—especially because my behind-the-scenes experience often paralleled my public disappearance.

At a certain point in the kidnapping, family members of the hostages exchanged contact information. I kept my name off the list. I worried that knowing about Jim's queerness might cause other families to worry unnecessarily. Even in the very small world of the hostages' families, I chose not to exist, at least for a while.

When I went downtown for the vigil following Tom's death, I watched from a distance of a hundred yards until the vigil was well under way. The media were there and so were my friends. I did not want them to pay undue attention to me in front of the media. The myth became my reality over and over. I could not exist, therefore I did not exist.

My experience of being disappeared gave me a window into the experience of people who are discounted altogether by the media version of the world. At one point in the kidnapping, I could not hold back. I wrote a letter to the editor of the Globe and Mail "as a dear friend of Jim Loney" about an article that referred to the "alleged abuse" of detainees in Iraq. I was amazed that even after Abu Ghraib, which CPT played an important role in helping to expose, the word "alleged" could be used. The very existence of detainees and the torture that defines their lives was subtly and insidiously questioned, an example of the power of the mainstream media to disappear something and shape a different reality.

Throughout the kidnapping, as Jim's community and I prayed in our nightly vigils, we came to be in solidarity with everyone who had loved ones imprisoned in Iraq and were powerless to effect any change whatsoever. We were, with them, suspended in a limbo of grief and terror. We knew what it was like to fear that a loved one might disappear, to never know what had happened to him or her. We had our own taste of utter marginalization and powerlessness.

Ironically I suspect that the secondary ordeal for Jim's family was contending with their media experience—being exposed, their family life suddenly a public matter, their emotional reaction to the kidnapping fodder for front pages and nightly news. They shouldered this work effortlessly, sharing their lives and their grief so that it might help Jim come home. The entire community of Sault Ste. Marie united around them. Under the pressure of this intense scrutiny, they maintained the dignity of their lives and managed elegantly to live as themselves.

I know they worked during the kidnapping to overcome our awkward history, to keep their hearts open to me. In the period after Tom's death, Jim's mom checked up on me. I had many good conversations with her. A member of Jim's family e-mailed me to apologize after the conversation with the Minister of Foreign Affairs. Sometimes I allowed my anger to overshadow the positive movement taking place, and I did not always keep a space open within myself for Jim's family.

In the end, Jim came home to all of us who love him. The extended Catholic Worker community crowded into our living room and welcomed him home. In the long drive to the Sault, Jim was able to tell me his story from beginning to end. In the Sault, people didn't disown him when they learned he was gay; they kept their welcome signs up in windows and storefronts everywhere. At church that first Sunday, everyone who gave Jim a welcome-home hug gave me one too. We received only one hate call, though the CPT office received many.

We deferred the press conference as long as we could. When it finally happened, Jim's mom thanked everyone who had given help and said she was proud of all of her children and their chosen partners. The evening prior in Jim's sister's home, we squeezed around one table for supper. During grace, someone gave thanks that we were all, all of us, finally together.

At that press conference, when I spoke publicly for the first time, I read a poem that I dedicated to Jim's family. It was the one I had sent to Baghdad in December, via a letter the RCMP said would be given to Jim in the event he was released. It's one of Jim's favorite poems, "The Great Day" by Carl Dennis. It reads in part:

Can you will yourself to see a common day
The way... the dead might see it...
The day their ship, long given up for lost,
Steams into the harbor, all flags flying...
Down the gangway they come,
A little thinner, a little unsteady,
Eyes wide in wonder at their rare good fortune.
Can you see what they see as they look around
Or feel what their friends waiting on the dock
Must feel as they run forward?
"Let me look at you," they keep saying,
Suspending their formal speech of welcome.
"You look good. You look wonderful."[9]

I sometimes wonder if the diminishment and debasement I endured would have been washed away in a single moment, had Jim and I held hands, walking towards the thousand cameras, when he arrived home at the airport, or if we'd embraced in front of everyone. But we didn't. It would have been unnatural for us. Our own coming out hadn't brought us that far. The terrible violence of being silenced was more dominant than the freedom we had thus far acquired.

"Silence equals death." It was the rallying cry of the queer community as it faced the AIDS crisis. It's a statement of truth. Non-recognition, disappearance, invisibility are violence that can eradicate one's very being.

"Let me look at you," the poet says. We must, all of us, learn to have eyes that see, and ears that hear, lest we condemn those we do not see or hear to a living death. It will only be when everyone is finally held with the words, "You look good. You look wonderful," that the Great Day will have arrived.

Dan Hunt lives in Toronto, Ontario, as a neighbor to the Catholic Worker community. Following the kidnapping and return of his partner Jim Loney, Dan took some time away from his work as a director of finance and administration in a Community Health Centre. He is currently working in Canada's largest shelter for homeless men where he is supporting the startup of a unique model for the provision of medical services to men in the shelter.

---

[9] "The Great Day," from RANKING THE WISHES by Carl Dennis, copyright ©1997 by Carl Dennis. Used by permission of Penguin, a division of Penguin Group (USA) Inc.

11

When Harmeet Is Free

Donna Mulhearn

"I will be good," I promised God as tears fell down my cheeks. "If you let Harmeet live, I will do what I have to do. I will do the right thing. Anything."

On my knees through those long, restless nights, I wondered what others had pledged to God, what deals had been made in desperation to see their loved ones free. I had spent much of December numb, January with red, swollen eyes, February and March in a daze.

Harmeet went to Iraq after I had suggested CPT as the safest way to go, based on my own experience of living as an activist/aid worker in Baghdad. He trusted my opinion. Because of this, he was sitting in chains somewhere in Baghdad. My only postcard of his trip would come from the hostage takers, in the form of a grainy televised image of Harmeet, pale and thin.

I knew he wouldn't blame me, and that he would be okay. That's what I told myself anyway, a hundred times a day—for 118 long, dark days.

Though Harmeet was in captivity in Baghdad, I sent him e-mails every few days from my home in a quiet monastery in the Australian countryside. He was suffering the cold of an Iraqi winter; I was suffering the heat of an Australian summer. We were thousands of miles apart, but I had never felt more connected.

In the e-mails I updated Harmeet on what was going on, what people were saying, what I was feeling. At times perhaps I went too far, said too much; such times made me wonder if he would ever read the e-mails at all. I regretted not saying these things to him in person. Why hadn't I? Why hold back until death hangs over us?

When death hovers, one re-evaluates life. I started phoning friends I hadn't seen for a while, started being nicer to my mum. I started appreciating more the beauty around me, saying things from my heart to loved ones. The time was intense, disturbing yet profound.

Harmeet was a friend because he was a kindred spirit, someone who inspired me to be more peaceful. He challenged me. Even held captive in a room in Baghdad, he still challenged me. I couldn't cope with the thought of not having him around in the future. The thought was too dark to entertain. The times I did contemplate it were the times when I lost it.

I first met Harmeet in the West Bank of Palestine. He was sitting across the table from me at the start of a nonviolence training session in Ramallah. It was December 2004; we were both in Palestine as volunteers with the International Solidarity Movement, eager to learn more about the occupation of Palestine and how to help the Palestinians in their nonviolent resistance to it.

I remember thinking he had a beautiful face, like a pixie: a permanent grin and a twinkle in his eye. Everyone had to tell him "speak up" because his voice was so soft, an expression of his amazingly gentle nature.

I remember how, when we shared our hopes and fears about working in Palestine, my fear included my impatience. I was worried I would get angry at soldiers and settlers. Harmeet feared not being forceful enough! Because we seemed to complement each other, we stuck together. One day I captured a beautiful picture of Harmeet with Palestinian children near Jenin, his smile as wide as ever.

When he left Palestine, he e-mailed me every few days with messages of support from New Zealand: I still have the smell of Palestine on my blue shirt... and I won't forget my duty while I'm here.

When I got home, we stayed in touch. Harmeet sent me all manner of interesting messages: articles, Buddhist prayers, stories about his life. Once he sent me a photograph he had taken of a kettle (yes, a kettle), with the caption "Something to make you laugh." Looking at the picture of an elegant, shiny old kettle sitting on a stove, thinking of his care in taking the picture, the simple beauty of it, his appreciation of the kettle, and his desire to share it with me, all had the desired effect—it made me laugh all day.

When, in May 2005, I sent out the story of my friend Marla Ruzicka, who had been killed in Iraq, Harmeet responded: I am sorry for the loss of your friend Marla. I have a candle here, in my room. It is for all the forgotten. I will light it tonight and every night.

Harmeet's peaceful nature was a guide for me. I considered Harmeet an enlightened soul and wise beyond his 32 years. In an e-mail he sent me from Iraq a day before he was kidnapped, he expressed more care and concern for me than for himself. Typical.

I had a brief visit with Harmeet in Auckland in August 2005. It was then that he told me he had decided to go to Iraq. I was surprised; it had been months since he'd first asked me about it. He had obviously thought it through and made a careful decision.

Harmeet's small university apartment was cluttered with all manner of artifacts: African art and masks. His life was busy with studies, playing squash, and helping to establish a Palestinian solidarity group on campus.

Despite his full schedule, he invested time maintaining friendships with people all over the world. I left him feeling hopeful and invigorated.

The next time I saw Harmeet was on the six o'clock news.

His face was pale but calm as he stood with his captors, the Swords of Righteousness.

At first the kidnappers accused the four of being spies and threatened to kill them within days if all Iraqi prisoners were not released from U.S. and Iraqi jails. Knowing firsthand the work of CPT, I found this claim frustrating. I had worked alongside CPT during my trips to Baghdad and have always admired their courageous and effective work.

I knew three of the four men taken; I fondly remembered Jim Loney asking if he could spend time with the street kids in our Baghdad shelter. He would come to play soccer with them and hang out.

These men—Harmeet, Jim, Tom and Norman—were compassionate peacemakers. They could not be spies.

So what we had, I figured, was a misunderstanding.

I watched as Arab and Muslim brothers and sisters across the Middle East and around the world mobilized in a bid to correct the misunderstanding, to show support for the men, and to appeal to their captors. Three of the four men had spent time in Palestine.

The International Solidarity Movement used its networks to try to influence the captors. I sent them my picture of Harmeet in Jenin, apparently the most recent photo of him. It was used on their website; then I saw it in newspapers, TV news reports, and websites around the world. After sending it out from my monastery in the countryside, I smiled each time it came back to me, which felt like a thousand times.

"When Harmeet is free, we will laugh about this," I told myself. "We will laugh and then demand a commission for every picture."

"When Harmeet is free." I preceded so many thoughts with these words, thoughts of what he might do ... "when Harmeet is free."

As we prayed for Harmeet, Jim, Tom, Norman and their families, I felt it was crucial to pray also for their captors – for their transformation and for the transformation of all of us to see beyond "us and them," to recognize the humanity in the other.

It was hard to think of anything I could do in the situation, but I prayed and urged others to pray. In January, at the end of my tether, I organized to send a personal appeal by video to Al-Jazeera. I had appeared on Iraqi TV before in my capacity as a human shield and aid worker. Some Iraqis thought it might help.

The cost of sending the video via satellite to the Middle East was funded by the Islamic Friendship Association. Appearing with me on the video was Australia's most prominent Muslim, Keysad Trad, who had never met Harmeet but had heard of CPT. He wanted to show support and spoke directly to the hostage takers in Arabic, and in no uncertain terms.

After we sent the video, my state of numbness returned. I knew people would ask, "How are you? Any news of your friend in Baghdad?" I wanted to yell back, "How do you think I am? If there was news, don't you think I would have told you?"

But Harmeet would not have wanted that. The thought of his gentle nature helped tame my fiery one. I felt I would have to tell him all this, to be accountable to him, so I answered quietly, "There's still no news. Please keep praying."

I did many media interviews, especially with New Zealand media who were eager for a contact who could talk about Harmeet as a friend. I was happy to oblige. It gave me the chance to highlight issues Harmeet was concerned about.

"What would he be thinking right now?" the reporters asked.

I had often thought about this. I answered, "He'd be very embarrassed about the fuss and attention on him, but he'd want us to think about the Iraqis held captive in prison cells or captive by the violence of Baghdad. He'd also be deep in thought as to how he might use this experience to further peace in the world."

Talking about Harmeet helped me. I wanted everyone to know about him and what he was like. At the dinner table I told stories over and over, so that my friends came to know Harmeet themselves. His candle was beside my bed, along with the now famous picture and an African mask he gave me. I lit the candle every night.

I was also keen to connect with others who knew him. Edwina, a peace activist called regularly from New Zealand to mull things over, to talk about Harmeet, to plan what we would do when he was released.

She called me with news one night in March.

I didn't believe it at first. I wanted to see it in print, in black and white. With shaking hands and a pounding heart, I raced to my computer. Thanks to the Internet, the news was confirmed within minutes: Harmeet was free. He was alive. I was free, too.

Several tearful phone calls to friends and many hours of jumping up and down followed. I went outside to be alone. Gazing at the stars, I smiled and wept.

I heard Harmeet's voice in a phone call from the Middle East a day or so later, and I prepared to travel to New Zealand for his return.

There he was: thin, cautious, but with a smile ever ready.

He was barraged with media. He seemed shell-shocked, but ever calm. I listened to his stories and looked through his captivity diary. He shared many experiences from his time "in the can," as he described it—

some of them funny, all profound. But there was one topic he could not discuss easily: Tom. His silence revealed the pain he felt at Tom's death.

I was right about what Harmeet was thinking "in the can" and what he thinks now. As he lights a candle for the forgotten in the world, he wants us to remember those whom he remembers, those who are still in captivity. He wants us to ask ourselves how we can further peace in the world.

He inspires still.

Former journalist and political adviser Donna Mulhearn served as a human shield during the war in Iraq. She later returned to Iraq as a humanitarian aid worker to set up a shelter for street kids in Baghdad and to support refugee families. She also spent four months in the West Bank of Palestine with the International Solidarity Movement. Donna is now a writer and speaker on nonviolence, contemplative spirituality, and politics. She recently faced trial and prison time after breaking into US Spy Base, Pine Gap, to do a Citizen's Inspection.

12

Reflections from the Edge:
The Friends and Supporters of Norman Kember

Pat Gaffney

What a difference a day makes in our work for peace. On March 22, 2006, we held our weekly vigil in solidarity with our Christian Peacemaker Team friends held captive in Iraq. The following morning they were released, without word or warning. One hundred and eighteen days of captivity had ended with tears of joy and prayers of thanksgiving.

Norman Kember, the British man who was held with Jim Loney, Harmeet Sooden, and Tom Fox, is a friend and partner of Pax Christi and a trustee of our Peace Education Committee. In August 2005 I heard of his plans to visit Iraq to learn more about the on-the-ground work of CPT and that his visit was undertaken in part on behalf of the Fellowship of Reconciliation (FOR) England.

With so many others, I was stunned when, on November 26, news of his kidnapping broke. Bruce Kent, a mutual friend and one of the most prominent voices for peace in the United Kingdom, relayed the news to me. I immediately called Chris Cole, director of the FOR England, asking if he could shed light on the unfolding story. Why had our friends been taken? Who had taken them and what was their motivation? I kept my radio on through the night.

As friends of Norman, my and others' first thoughts were for his safety and for the peace of mind of his wife, Pat. But where to begin supporting her? The press was providing us with the little information we had about the kidnapping. Was there a distinct role Pax Christi should play at this time? We knew of Norman's commitment to peacemaking and nonviolence, but little about the terms and reality of his visit to Iraq.

Circumstance soon set the agenda for our responses. On November 29, the first video footage of the hostages appeared on Al Jazeera television and was broadcast throughout the United Kingdom. The blurry images of the four men served as a reality check. The footage brought with it another wave of media contact. We were riddled with questions: "How do you think Norman is coping?" "How do you think he looked?" "What do you feel when you see the men?" But how were we to answer? We could do little more than speculate and hope.

By this time, friends from other Christian peace organizations were in contact with us: Sue Claydon from the Anglican Pacifist Fellowship, Gillian Collins, the secretary of the Baptist Peace Fellowship (BPF) and a good friend of the Kembers; and Tim Nafziger, the CPT link at the London Mennonite Centre.

On December 2, we held the first national vigil for the four men, bringing together Christians and Muslims on the steps of St. Martin in the Fields in Trafalgar Square, London. Similar vigils were held in Bradford, Derby, and Oxford. These first vigils took place during Advent, and the Scripture themes and timing of Advent provided a fitting spiritual focus for our work—waiting and watching in the hope of something good, something new.

That night another video appeared on Al Jazeera. It announced the first deadline for a response to the kidnappers' demands: December 8.

Keeping hope alive

Around this time, we realized we needed to join energies—to support one another, to share our reactions and responses, and to determine how best to work. Sue and Gillian along with Steve Whiting and Marigold Bentley of Quaker Peace & Social Witness joined this first "core group" meeting in early December. Our common denominator was our personal connection to Norman and the fact that we had all worked with him in various ways over the years.

The meeting was like piecing together a jigsaw puzzle, trying to form as complete a picture as possible of what was happening. We discovered that Norman had undertaken a radio interview with the Christian Premier radio station prior to his departure. The interview, in which he spoke of his motivation for going to Iraq and of his understanding of the reality he might face, proved helpful. Tim tracked down photographs and biographies of the other hostages, which were added to leaflets we handed out and briefings posted on the Internet.

We became aware that the Muslim communities in the United Kingdom and Palestine were prepared to offer support and solidarity. Anas Altikriti, the former president of the Muslim Association of Britain and himself an Iraqi, planned a visit to Baghdad to try to persuade the captors that the four hostages were not spies. Mufti Ikrema Sabri, a top-ranking Palestinian cleric, issued a statement calling for their release. And through our international links, Pax Christi secured a message and call for release from the Latin Patriarch of Jerusalem, Michel Sabbah, himself a Palestinian and president of Pax Christi.

Clarity began to develop from this meeting. Out of the tragedy of the kidnapping, many people were given an opportunity to communicate a message about nonviolent peacemaking, accompaniment, and witness in Iraq. We all worked to convey the message that Norman, Tom, Harmeet, and James were men of peace, committed to nonviolence, to convey their and our continued concern for the people of Iraq and the violence and injustice they are exposed to on a daily basis as a result of war and occupation.

We needed to "locate" Norman's peace work, both within the organizations he supported—the BPF, FOR, and Pax Christi—and within his family and church community. We were aware that whatever we communicated through the press and media could make its way, via Al Jazeera and other press networks, to Iraq.

A loose plan of action and response was established. We would log approaches taken with the media, and coordinate vigils and press work. We would produce a common resource—a leaflet—for use at vigils and gatherings. We would maintain contact with Pat Kember and Norman's church community. All this was a tall order for a small group of people working within fragile and under-resourced organizations!

Support and solidarity grow

With the airing of the third Al Jazeera video, which set the first deadline, anxiety grew. We were in for a long haul. Despite Tim's best efforts as the CPT contact in London, the lack of a stronger, authoritative voice from CPT in the United Kingdom updating us and the press on CPT's work in Iraq and the hostage crisis, we found it difficult to set Norman's involvement in the Iraq delegation in its correct and full context.

We produced a new leaflet including photos of all four hostages and basic information about CPT's work in Iraq. We used the leaflet to multiply our efforts. We invited people to organize public vigils in their town centers, which happened in many places. Our websites became an important channel of communication and support around the country.

Talking with Pat on the phone one day, following one of her own broadcasts on Al Jazeera, I became aware of the depth of public concern for the hostages. She was overwhelmed by the volume of messages, cards, and flowers she was receiving from the United Kingdom and beyond— some from friends with whom she had lost contact and many from strangers who wanted to express concern and support.

We relocated our weekly London vigil to the north end of Trafalgar Square to allow more people to join and to be more visible to passersby. The winter nights were bitterly cold, yet a faithful core gathered each week to stand in silence with torches for light, holding images of the men and colorful rainbow peace flags. We would end our time in reflection, perhaps using the Litany of Prayer for Peace and the Four Men from CPT or an interfaith prayer or words taken from the writings and reflections on peacemaking by Tom and Norman.

Friends and parishioners from Norman's home church joined each week and relayed messages and encouragement back to Pat and their wider congregation. We knew that Rob Gardiner, the minister at Norman's church, was himself fully taken up in supporting Pat, fielding the press, and engaging his own church community in times of prayer and support.

The first deadline passed, then the second, and still no news. Christmas was approaching, and the twenty-fifth day of the abduction of the men fell on December 21. On this night, our vigil and others around the country attracted a great deal of media attention. We stressed that our gatherings were a reminder of the people of Iraq and of all the people of good will—regardless of faith or tradition—who work for peace in that country.

During Christmas week, a daytime vigil in Trafalgar Square attracted more people than usual, and it was at this meeting that our Muslim friend Anas Altikriti spoke of his visit to Iraq and the work he had undertaken there, setting up phone hotlines by which callers could share information about the men and their whereabouts. It was not until much later that we discovered his visit had entailed great risk. One of the group accompanying Anas had been killed. Anas's support and the encouragement from the Muslim community were greatly valued.

The markers of Christmas and New Year had come and gone. Our concern for Pat and Norman's family was growing. We knew they had contact with the Foreign and Commonwealth Office (FCO) and with a police support team, but had little sense of how this was helping or supporting them. It seemed strange that neither the FCO nor the police support team attempted to contact us. We, the group of spokespeople from three or four Christian peace groups, had no idea of whether the actions we were encouraging and the statements we were making were of help or hindrance. I did at one point make contact with the police support team, but received little feedback on what we were doing. Neither did we receive much guidance from CPT itself. So our discernment in the crisis response group became more important, as did the personal support we could offer one another.

In mid-January religious leaders in the United States issued an open letter on the plight of Iraqi detainees, challenging the abuse of prisoners. It also called for the release of the four men. This letter sparked the idea of drafting something similar in the United Kingdom. We wrote a short open letter to Tony Blair that focused on the conduct and actions of our own military in Iraq and a plea for Iraqi detainees and our four friends. We circulated it to religious leaders for their support. This caused a flurry of activity as we identified sympathetic leaders and planned a press conference. Our particular aim was to use the letter for media work within the Middle East, to have it shared there in the hope that those holding the men would see people working for peace and justice for Iraq.

In just a few days, we secured forty names: Anglican and Catholic bishops, free-church leaders, Muslim leaders and academics, and more. The press conference took place on February 6 at the Foreign Press Association in Central London. Al Jazeera covered the meeting, as did an Iranian reporter, the Voice of America, and an international Christian weekly. The open letter became a useful resource when talking to national, local, and church press contacts.

Weekly vigils and acts of witness and worship continued around the country. In addition, we heard of other initiatives: the communities of elderly sisters holding the men in daily prayer; the school children sending letters to Pat; the churches where photographs of the men were prominently displayed as a focus for candle lighting and prayer. Norman, Tom, James, and Harmeet were very much in the public mind and heart.

One hundred days

How to mark the one-hundredth day of our friends' abduction became our next focus—as an important day in itself and as another "hook" to engage public and press interest. Could we release a hundred white doves? Could we project images of the men onto buildings in Trafalgar Square? Could we mobilize thousands of people to join us? Our imaginations and humor carried us away and a plan developed.

Gillian Collins of the Baptist Peace Fellowship proposed that we engage every Baptist church in vigils and prayer on Saturday, March 4, the day before the hundred-day anniversary. On each of our websites, we offered a special hundredth-day leaflet that could be downloaded for use at local vigils. We planned a vigil in Trafalgar Square for the afternoon of the hundredth day, March 5, with the focus on hope and release. We produced a hundred white cutout doves for children and adults to hold and wave. We produced a massive 100 DAYS banner as a focal point. Pat sent a message to those supporting vigils around the country.

We had all made one hundred days and were in for a long haul.

Broken spirits

When Tom Fox was missing from the images on Al Jazeera March 7, our hearts sank. What did this mean? Another round of second-guessing began.

News of Tom's death broke early on Saturday, March 10. It left us numb. Concern for Tom's family and for Pat was uppermost in our minds.

111

We later discovered that the FCO had contacted Pat prior to the story breaking in the press—this at least would have saved her the shock of hearing it via the media. But then I knew that part of Pat's preservation mechanism was not viewing or listening to the news.

Once again, we were aware of the vulnerability of the four men.

Taking nothing for granted

Like I said, what a difference a day makes. On March 22, the usual crowd gathered for the weekly vigil, the only change being that the evenings were getting brighter. We left with the usual greeting, "See you next week."

Imagine the joy, disbelief, excitement, and bewilderment that followed the next morning! The men had been released. Still at home and hardly able to watch the news unfold, I tried, as did other members of our crisis group, to field constant press calls for interviews. As before, it was the press who were informing us of what had happened. All we could do was share reactions of joy and thanksgiving.

However, another surprise was in store: the about-turn taken by the press in less than twenty-four hours. Following the release of the three men, the media turned from being sympathetic and understanding to downright hostile. I found it hard to keep my cool when interviewed by U.S. TV and the U.K.'s Channel 4 News. Norman had not even arrived back in the country and the media were trying to humiliate him and his project, to charge him with being foolish and naïve, and to accuse him of being ungrateful.

Why was this so? Was it because Norman still challenged the legitimacy of the occupation of Iraq? Was it because, while Norman thanked the military personnel and diplomats involved in securing his release, he still affirmed that real peace cannot come by military means or armed force? Norman expressed some of this in the statement he read on his arrival at Heathrow airport: "It is the ordinary people of Iraq you should be talking to—the people who have suffered so much over the years and still await the stable and just society they deserve."

This hostility offered another opportunity for members of our group to talk about the nonviolent Christian witness of these men and of the CPT approach to peace work. Having lived through 118 days of fear, loss, and anxiety in hopeful prayer and fellowship, we knew we must also give thanks with prayer. Thousands of people had been touched by this experience, new friendships and alliances had been forged—among the most significant being those with the Muslim community. So it was that our last vigil was held in Trafalgar Square on March 29. To our surprise, more people turned up for this vigil than ever.

What have I learned?

First, I learned that we need one another in the work for peace. No matter how long we may think we have "been around," new things will arise to surprise us. The crisis response group became an important point of reference for support, encouragement, discernment, and humor, and was extraordinarily productive. We accomplished a huge amount with little backup. Much of the ordinary work of our already small and overstretched organizations was put on hold or took a back seat during this crisis. We would not have had it any other way. But could we have sustained this had the crisis continued or worsened?

My second bit of learning is that things could have been different. We need not have been "surprised" and unprepared. Perhaps we should have been more quizzical of Norman before his departure, talking with him about his expectations and the various "what if" scenarios that such a visit could bring.

Which leads to my third bit of learning, that CPT missed an opportunity by not being more "on the ground" in the United Kingdom to raise the CPT's profile throughout the crisis and to so build a stronger base for itself here. But CPT is small and did not have the resources to respond. We all have much to learn and communicate to others about what it means to "give of oneself" in the CPT model of "getting in the way." Perhaps the time is ripe to bring together different models of witness and accompaniment that are now offered from within the United Kingdom.

Finally, I have had affirmed that the media are fickle. We must not allow them to set our agenda as we work for peace. We were well aware of the game that is played: news makes news and creates its own spin. What is "good news" one day is ridiculed on another. Without a press office, without spin doctors or PR people, I believe we did a great job in maintaining the integrity of the witness and message of Norman, Tom, Harmeet, and James.

Perhaps our weakness was, in the end, our greatest strength.

Pat Gaffney has been general secretary of the British section of Pax Christi, an international Catholic movement for peace, since 1990. Her role involves advocacy and education work on issues of violence, war, nonviolence, and peacemaking. Pat's work has taken her on solidarity visits and exchanges to Russia, East Timor, and Israel-Palestine. She has also been involved for many years in acts of nonviolent resistance to nuclear weapons, which have led to arrests on twelve occasions and imprisonment on three. In 2005 Pat was one of the 1,000 Women for Peace nominated for the Nobel Peace Prize.

13

Revisiting Courage Inside San Quentin State Prison

Watani Stiner

Before getting up from my narrow prison bunk, I reached toward the wall
and pushed the button on my radio. My cellmate had already gone, working
as an infirmary clerk and having been released about twenty minutes before.
Conveniently our work schedules allowed us enough individual cell time
(and space) to privately prepare for work. I made my way toward the small,
stainless-steel sink to wash my face and brush my teeth. While letting the
hot water run in preparation for my ritual morning coffee, I listened to the
news on KPFA, an "alternative" radio station.

Radio talk show host Amy Goodman of *Democracy Now* reported on
the escalating violence in Iraq and four recent kidnappings in Baghdad.
Along with a rising demand for foreign-troop withdrawal from Iraqi soil,
there had been several graphic videos of decapitation.

I listened carefully as Amy named the four men: Harmeet Sooden,
Jim Loney, Norman Kember, and an American named Tom Fox. All four
were abducted by a group calling itself the Swords of Righteousness
Brigade. And Amy said, "The kidnappers had threatened to kill their
hostages unless all prisoners in U.S. and Iraqi detention centers were
released by December 8." That was three days ago.

Interestingly these four men were not armed soldiers, occupying
the streets of Baghdad. They were not journalists, seeking to secure a major
story. Nor were they contract workers, lured to a volatile war zone by
prospects of higher-paying salaries. These four peace activists traveled to
Iraq with a commitment to work with families of prisoners and to promote
peace.

My immediate thoughts upon hearing of these four seemingly
adventurous "religious zealots" going to a Muslim-dominated country to
voluntarily inject themselves into a violent situation was that either they
were foolhardy or suicidal, or both. Nowhere in my mind could this foolish
act of "peaceful" intervention be construed as courage. For me, courage is
about meeting challenges, persevering in the face of difficulty, danger, and
even death—not voluntarily jumping into a quagmire in a fanatical effort to
"convert the heathens."

It wasn't until listening to and participating in a conversation with two incarcerated friends that I realized I had overlooked an important attribute of courage.

After the prison population count had cleared and the bars were pulled for our release, I met up with two of my back-in-the-day friends, one of whom is currently serving a twenty-five-years-to-life sentence on a nonviolent third-strike conviction. For the purpose of this story, I will call him "Butch."

Butch is an abrasive individual who prides himself on being a self-proclaimed prison philosopher, full of witty sound bites and sweeping positions on every aspect of life. Butch was found guilty of cashing a stolen 250-dollar check. "Can you believe that, man!" Butch will say. "Twenty-five years to life for one lousy stolen check! I didn't kill anybody! I'm a damn political prisoner!"

My other friend, "Jamie," is sixty years old, Hep-C positive, diabetic, and suffering from high blood pressure. Jamie has been incarcerated for over twenty-seven years and, following a medical diagnosis, swore never to allow himself to die in prison. Over the past decade, the three of us have become close companions.

My own journey to and from prison (and back again) is perhaps an unusual one. After graduating from high school, I was taken with the idea that I could make a difference in the world by challenging an unjust and racist society. Subsequently I joined Maulana Ron Karenga's Us organization, a Black cultural nationalist group. Maulana's oratorical style, leadership skills, and comprehensive "Kawaida" doctrine captured my rage and fueled my imagination. Without question, I considered myself a dedicated and totally committed member, willing to sacrifice anything for our cause. According to my revolutionary belief system at the time, "self-defense" legitimized acts of violence committed for the cause.

I am currently serving a life sentence for conspiracy to murder in the 1969 shooting death of two Black Panthers on the UCLA campus. Although I was not convicted of the actual shooting, my affiliation with the militant Us organization, coupled with documented acts of FBI provocation, enabled the district attorney to implicate me in an elaborate conspiracy theory.

In 1974, I escaped from San Quentin State Prison to save my life. The violence and racial tensions in the prison at that time had resulted in more than one attempt on my life. I fled the country to South America, where I lived in exile for twenty years. After an outbreak of cholera, malaria, and civil war, bringing economic devastation to the small, "structurally adjusted" country of Suriname, I entered the U.S. embassy and negotiated my surrender. I agreed to give myself up in exchange for U.S. assurances that my destitute family—six children, all American citizens by virtue of my citizenship, and a Surinamese wife and her son—would be cared for and allowed to emigrate to the United States. Upon my signature, the agreement was supposedly sealed.

Weeks after my voluntary surrender and subsequent reincarceration, however, I learned that the United States government had reneged on its part of the deal. It would be another twelve years (from the time of my surrender) before I would see my family again. Thus, throughout my life's journey, I have formulated justifications for hatred and the use of violence. I have also revisited different ideas of courage.

About a year and a half ago, and with some begrudging on Jamie's part, Butch and I entered into a pact regarding Jamie's health: We would see that he controlled his diet and monitored his daily consumption of water. Butch and I also agreed to keep Jamie company on daily walks that we cajoled him to take on the lower yard, committing ourselves to certain days. Monday, Tuesday, and Wednesday were Butch's days to walk with Jamie. Thursday, Friday, and Saturday were mine. Sunday was designated church-and-rest day. Jamie's end of the deal merely required him to show up.

"ID cards!" demanded the guard standing at the security gate. The three of us passed the small guard post and headed down the concrete stairs to the lower yard.

Seemingly out of nowhere, in an angry, harsh tone, Jamie blurted out, "Why do these people like to stick their noses in places where they ain't welcome? That's just plain stupid!"

My eyes connected with Butch's; both of us were baffled by Jamie's comment. We waited a few silent seconds for more information.

"A bunch of idealistic fools, that's what they are!" Jamie continued. Still no hints. "They should have known better!"

More silence.

I'd had enough suspense. "Man, what are you talking about, Jamie?" Both my curiosity and frustration were rising. "You're getting yourself all worked up about something, and we're supposed to guess what it is? Now you know that ain't good for your blood pressure."

"I'm talking about the news, man! The news!" he shouted. "Don't ya listen to the news?"

"One more time now," Butch said. "What are you talking about?" He guessed, "Rachel Corrie?" a news story we were quite familiar with, having debated the subject at length two or three years ago.

"No! Not her!" responded Jamie, noticeably frustrated that we had no idea what he was talking about. "I'm talking about those four people who got themselves kidnapped in Iraq. Those Christian peacemaker people. Now, why would anyone just voluntarily walk into a trap like that?"

It was not at all surprising that Jamie held the same views about the four Christian peacemakers that he'd held about Rachel Corrie: theirs was a fruitless mission. "Anything could go wrong, and usually does," attested Jamie, drawing from his own experience.

A spirited young peace activist with the International Solidarity Movement, twenty-three-year-old Rachel Corrie had volunteered to travel from the United States to Israel to help promote peace and ensure justice for the Palestinian people. Defiantly opposing the bulldozing of a Palestinian home, young Rachel nonviolently intervened and was callously killed.

"Aren't those kidnapped men Christians on some religious mission?" I asked.

"No, they are idealistic fools, they're on a suicide mission!"

Butch finally connected, recalling the broad news coverage. "Oh that! I saw that on the news too. Why didn't you just say that in the first place? Those Christian Peacemaking Army—or something like that."

"That's what I've been talking about. Haven't y'all been listening?"

"You think they're all dead?" inquired Butch.

"Nobody really knows," Jamie answered. "They're still missing. One of them, I think the one from the U.S., was the only one shown in the video. He had a hood over his head."

"Oh, yeah, I saw that too," I said. "They were talking about it on KPFA last week. They don't know where the other three are. They could be dead. Plus the deadline for the U.S. to release all Iraqi prisoners in U.S. and Iraqi detention has already expired."

Jamie started to increase his pace, more out of anger than for exercise. The tone of his voice commanded our attention. "Why would they go all the way over there in the first place?" Jamie could not shake the question. "So many ways to lose your life. Why give it away voluntarily? Once you're dead, you're dead!"

Realizing that history is replete with Christian missionaries going about trying to "civilize the heathens," I had formed my own opinion about the four Christian peacemakers: "People should have the right to believe in whatever they want," I said. "Christians shouldn't be in Iraq trying to convert Muslims."

"What I think the problem really boils down to," Butch stated with certainty, "is that those peace activists are nothing but pacifists. They wouldn't be in the situation they're in if they'd stop praising the Lord and start passing the ammunition." Butch thought that statement was truly profound.

Thoughts, not intended for words, slipped out of my mouth. "What would cause someone to take another person's life?" At the end of those words, an eerie silence settled among us. For the second time, we reached the out-of-bounds line and turned around to continue our walk in the opposite direction.

After careful consideration, Jamie spoke somberly about his crime. "I'm in here because I took another man's life," he said. "I didn't intend to do it, but it just happened." Butch and I listened. "I could never give that life back. If you ask me, sometimes it has to do with being in the wrong place at the wrong time."

Although I hadn't particularly understood or agreed with the nonviolent philosophy and tactics of Christian Peacemaker Teams in going to Iraq, what I'd read and heard over the radio compelled me to revisit my assumptions about courage.

I suddenly realized we were slowing down again. "Walk-up!" I urged, seizing the opportunity to pick up the pace—and the controversy. I wondered about this word *courage* and what Butch and Jamie had thought about it. After all, it does take a lot of *something* to peacefully venture into a violent situation. I decided to provoke some answers by playing devil's advocate.

"Peace by any means necessary!" I declared with my two fingers displaying the peace sign.

"Peace? You can't get no peace without some firepower. That's the only lasting means to achieve peace." Jamie was certain. "Because those who have the weapons are the ones who decide whether there will be peace or not."

"They went over there to break the cycle of violence, not add to it," I said.

"Stupidity!" shouted Jamie with greater emphasis. "Peacemaking! How can anyone make—let alone keep—peace without weapons?"

I decided to personalize my line of questioning: "Is there anything in this world that you would have the courage to sacrifice your life for?"

Butch, who had been quietly listening until now, decided he could answer this one. "My daughter," he said. "I know I would have the courage to sacrifice my life for her, if I had to."

"Courage!" Jamie bit, turning to me, but clearly directing his question to the two of us. "What those Christian peacemaker people are doing in Iraq has nothing to do with courage. That's just foolhardiness."

"Okay then... " I had another question. "What about a military soldier who decides to pick up a weapon and fight in a war. Is he brave; is he a coward; or is he just plain stupid?"

"It all depends," said Jamie, careful not to provide a quick answer.

Realizing he was being evasive, I moved to my next question. "So, then tell me this, Jamie. What would you call a man or woman who jumped into a raging river to save a child: hero or fool?"

"Well, if he or she was a good swimmer, and it would be of minimal risk to the rescuer's own life," Butch paused as if to give his answer deeper consideration, "I would have to say neither hero nor fool."

"But what if that person could not swim and yet jumped in anyway?" I asked, turning our tit-for-tat dialogue on courage into a series of questions and answers.

After what seemed a split second, Jamie answered, "Then I would have to say fool."

"Well, what if—"

"Hold on," he interrupted. "Now let me ask you a question. What would you call someone who would jump into a raging war zone without a weapon?" Without waiting for my answer, "A zip-damn fool! That's what!"

Remembering the "revolutionary" challenges facing us in the 1960s, I reflected on parallels between CPT and "the movement" I had been involved with: courageous participants on both sides willing to sacrifice their lives for what they believed in. There were those of the civil rights movement, exemplified by Martin Luther King Jr., who had the courage to stand up "nonviolently" for racial equality and social justice.

Then there were the defiant young radicals and Black revolutionaries who were angry and courageous enough to meet violence with violence, who were not afraid to go to jail or die for their various causes. Malcolm X was the chief proponent of this "By Any Means Necessary" strategy in Black America. Malcolm had the courage to transform his life and challenge—peacefully if possible, violently if necessary—unjust and racist policies and practices. I wondered, What was the difference between the "nonviolent" courage of Martin and the "self-defense" courage of Malcolm? Or was there one?

My reason for being in prison today has a lot to do with this question of violence. It's an age-old question. "Violence begets violence," as the saying goes, and since Blacks were merely responding to the systematic violence perpetrated against us as an oppressed people, we were the good guys convinced of our justification to defy and defeat the bad guys "by any means necessary." Martin Luther King's nonviolent approach was not as "courageous" or glamorous as Malcolm's when reduced and simplified. In a world of diametrically opposed roles and images—good guys and bad guys, or bullies and underdogs—the passive protagonist seemed too weak. To emulate him seemed like cowardice. However, history has shown time and time again that when violence meets violence, the end result is inevitably more violence, and subsequently more deaths.

Jamie elected to set the record straight. "Unlike Malcolm X, Martin was a coward; he didn't want to die."

"Malcolm didn't want to die either," Butch let him know.

In an attempt to avoid agreeing with either one of them, I gladly stated my opinion. "But the truth is, and you both have to admit this, nobody sane really wants to die for nothing. And unless they value something greater than themselves, they're not going to put their lives on the line."

My thoughts wandered: Is CPT following in the nonviolent tradition of Martin Luther King? Was the action of Rachel Corrie standing before that bulldozer in Palestine a defiant reflection of Malcolm X? Can "nonviolent intervention" really make a difference?

I tried to step into the heads and hearts of those four peace activists, imagining the dusty, dark dungeon where they may have been hidden and the terror they must have been experiencing, wondering if any of them had regrets. I pondered the state of their courage now.

"So," Butch asked, "how would *you* define courage?"

"Well," I began thoughtfully, "let's look at the action of those four peacemakers who went into Iraq and ended up kidnapped—maybe even dead."

"Plain stupid!" scoffed Jamie. "They knew very well that they were entering into dangerous waters by going to Iraq, and yet they went anyway!"

"Precisely the point," I said. "They knew and yet they went anyway. How much courage does it take to go into a dangerous situation, not out of a sense of patriotic courage, but out of a sense of moral courage?"

I could see Jamie looking around. "Why don't we sit down over there in the baseball dugout and rest," he suggested. "Just for a few—"

"Keep walking," I said, forgetting my point. "You ain't slick. We still have, ummm," checking my watch, "thirty-five minutes to go."

"Moral courage," reflected Butch, clearly interested in the concept. "Now, that definition does have a certain resonance to it. But exactly what does it mean, professor?" The note of sarcasm was unmistakable.

"Having the *courage* to say and do what you believe is right, even when power and popularity oppose you."

"So, I suppose in some broad and twisted way," remarked Butch, "we can say the same thing about those four men."

Jamie didn't appear pleased with the sudden consensus between Butch and me. "I'm not sure I agree with that."

Butch continued, "Then are you saying that it depends more on *how much* you believe in something than *what* you believe in?"

"Or maybe *how much you believe in what you believe in*," I told him.

"It's not sane to want to die!" exclaimed Jamie, trying to insert himself back into the conversation. "There's no way in the world that those people didn't know their lives were in danger by going over there!"

"I don't think it's about wanting to die at all," I said. "It's about the type of humanity you want and the belief that you can make a difference, in spite of the challenges and difficulties you must overcome. Courage doesn't necessarily have to be measured by one's willingness to stand firm in the face of death. In fact, courage could also be realized by one's unwavering commitment to something despite the possibility of humiliation or being viewed by others as cowardly or foolish or traitorous."

The three of us seemed to have lost track of time, immersed in our discussion about courage. "SEVEN O'CLOCK IN-AND-OUT!" shouted the voice over the loud speaker.

"Okay! Time's up!" beamed Jamie. "Our walk, gentlemen, has unfortunately come to an end." He claimed he was exhausted. Butch too was ready to leave the yard, wanting to get back to the novel he had started.

I was thirsty for more information about these Christian peacemakers. There was something admirable about people who would put their lives on the line for something they believed in. Being a child of the Black Power movement, that idea was quite familiar. I understood and had respect for Christian Peacemaker Teams for being passionate about what seemed a just cause. However, I still wasn't sure how I felt about their nonviolence, their pursuit of peacefulness in a violent situation.

"I think I'll drop by the church and library to see if they have anything on the peacemaker organization," I told my friends. I had many unanswered questions.

Over the following days, my friends and I continued our routine walks and discussions. We kept abreast of the developments concerning CPT, and we continued to have our differences.

I was able to solicit and receive several CPT newsletters and articles regarding the plight of the four kidnapped peace activists. I read about the group's history and the international work they have been doing since 1984, the year they were formed. I was both intrigued by their discipline and moved by their determination and self-sacrifice. But over the years, I have become somewhat cynical, leery of people willing to give up their lives for what they believe to be a "just cause." In my experience, what is "just" today becomes "unjust" tomorrow.

My initial assumption about CPT's purpose for being in Iraq was dispelled. I read that their organization does not participate in missionary activities abroad. "So they weren't in Iraq trying to Christianize the natives." Instead the four men were, as their motto suggests, "getting in the way" of injustice. This was an interesting concept, I thought. One can fight against injustice—I was well aware of that concept and practice. But exactly how does one get in the way of injustice? I began to immerse myself in the materials and literature available to me, searching for the real meaning of courage and how it is defined by the actions of folks like CPT.

Fueled by news of Tom Fox's cruel death and the rescue of the three remaining kidnapped members of CPT, my friends' and my conversation continued on the lower yard. "Man, when I first saw the video of those four Christians in orange prison jumpsuits, I kind of felt sorry for them," confessed Butch. "All tied up and blindfolded and—"

"But don't forget," interrupted Jamie, "they had to be rescued by U.S. soldiers. If they hadn't intervened, those other three Christians would have been shot in the head and chest, and their bodies dumped on the streets of Baghdad—just like their companion Tom Fox. So don't ignore that fact either!"

"Man, all I know is that those dudes sure are lucky."

"Lucky?" Jamie asked as he veered off the track and up the concrete slope toward the water faucet. "I need some water," he said, causing us to follow. Jamie hesitated for a second after he'd had a drink, then added, "Well, at least three of them are lucky."

Butch acknowledged he had not actually seen the video of the four, but had heard the news of the one found dead. He knew authorities were searching for the others.

"I'm telling you," Jamie said confidently, "if it hadn't been for the soldiers with guns, they all probably would have ended up like their companion, Tom Fox."

Butch mumbled to himself—but loud enough for Jamie and me to hear, "Sometimes even the show of force can eliminate the need to use it. But you have to have it." I pondered his words.

"Without some means of punishment, why would anyone fear doing wrong?" I asked, as Jamie took his turn at the fountain.

"Yeah," both Jamie and Butch uttered in agreement. I was the last to drink and the one to lead us back to the track.

"Just what I was saying," Jamie spoke quickly. "Even God relies on fear."

Butch clearly welcomed Jamie's support of his argument. "That's what I said. The fear of burning in hell is a very powerful deterrent against evil. Without it, why would anyone want to do good?"

"That's right," I agreed, then added, "history is full of accounts of people killing and doing exceedingly cruel things in the name of their gods."

I looked up and saw two armed guards walking along the narrow gun rail. "Hmmm—" I reflected, "and you think that's the only way to keep people in check, fear? What about the power of love?" More out of my own confusion than for controversy, I added, "What about those people who are motivated by the love and compassion of their gods?"

Equipped with more information about CPT, I was becoming more informed in my role as devil's advocate. "My opinion of Christian Peacemaker Teams' mission in Iraq has changed," I acknowledged.

Checking his watch, Butch decided to shine the spotlight of courage directly onto me. "What about Watani?" The question was directed at Jamie. "He decided to come back to prison because he wanted a better life for his family. Now, was that an act of courage or just plain stupidity?"

Not wanting to sound insensitive, and no doubt subdued by our friendship, Jamie was reluctant to comment. "Well, that's different," he said.

"Different?" Butch refused to allow any sensitivity or solidarity to linger between us. In a tone of outrage, he asked, "How can you call choosing to come back to prison with a life sentence different? Stupidity is stupidity!"

"Well, Watani had his reason. His children."

"Would you have done that, huh?"

"No, but—"

"But nothing!" interrupted Butch. "That doesn't sound very smart to me," he chided, knowing that he was forcing Jamie into a corner. "How does what Watani did make him any less stupid than those four peacemakers?"

I felt somewhat attacked, stunned by the directness and direction of Butch's questioning. And I certainly didn't see my surrender as either stupid or courageous. Given the situation, it was the only rational decision I could make. My freedom, which is what U.S. authorities wanted, was the only thing of value I had to trade for the safety of my family. Consumed by fear of what could happen to them, I realized that I loved my children more than I hated my incarceration.

Tom Fox, Harmeet Sooden, Jim Loney, and Norman Kember must have loved peace more than they had hated war. Why else would they nonviolently put their lives in harm's way? I was beginning to realize that a sense of unconditional love was the main ingredient in all acts of courage.

I also thought about the "courage" of suicide bombers who are motivated by a kind of religious fervor. Their actions are rooted in the strategy and tactics of vengeance, not love. Courage, I determined, cannot be associated with acts that destroy or diminish human life.

Butch was making it difficult for me to continue as devil's advocate. "Watani, Jamie just called you and those peacemaking people stupid, not courageous," he said. "Now what do you have to say about that, huh?"

Actually I had plenty to say. Still I decided to save it for another day. Playing along with Butch's humorous instigation, I got in Jamie's face. "Who you calling stupid, dude?" I said, laughing loudly. Inside I knew I had embraced a new understanding and appreciation for the meaning of courage. "Where is the love?" I blurted out to both their surprise. Suddenly

CPT's slogan, "getting in the way" of injustice, was making a whole lot more sense.

Larry "Watani" Stiner was born in Houston on January 30, 1948. After spending twenty years in exile as an escaped fugitive (1974-1994), he voluntarily surrendered to U.S. authorities in exchange for the safety of his family. Watani is a soft-spoken, conscientious father who "loves his children more than he hates his incarceration." He is currently resuming his life sentence at San Quentin State Prison.

14

On Silence, Closets, and Liberation

William Payne

It was a few days after Jim's abduction. Media people were swarming our little corner of Parkdale, the rundown west Toronto neighbourhood where we've lived for over a decade. Dan and I had already agreed it would be best to suppress any information about Jim's sexual orientation: publicizing that he was gay would not improve his chances of surviving. There was a knock at the door of Dan and Jim's house. Through a crack in the rainbow-colored paper that another housemate, Jo, had pasted over the window, I spotted a television camera. Another knock.

I opened the door to a twenty-something woman, microphone in hand, cameraman at her side. She asked, "Are you Dan Hunt?"

"No."

"I'm looking for Jim Loney's partner. Are you his partner?"

I inhaled. "If you mention in your story that Jim might be gay, whether he is or not, you'll get him killed." It was time to be blunt, and it worked.

She stumbled on her words. "I'm not homophobic. My boss is gay."

"That's not the point. We don't know who is holding Jim, but if they are homophobic, any suggestion that he might be gay could lead to his death."

I could see her backing off the storyline. I exhaled. And so, in the hope it would help bring Jim home alive, our collective return to the closet began.

Along with Jim and his partner, Dan, I live in the Toronto Catholic Worker community, a loose collection of households west of downtown, part of a faith-based and social-change-focused, anarchist tradition begun in the Depression. For a couple of dozen people, these sagging Victorian-era houses have become our village, our family. As well, amid the pain and suffering Christianity too often provides those who are gay, lesbian, and bisexual, our community is a safe space for people of all sexualities.

I am one of several members of the Toronto Catholic Worker community who have discovered in CPT a home for our peacemaking work. This past decade, a time of rapid expansion for CPT has also seen the organization more fully embrace the contributions of out queer Christians in its work. But in the midst of our lived experience as people struggling for wholeness and social justice in a broken world, our brother Jim was snatched up. In the time it takes to jam on the brakes of a car, bringing it to a too-rapid standstill, we stopped being activists and joined millions of others throughout the world who are victims of war.

For the sake of Jim's safety, those who love him took great pains to reconstruct the closet walls he had so painstakingly torn down a decade earlier. As we worked to devise a media strategy designed to communicate to the kidnappers that these men were people of faith working for an end to the violence experienced by Iraqis, we also had to carefully manage personal information that might be misunderstood or misused.

And so we felt compelled to include a clear directive not to mention anything related to Jim's marital status or sexual orientation in the guidelines sent to CPTers and others involved in media work related to the kidnapping. As well, Dan's face was carefully edited out of photographs of Jim shared with the press. Even Toronto's Now Magazine and Catholic New Times agreed to remove from the Internet articles Jim had written on related themes. Reversing years of closet dismantling is hard to do, but we were amazingly successful.

This chapter is about queerness and about how the sexual orientation of one of the four CPTers kidnapped in Iraq must be seen as an intrinsic, even central part of the story. For Jim's queer family, his circle of LGBT-identified friends, the narrative of the hostage-taking is incomplete without an account of how homophobia played a leading role in this drama. This chapter is also about the crossroads between sexual orientation and religion. Yet it is with sadness that I even use that metaphor. I believe profoundly that the way to wholeness in the realms of sexuality and spirituality should not be separate journeys. But too often they are. Finally, while this chapter is about the impact Jim's gayness had on the story of his kidnapping, this is not Jim's story. And though this story is very much about Dan, nor is it his story. Their stories are theirs to tell, in the time and place of their choosing.

Reassembling the closet

One of the many miracles CPT experienced during this time of horror was a torrent of support from throughout the world. In Toronto, this outpouring manifested as practical assistance, largely from people who have come to know and love Jim and the Toronto Catholic Worker community through the years. Many of these were gay, lesbian, and bisexual people who have found on the fringes of organized Christianity a spiritual home. For those four months, my own life shrank to include only the CPT office, the Catholic Worker community, and the streetcar tracks between. Community was for me a salve in the midst of existential pain.

Gay, lesbian, and bisexual people used the gifts of their lives to do whatever could be done in a situation where there was very little to do. We are used to surviving despite the closet. Though it's not a place we want to go, we know how to craftily navigate the waters of deception when we need to protect life and limb, and we did it again for four months. The gift of levity was one I particularly needed amid my growing fears regarding Jim's well-being. I was on the phone frequently, so when Joseph brought me a pink telephone shaped like a nymph, calling it my "radical fairy telephone," I almost died laughing.

Four months after Jim came home, many of his lesbian, gay, and bisexual friends affected by his kidnapping gathered together at the farm of Joseph and his husband, David Martin, for what we came to call the "queer weekend." We laughed and cried, ate and played, and we shared with each other how queerness affected our experience of Jim's captivity. We made rainbow-colored, tie-dyed T-shirts, and we developed the "sissy serve" — the second chance to get the volleyball over the net when one's first serve fell short. During that weekend, we took time to sit in a circle to remember.

David recalls how he and Joseph first learned of the abduction while driving home from a family gathering. "We heard it on the radio—two Canadians had been kidnapped. We wondered [pause] and hoped not. Then we got the call from Dan that confirmed it, and the panic set in."

David's memory of Jim from the eve of his departure for Iraq took on great importance. "We were at their house, and Jim and Dan were sitting on the couch. Jim was caressing the back of Dan's head, twirling his hair. Joseph and I mentioned later, 'Wow, we haven't seen Jim that affectionate.' I remember thinking that it was such a beautiful, tender thing that we were part of, and it became this thing that sustained me."

In the rush to find a photo of Jim, Dan suggested we use one taken by Joseph the night before Jim left. David comments, "It was my favorite photo from that night, Jim with his arm around Dan's shoulder, both smiling, with Jim's head tilted toward Dan's head."

Robin Buyers, the CPTer who coordinated the media response to the kidnapping, also remembered that photograph. "The defining moment for me as a queer woman during the crisis was when Dan's image was cut out of that loving photo taken of Jim and Dan the night before Jim's departure. I watched the process of the photo editing from my desk, and cried quietly. In the days that followed, I worked ferociously to protect Dan, and Jim and Dan's relationship, from an already knowledgeable media. At the same time, my active role in making Dan invisible broke my heart."

That image we carried to countless vigils, and that was flashed around the world, was a constant reminder of Dan's invisibility. He had been literally "cut out" of the picture.

David remembers, "That is how I experienced Dan during the time of captivity. While other spouses and family members were in the media spotlight, Dan was explicitly missing."

That photo became symbolic of the act of re-closeting in which we all participated to help preserve Jim's life.

On silence and silencing

Helyn Fisher, a lesbian in our community who often prepared food for Dan during the crisis, remembers her first reaction to the kidnapping. "My biggest concern was Dan, as there wasn't much I could do for Jim other than pray and worry, which I did."

Joseph described how this situation affected Dan. "The silencing was horrible. On a rational level I understand why we didn't talk about Jim's sexual orientation, but it was not a healthy place for Dan to be in. I watched Dan slipping into more and more invisibility."

Joseph's husband, David, also remembers their concern for Dan. "Our first thought was we've got to be with Dan; we need to support him; we need to be there. We decided that we would travel into Toronto as soon as we could."

David and Joseph are teachers living outside Toronto, but spent the four months of the kidnapping crisis traveling back and forth between their rural life and the city to offer support to Dan and to the CPT office.

"Annihilation is a word I think describes the experience for me," said Dan, as he recalls the pain of facing repeated homophobic exclusion by officials of the Canadian government throughout the four months of Jim's kidnapping.

Many of us were angered by how government officials repeatedly negated and ignored Dan. For Joseph, this brought back memories of the homophobic treatment of lovers and friends during the early days of the AIDS crisis. "We had seen partners being excluded again and again until some of these laws finally came through that protected gay spouses. So when Dan had to go to a lawyer to speak on Jim's behalf, I went to that place of sorrow. Why does Dan have to fight for the right to speak on Jim's behalf?"

To continue CPT's efforts to shine light on the situation of ordinary Iraqis, a series of public vigils and marches were held during the crisis to draw attention to the horrific suffering occurring in that country due to military occupation. This was the work Jim and the other kidnapped brothers were doing when they were abducted, and we felt it was right to continue their work. We also felt that it was an important element of our strategy to continue clarifying in the Iraqi media who these kidnapped people were as peace activists, hoping this would help keep them alive. Queer people, among them longtime friend of our community Rory Crath and his partner Mark Chilton, were prominent among those who organized these efforts.

Rory describes his experience of the hiding of Jim's sexual orientation through this time: "There was just silence, and it was haunting. It was just haunting." Rory also spoke of the effect of the silencing on himself. "I think that I split. In private, with my partner and people with whom I was very intimate, and then in conversation with Dan and with queer people at the Worker house who are foundational to Jim's chosen family, I felt I could have full emotions. ... It felt very full and rich. And then when I moved into public space, ...conversations were haunted by the stripping away of people most intimately connected to Jim. There was something terribly wrong with those conversations."

David comments that the pervasiveness of the silence also silenced him. "I remember going to school and telling people that James is a very good friend of mine and that I'm very upset, but I couldn't talk about Dan, and it all became this veil of secrecy." This brought up prior personal experiences. "This is how I've lived my life in the past, when I wouldn't tell people the full story about me because I was afraid."

Ryan also talks about this experience of silencing. "I knew right away that it had to be kept private. It made sense, but it was hard to then talk about this situation, because I couldn't talk about that aspect, our relationship to each other. I would tell people very calmly, nonchalantly, 'Oh, my friend's kidnapped,' and they would ask about it, but I didn't have anything else to say. I found it very isolating."

Fragments of hope and joy

Many people at the gathering also shared moments of hope and joy amid this time of crisis. Dan contrasts his experiences of homophobia by government people with the unassuming question of one of the children in our community. "Tonnán, Richard and Madeline's son, age five, heard there was going to be a televised family appeal and asked, 'Is Dan going to be on TV?'"

David found something in the cropped photograph to hold onto. "I noticed...a little red triangle in the bottom right corner, Dan's shirt. I thought, 'There's Dan. You're silent, you're invisible, but there's the visibility.' It was the weirdest thing. I don't know why but it comforted me to know that even though Dan was cut out of the picture—at least to the few who knew—that little bit of red shirt was actually Dan. That was beautiful to me."

Dan remembers that the support of his housemate Michael and other gay people was crucial for his survival through the ordeal. "I was carried through this by people who loved me, and I drew just unbelievable strength from the queer people who supported me, because I felt that they understood what was happening to me. It was the most important thing that happened—having my queer friends."

As part of the struggle to walk a path uniting sexuality and spirituality, communal prayer took on great importance for many of Jim's queer friends living through the ordeal of the kidnapping. Of particular importance were the private vigils held at the Toronto Catholic Worker. Likewise, participating in and organizing times of public vigil was significant for many.

Both David and Joseph organized daily gatherings in their schools. "I run a gay-straight alliance group in the public high school where I teach. Our students had met Jim, because he spoke at our school, so when the story broke and Jim's picture was in the paper, I announced I was going to start holding daily vigils. The students who came were the kids who were connected to the GSA group," recounted Joseph.

David adds, "We started a vigil as well every morning at my school. We had a big poster that people signed, and I had printed off pictures of all the hostages. We're not supposed to light candles but I lit a candle. I'm in a public school and I didn't want to bring God language into it, so what I did was a silent vigil. It was powerful. In this case, the silence was beautiful, as we were in solidarity with getting Jim and the rest released."

It seems impossible now to describe the day after day, week after week of waiting and hoping against all hope, the throbbing sensation of moving closer and closer to accepting the likelihood of a dear friend's death. Then I was yanked back to the world of the living through the ring of my telephone in the middle of the night. Jim was free!

While I would eventually come to joy, the first response at the core of my being was intense relief, the kind of release you experience after carrying a heavy load far longer than you had thought yourself capable. I cried. Michael, our community's elder and gay mystic, had called us to believe that somehow an "explosion of goodness" would come of this horror. That was the expression he used, "explosion of goodness," reminding us that God can work miracles amidst a vale of tears.

And then we danced! At four o'clock in the morning, David and Joseph jitterbugged around their kitchen and again with their students a few hours later. Rory and Mark had the queer contingent over to their comfy digs that evening, and did we boogie! Jim was in the Green Zone. Jim was in Dubai. Jim was on his way to Germany. Jim was coming home! "No more prisons," Jim told Dan at the Toronto airport after his plane touched down. "We will meet the press together." The closet doors were ripped from their hinges.

A couple of weeks later, a group of us went to the Retro Queer Party at Buddies in Badtimes Theatre (a Toronto gay landmark), and again we shook our hips. Joseph commented that not until that night, when Jim gave the DJ a CD with his and Dan's song, "Walk Five Hundred Miles," and Jim and Dan danced together, was it finally over.

Dan speaks of his delight in being unreservedly welcomed when he and Jim visited Jim's hometown a couple of days later. "A hopeful event for me was going to the church on that first Sunday in the Sault. Everyone who came up to congratulate Jim gave me a hug and congratulated me too. That was in a Catholic church, and that's just not expected."

But they still don't get it

Of course Jim's coming out was sensational news for the press, and for them an unanticipated angle of the story. Too often though, they didn't really get it. The mainstream press seemed incapable of understanding the depths of homophobia that queer people deal with on a daily basis.

Ryan comments, "It was really profound that keeping quiet, that keeping everything to ourselves was very central to those four months, but for other people it seemed an interesting tidbit at the end. I found that very difficult."

Mark recalls a similar experience. "The woman who sits next to me at work mentioned that she found it a bit annoying that the story was going on so long in the media. I tried to explain …that it wasn't so much keeping the story in the news as telling an untold and essential part of the story, filling in gaps that needed to be filled."

Rory also reflects on this incapacity for public discourse to truly grasp what the silencing was all about. "It was almost like …a curiosity that Jim was gay. That was what registered. There was a surface acknowledgement, 'Ah, there was a partner, and they were gay,' but my reading of it was that it wasn't hitting people at a deeper level." Rory observed, "at times we're just so thankful that we're being accepted at a surface level that we don't expect people to love us enough to think deeply about the institutional homophobia that prevents us from being human to each other as well."

His partner, Mark, adds that this experience has pushed him to look at how he lives in the world. "I think what it did for me as a queer person was to make me more intentional about being out. There are times you have to blurt it out or be intentional about making it a topic."

Dan reflects that even after the veil of silence over Jim's sexual orientation was lifted, other essential aspects of our shared experience continue to be ignored. "Once I started to speak, this superficial gay label took over, and then people didn't want to hear about how I live communally. There's no category, so people don't understand it. I have really felt that the most beautiful thing that was silenced was our life together in community, and what that is."

Where faith and queerness cross paths

One week after Jim, Harmeet, and Norman were released, CPT issued a press statement explaining why we had not divulged Jim's sexual orientation during the kidnapping. "In consultation with Jim's partner Dan Hunt, CPT decided not to mention Jim's orientation for reasons of his safety." The statement included a quotation from CPT's director, Doug Pritchard: "It's a sad fact that around the world gays and lesbians are more vulnerable to attack than straights. When Jim was already in a vulnerable position we didn't, nor did his family, want him exposed to further danger. Those of us who have worked with Jim consider him a brother in Christ, with a strong spiritual core that empowers both him and his teammates to do the work they need to do."

For many of the gay, lesbian, and bisexual people involved in the response to Jim's kidnapping, this experience has resulted in a closer look at our spiritual lives as sexual outcasts. For example, Denise commented that joining with two other lesbians for weekly prayer vigils in Vancouver provided a place to share how they were feeling about having to hide Jim and Dan's relationship. "As a faith-based person, this experience made me feel queerer," she wrote. "We could pray for Jim and Dan, and talk about ourselves and who we are as queer Christians. In the end, the CPT hostage experience has become the first time my queerness and my Christianity have come together."

There has been homophobic backlash. A short while after Jim's return, using homophobic epithets, a young man yelled threats of violence outside of Jim and Dan's home. Others have contacted CPT to say they felt duped into praying for someone they later learned to be gay. The response of the hierarchy of the Catholic Church has been horrible. Organizers of a social justice event in the diocese of London chose to un-invite Jim as their keynote speaker when directed to do so by their bishop. In addition, the Bishop of Peterborough directed the churches and schools under his jurisdiction not to extend invitations to him to speak, the diocese of Hamilton withdrew its sponsorship of an ecumenical event due to Jim's presence, and the bishop of Winnipeg blocked Jim from speaking at a social justice event there. This is probably but the tip of the iceberg, as there are likely many other churches and individuals who will not invite Jim to speak simply because he is gay; but we will never know.

For CPT however, this journey has also assisted us in gaining clarity regarding what full equality means. Robin reflected, "When so many of us walked together with the CPT banner in the Pride parade last June, I felt that CPT itself was healing, not only from the crisis of the kidnapping but from longstanding wounds within the organization itself."

A consensus has arisen among the gay, lesbian, and bisexual Christians involved in the response to the kidnapping. This has not been about the homophobia of Iraqi culture or of Islam, but rather about the pervasiveness of homophobia throughout the world and the particularly virulent strain within religious contexts of many stripes. Ironically the very day the picture of Jim and Dan first appeared in newspapers across Canada, the image was juxtaposed with the announcement of Prime Minister Stephen Harper's intent to reopen the same-sex marriage debate. This proved an interesting bookend. The date of Jim's kidnapping had coincided with the publication of instructions by the Catholic Church to bar gays from the priesthood.

Another member of the Toronto Catholic Worker named Rob Kleyson observes, "Whether having to do with the fears regarding the kidnappers' possible extremist Muslim background that led to the silencing of Dan's voice ...or later the Catholic Church's distancing itself from Jim upon his return and his coming out, the issue that most stuck out in my mind was the hostile and violent effect of religion on queers."

Religious fundamentalism will most certainly be overcome through acts of solidarity, and there were many during this crisis. Denise remembers a call she received from Dan during the crisis. "One night Dan phoned me somewhat frantic, and asked me if I knew a Muslim scholar. I think he was considering how to handle revealing his own existence were it to come to that. I knew two Muslim women who had progressive positions on LGBT issues, so I called them that night, and they both responded immediately to help Dan. One went over to his house within twenty-four hours to talk to him, while the other phoned him from Vancouver and maintained contact with him over the rest of Jim's captivity." For Denise, this response was profoundly important: "This was a cross-religious solidarity in the face of homophobia that marked me deeply. This was not about homophobic Islam versus progressive Christianity. This was progressive Islam and progressive Christianity challenging fundamentalist religion, and it was straight Muslim women of color allying with white queer Christian men and women."

I think my favorite queer moment of the crisis happened in Toronto's Catholic cathedral. A few weeks after the kidnapping, religious leaders from several different Christian denominations gathered together to pray for Jim and the others. St. Michael's was packed. As I sat, I remembered that the last time Jim had been to Mass at St. Michael's he had held up a banner calling for an end to the church's homophobia. On that occasion, during a homily in which Toronto's bishop was exhorting

133

Catholics to oppose equal rights for sexual minorities, Jim and a friend named Tom Harrington tried to unfurl a bed-sheet stenciled with a call to end the homophobia of the church. Alas, they had arrived a bit late and only found seats amid the scaffolding in place to repaint the cathedral's ceiling. Thus most people's view of the banner was blocked.

I joked that this time Jim had gone to rather great lengths—getting himself kidnapped—to make it possible for Fr. Bob Holmes and me to hang two twelve-foot banners on the very altar of that same cathedral. This time the banners called for an end to the occupation of Iraq.

Several months after Jim's return, he is now swamped with speaking requests. However some—most notably church people—have withheld or withdrawn invitations precisely because of his gayness. "Have we forgotten that we are all members one of another?" read that banner held amid the scaffolding in St. Michael's cathedral a decade ago. We have come a distance, but the journey is not yet finished. Two years later and the Iraqi death count continues unchecked.

I am so thankful Jim came home alive.

William Payne recently completed a masters thesis entitled "Homophobic Violence as part of the Colombian Conflict." He has been active with CPT since 1998 and has served with teams in Chiapas, Esgenoopetitj, Colombia, Palestine, and Algonquin territory. For the past sixteen years, his home community has been the Toronto Catholic Worker.

15

Writing Peace out of the Script

Simon Barrow and Tim Nafziger

This article describes the story of media coverage of the CPT hostage crisis from two different but overlapping perspectives, that of Ekklesia (www.ekklesia.co.uk), which runs an independent Christian news service, and a small group of CPTers, peace activists, and friends of Norman Kember who handled media enquiries in the United Kingdom during high-interest times, sending out press releases at others.

Simon: It's really not the story, I'm afraid

There was a brief pause in the conversation, just after I had started to explain what Christian Peacemaker Teams was and the thinking behind its practical methods of "getting in the way" of self-reinforcing violence.

"Well that's very interesting," the journalist responded. "It raises a lot of important questions, I can see. It's just that in terms of what my news organization wants right now, it's really not the story, I'm afraid."

The reporter in question was based in the United Kingdom and freelanced for a newspaper syndication service. He wanted some background on the latest Iraq hostage crisis, because people were asking his agency for "news and updates" about the situation. He knew something about the region and the increasingly fractured post-war context, but his antennae failed to picked up the issue of who these "peace activists" were and why they were caught up in a dangerous situation.

So after a few fruitless telephone calls, he decided to type "Christian peacemakers + Norman Kember" into his news search engine. Lo and behold, several stories from Ekklesia came up. He figured this "Christian think tank and news service" might know something he didn't and that it could be just the information one-stop he needed. Thus, he gave us a call. This pattern repeated itself many times during the long four months before Harmeet, Jim, and Norman were freed on March 23, 2006—following the tragic killing of Tom.

From November 28 through to the end of March, Ekklesia found itself considerably preoccupied with the Iraq kidnap story. As a U.K.-based Web agency with a global reach, we had a range of reasons for our interest. Our work involves promoting alternative Christian perspectives on policy issues and reporting concerned with religion and public life. In this, we increasingly work with both the mainstream secular and church media. Our viewpoint is shaped by commitments and insights directly sympathetic to the outlook of the "historic peace churches"—the Quakers, Mennonites, and Church of the Brethren—who founded CPT. We also have links with CPT first established through the British "Root and Branch" alliance, which includes the Anabaptist Network UK and the London Mennonite Centre.

It was natural, therefore, that we would take a particular interest in a news story where the practical possibilities of nonviolent direct action, conflict transformation, and peacemaking were at issue—and where the lives of friends well regarded in our broader circles of collaboration were at risk. Between November 26, 2005, and April 2006, we ran more than a hundred and fifty news reports and comment pieces related to the crisis, alongside two specific briefings, one on CPT itself and one tackling the growing number of confused or unfounded media allegations against both the captives and those supporting them.

As we became more observant of and involved with media coverage of the CPT-Iraq hostage situation, the questions grew larger. How was "the story" developing? What shaped the way people saw these events? What were the turning points in perception? And what longer-term lessons could those concerned for peace with justice learn about handling the media circus? In short, what writes peace in and out of the script?

Tim: The first calls from reporters

As we try to understand the media coverage of the CPT hostage crisis, we can learn from people interviewed by reporters in the first few days of the crisis, and the quotes major news sources published. As a coordinator for CPT-London and a press contact for CPT-UK, I discovered quickly that reporters shape the story by using only a few quotes from a longer interview. To get a closer look at this process, I talked with some of the people who were interviewed by the British press.

Bruce Kent first heard about Norman's kidnapping when he received a call requesting an interview on the evening of Sunday, November 27. Bruce, director of the Campaign for Nuclear Disarmament (CND) through most of the 1980s, left the Roman Catholic priesthood as a result of his political work. He is well known in the United Kingdom for his peace work, which made him an obvious choice for the media when they heard a peace activist had been kidnapped in Iraq.

During the first days following the kidnapping, Bruce spoke with copious journalists and felt strongly that most were sympathetic to Norman and his friends. On Tuesday, November 29, a video of the hostages was broadcast widely in the United Kingdom. Media interest increased dramatically.

In an article on the twenty-ninth, the Guardian's quotes from Bruce focused on Norman's motivations for going to Iraq:

> [Bruce Kent] said the campaigner was in Iraq "to show that people in the west are not all Bush and Blair." Mr. Kent said Mr. Kember would have been aware of the risks in Iraq and talked them over with his wife but decided to go whatever they were. "People with a vision for change in the world will always take risks."[10]

On the same day, the BBC ran similar quotes from Bruce on Norman's awareness of the risks and his motivations, but also included quotes from Bruce that focused on Norman's personality and his abilities: "Mr. Kent, who is vice-president of CND, said his friend was 'a lovely man' with a 'twinkly sense of humor.' 'He's a very deep, sincere man. A man whose whole life has been dedicated to peace,' he added."[11]

Reporters were always interested in Norman's age and asked Bruce how he thought Norman was holding up. "I think he'll be probably the strongest member of that group," the BBC quoted him saying.

Pat Gaffney was another frequent recipient of calls from the media during the first days after the kidnapping (see chapter by Pat Gaffney). After a video of the men was released on the Tuesday following the kidnapping, Pat focused on refuting the allegations by the Swords of Righteousness Brigade that the four men were spies. "Having known Norman for such a long time and his deep conviction that war is never a way of solving problems, ...I was very disturbed that his intention and reason for being there is ...misunderstood," quoted the Guardian.[12]

Maureen Jack heard about the kidnapping while in Hebron with CPT. Maureen is a retired educational psychologist from St. Andrews, Scotland. She joined CPT as a reservist in January 2003 and spends three months a year working with CPT. Most of her time is spent with the Palestine team, but in 2003 she spent two-and-a-half months in Iraq before and after the invasion. She led a delegation to Iraq early in the spring of 2005.

On December 1, Maureen returned to Scotland to find her answering machine overflowing with messages. "That was the first I realized what a big story this was in the U.K." Maureen said, "I spent the evening returning calls and doing an interview. For some days there were frequent calls." Maureen felt that the questions from the press during those

---

[10] Source: www.guardian.co.uk/international/story/0,,1653588,00.html.

[11] Source: news.bbc.co.uk/2/hi/uk_news/4483184.stm.

[12] Source: www.guardian.co.uk/international/story/0,,1653588,00.html.

first weeks were reasonable and that, for the most part, reporters did their best to represent what she said to them.

On December 3, the Guardian published Maureen's explanation of CPT's work in Iraq:

> Maureen Jack, from CPT, who has spent time in Iraq, said the group had been campaigning on behalf of a number of detainees held by the US in Iraqi jails. "These are all men who have been in strong opposition to the invasion and occupation of Iraq and the human rights abuses that it has entailed," she said.[13]

The article also included Maureen's description of a rally by Palestinians in Ramallah on behalf of the four men.

On December 4, 2006, the Scotsman did a much more in-depth article centered on quotes from an interview with Maureen. It used eight full-paragraph quotes from Maureen to convey her perspective on the situation, her experience of leading a delegation to Iraq, and how the Iraq team had dealt with the dangers. It went far beyond any of the other major papers in telling CPT's story.[14]

The quote that nearly every news source used was from Norman himself. It came from an interview with Premier Christian Radio on Remembrance Sunday, November 13, 2005. The interviewer, Rob Frost, asked Norman if he felt he was brave. He replied, "I don't know. I've done a lot of writing and talking about peacemaking. ...I've demonstrated ...but I feel that's what I'd call cheap peacemaking." When the interviewer asked if going to Iraq could be more costly, Norman replied, "It could be." These two excerpts were the closing paragraphs of countless articles in the British media.

Significantly the media ignored the sections of Norman's interview in which he spoke passionately and in depth about his views on the war in Iraq, his commitment to a spirituality of nonviolence, and his opposition to the just-war theory: "There's a myth that violence works and I think it's about time that we went away from that myth. The established church has been much too preoccupied with this theory of the just war, and it just doesn't apply in practice."[15]

---

[13] Source: www.guardian.co.uk/Iraq/Story/0,2763,1656929,00.html.

[14] Source: thescotsman.scotsman.com/index.cfm?id=2367842005.

[15] Source: www.premier.org.uk/streaming/news/normankember1.asx.

Simon: The "soap opera" view

For the western news media, North American and European hostages in the Middle East are big stories because they personalize and dramatize what can otherwise seem like one endless series of faraway, nameless tragedies. They become, in fact, miniature soap operas with their own recognizable cast of heroes, villains, victims, and clowns. Their stuff is the daily drama of hope and despair writ large. Their setting is an exotic but mostly unexamined stage. No one knows how long the mini-saga will last, but everyone realizes there can only be two outcomes: tragedy or triumph.

In the meantime, minute attention is paid to the twists and turns of the story—or, in the absence of any real news, what people think the story is or "should be." And it is in these terms that the conventions of "the narrative" and "the script" are written by those who have to keep people watching and reading. They are experts at their craft. They know what communicates and sells to a broad or narrow audience, and they know how to tailor the plot details to the kind of story that can be told—and the kind of story that cannot.

The "dominant narrative" (the generally accepted version of events) is frequently established in the earliest stages of an event, and this was certainly the case in the CPT-Iraq hostage situation. At its starkest, it went something like this: "A well-meaning but essentially naïve and ill-prepared group of peace activists—Christians who are fish-out-of-water in a conflict-ridden Muslim environment—have been kidnapped by a militant group after political advantage or money. Some admire their intent to bring peace, but realists know that they are at best misguided and at worst irresponsible. Their chances of getting out of this alive are limited, but if they do, it will be a warning to fellow activists that they should keep their idealism out of the real, grown-up world of politics and violence."

As the weeks elapsed, further refinements were added to this dominant script. CPT, a "previously unknown" group, was portrayed in many quarters as essentially "anti-American." The default presumption, based on little if any serious research, was that CPT had recently blundered into a situation it didn't really understand. That its impact on the conflict was minimal or zero. That its aim was to offer gestures of peace with little or no substance behind them. That it was either colluding with insurgents and terrorists or simply blinded to the reality of the situation on the ground. That its attitude toward the soldiers who had been sent to Iraq as part of the U.S.-led coalition was one of disregard, hostility, or ingratitude.

Of course there were contrary examples of good journalism that probed well beneath such simplistic stereotypes, but the overwhelming image was at least mildly negative toward "the peace activists"—with public opinion in Britain, for instance, running approximately 60 percent critical, 25 percent neutral, and 15 percent supportive. This was reflected over the four months, with a range of variances according to the scale of coverage and what was going on, in opinion surveys (of different degrees of thoroughness or reliability), print and broadcast reporting, online commentary (especially Web logs), and phone-in or discussion programs on radio and TV.

Tim: Reclaiming the initiative

On December 6, I met with Pat Gaffney and Chris Cole, director of Fellowship of Reconciliation UK, of which Norman is a trustee. We discussed how CPT-UK and other peace organizations could respond to the kidnapping. Though press coverage had been intense in the first few days, it had gradually tapered off, and we felt a strong need to keep the plight of Norman and the others in the spotlight. At an initial vigil in London on December 2 in Trafalgar Square, only a few reporters had been present.

Rather than reacting to the deadlines of December 8 (and then 10) set by the hostage takers, we chose to hold the next vigil on December 12. On the ninth, FOR and Pax Christi sent out the first press release announcing the vigil in London and one in Oxford. The press release focused on remembering the hostages, the families, and the ones who were holding the men. The release also included a call for peace and justice for the people of Iraq.

The BBC and other news sources covered the vigil. They focused on the drama of friends and family waiting to hear news after the final deadline set by the hostage takers passed two days earlier. The story quoted Chris Cole as saying, "We are looking for a miracle at this stage," and Bruce Kent saying, "I haven't given up hope at all. It's quite possible they may be preparing a video to say why they are releasing them."

The press almost completely ignored the call to remember Iraqis detained by the United States and United Kingdom that we emphasized in a number of vigils and in interviews.

Over the next weeks, we held regular vigils and found fewer and fewer press coming to them. If there was nothing to add to "the story," they weren't interested. Typical of most U.K. papers, The Telegraph ran eight stories through the first month of the crisis and then only three between early January and March 24: one story on each of the two new videos and one on Tom Fox's death. After the release, they ran ten stories.

In Scotland, Maureen Jack and fellow CPTer Jan Benvie arranged vigils in Edinburgh and St. Andrews, both of which were attended by about thirty people. Maureen continued to answer phone calls from the media.

Simon: Challenging distortions

Throughout the CPT-Iraq hostage crisis, Ekklesia's coverage of events was shaped by three realizations. First, we recognized that CPT's overriding priority would be to ensure that the possibilities of Harmeet, Jim, Norman, and Tom being released were heightened rather than imperiled—and that this would necessarily limit what they were able to say and do. We shared the core concern, but recognized (in a modest way) that we also had greater freedom and a different kind of responsibility. We wished to demonstrate that committed reporting could show a concern for the truths sometimes obscured by affected neutrality.

Second, we believed that it was important to put into the public arena facts and issues that were being lost or distorted by the dominant narrative. With up to twenty-five thousand unique daily visitors to the Ekklesia site—among them a range of journalists and commentators reaching much wider audiences—we had some capacity to do this, though Ekklesia is, of course, a tiny fish in a vast media ocean.

Third, we thought it might be possible for us to offer a direct challenge to false information from time to time. That did, indeed, prove to be the case. I'll share some examples. In the immediate aftermath of the news that Harmeet, Jim, Norman, and Tom had been kidnapped, a flurry of diplomatic activity and comment ensued. In early December 2005, a story circulated that a local Iraqi negotiator who was seeking to contact the previously unidentified kidnap group, the Swords of Righteousness Brigades, had been abducted. In the words of reporter Michelle Shephard in a story for the Toronto Star that was picked up by other agencies and outlets, "A source told the Toronto Star the local negotiator has not been heard from since Thursday [December 15] and had recently met face-to-face with members of the group believed to have kidnapped the activists."

This story was significant for a number of reasons. It was part of a pool of speculation, often derived from questionable sources, which those seeking the release of the men regarded as profoundly unhelpful. It suggested that direct contact had been established with the kidnappers, contrary to the experience and knowledge of everyone else involved on the ground. It also illustrated how the media is sometimes keen to make itself a protagonist in the story it is reporting—often at the expense of accuracy.

Ekklesia e-mailed a CPT worker with direct contacts in Baghdad who said the negotiator abduction story was unfounded. We then contacted the editorial teams at both the Star and one other Canadian agency to ask if (without revealing their sources) they could confirm that their claims had been corroborated by at least one reputable source. No such assurance was forthcoming, and in one case we received no reply at all. So along with SooToday, a paper in Jim Loney's local area that had a syndicated Web presence, we reported that there appeared to be no substance to this rumor and that CPT had denied it. This probably helped to stem its further circulation, though it did briefly resurface several weeks later (unqualified) in a London newspaper.

In general, media coverage tended to ignore or misrepresent why CPT was in Iraq (to support local civil and religious groups involved in peace-building and violence reduction); how long it had been there (well before western troops had arrived); and what it was achieving (modest but significant relationships and interventions which are only possible for those who come in without military-protection or commercial motives). Ekklesia was able to provide this information.

Similarly Ekklesia (along with other "alternative" outlets like Sojourners and Mennonite Weekly Review in North America) was able to point out that hostage taking was much more an issue impacting ordinary Iraqis than international visitors, that violence on all sides was proving demonstrably to be the problem not the solution, that the U.S.-led invasion and occupation of the country remained the backdrop to resistance and internecine disorder, and that "conflict transformation techniques" were not a new idea but formed part of a credible tradition of action and research.

We also tried to highlight the truth that Christians, Muslims, and those of good faith were finding unexpected common cause in the midst of this small human drama—and that this showed that efforts to build peaceful relationships and to resist violent resolutions in a situation of escalating low-intensity war were not "foolish," but rather offered tangible, small-scale hope in a context of otherwise deepening conflict. Moreover, there were many concrete stories that illustrated this and that also demonstrated why the "clash of civilizations" thesis (Huntington, 1996) is a self-fulfilling prophecy that feeds the forces of division it purports to expose.

For us, this was the real story. While one reporter claimed "nothing was happening," we knew that many efforts were being made to free the four men. Keeping the story alive through the dark days of silence from Baghdad was a major task in itself, so that those connected with the kidnappers would know international concern remained solid and those in captivity (not just Harmeet, Jim, Norman, and Tom, but all in detention or held hostage in Iraq) might know they were not alone, not forgotten. As far as much of the media was concerned, however, these concerns barely registered on their radar. With honorable exceptions such as Vatican Radio, the underlying story continued to be ignored. News is, predominantly, spectacle rather than perspective, event rather than process, and precipice rather than plain.

Tim: The Muslim world rallies

Some of the most important support for the hostages during the crisis came from Muslims around the world. Maureen Jack was on the Hebron CPT team when they began calling local Palestinians to gather statements of support. "We rang our Muslim friends first, and then our Christian contacts. People were so kind, shocked and desperate to do what they could to help." She recalls how one longstanding friend of the team called in all sorts of favors from friends and friends of friends and got widespread support from prominent Palestinian leaders for a statement in support of the missing CPTers. The statement reads:

> More than once [CPTers] placed themselves in front of [Israeli Defense Force] tanks, and they confronted Israeli occupation bulldozers with their bodies, defending Palestinians' homes against destruction. They accompanied our children when they were threatened and attacked by Israeli settlers on their way to and from their schools. Because of what they were doing, the CPT members were subjected to arrest, beating and pursuit by the Israeli soldiers and settlers in more than one location in Palestine.[16]

The statement went on to call for quick release of the four CPTers. It was signed by most of the major Palestinian political parties, including Fatah and Hamas, and was released on November 29, three days after the initial kidnapping and only hours after CPTers first began calling their Palestinian friends.

The statement was completely ignored by the British press.

In the United Kingdom, Muslim support for CPT was most visible from the Muslim Association of Britain. At the beginning of December, they sent Anas Altikriti as their envoy to Iraq to work alongside the CPT-Iraq team for the release of the four men. His departure received some coverage in the U.K. press. The December 1 BBC article also included quotes from the Muslim Council of Britain. "Secretary General Sir Iqbal Sacranie said: 'Norman Kember is a man who cares deeply for the people of Iraq, and his kidnap and continued detention is completely unjustifiable. Our faith of Islam holds in great esteem the peaceful bridge-building work that Mr. Kember was involved in.'"[17]

Three days later the Observer (the Sunday partner of the Guardian) reported Altikriti's apparent success in encouraging five Sunni parties in Iraq to call for the release of the hostages.[18]

---

[16] Source: www.cpt.org/iraq/response/palstatement.htm.

[17] Source: news.bbc.co.uk/2/hi/uk_news/4488498.stm.

[18] Source: www.guardian.co.uk/Iraq/Story/0,,1657512,00.html.

On Wednesday, December 7, when the kidnappers extended the deadline by two days, some reporters gave credit to British Foreign Secretary Jack Straw.[19] However, The Observer suggested that credit should go to Altikriti.[20] The same article surveyed Muslim responses from around the world, including the Muslim brotherhood in Egypt and twenty-three different Muslim organizations that signed a press release organized by the Muslim Association of Brotherhood.

Other prominent Muslim voices that came out during that week included Moazzam Begg, a Briton who spent nearly three years in the U.S. military prison in Guantanamo Bay before being released. He was joined by three of his fellow prisoners.

The highest-profile appeal from the Muslim community in the United Kingdom came from Abu Qatada, a prominent Muslim cleric imprisoned in England. He is a controversial figure wanted in Jordan for alleged terrorist activities. This was the only appeal from the Muslim community covered by the Telegraph. Both it and the Guardian quoted the same passage: "I, your brother Abu Qatada …beseech my brothers in the Swords of Truth in Iraq, who are imprisoning the four Christian peace activists, to release them in accordance with the fundamental principle of mercy of our faith. Our prophet said mercy should be shown unless there is a reason in Sharia [Islamic law] that prevents it."[21]

Personally, I believe that this outpouring of support may have played a critical role in avoiding the worst in those first few weeks.

Simon: Rescue and reaction

After the tragic news of Tom Fox's murder, there was great elation at the surprise freeing of Norman, Jim, and Harmeet, but once again, the dominant narrative asserted itself rapidly. When news broke that British SAS soldiers had been directed to the place where the three men were being held and had broken in to release the men, the media quickly responded with stories of "our brave boys" being required to save a group of peace activists who had been working against their presence. How very ironic, they argued. Once again, it is soldiers not anti-war activists who prove the most effective peacekeepers.

What was conveniently ignored in this account, as in subsequent vitriolic accusations that CPT had "imperiled" the soldiers who were "called

---

[19] See www.guardian.co.uk/international/story/0,,1663291,00.html.

[20] See observer.guardian.co.uk/focus/story/0,6903,1664639,00.html.

[21] Source:
www.telegraph.co.uk/news/main.jhtml?xml=/news/2005/12/08/whost08.xml
and http://www.guardian.co.uk/Iraq/Story/0,,1662102,00.html.

upon" to rescue them, was the fact that the freeing was actually achieved without violence. That the groundwork of intelligence was civilian, not military. That Christian Peacemaker Teams are explicit in asking the military not to risk themselves or to use violence to effect rescue should anything happen to them. And that the same soldiers who can from time to time engage in honorable actions to free prisoners or assist civilians are themselves victims in a hopeless cycle of violence where they are mostly powerless to stem the escalation of insurgent brutality and are (additionally) components of the tragedy they are asked to "solve." Those who disavow arms, on the other hand, can effect trust and cooperation through the same nonviolent means that make them unavoidably vulnerable—with the distinction that they are, in Gandhi's formula, part of the peace they propose.

It is important to acknowledge that truth is contested and that the powerful have a built-in advantage, but that integrity in reporting and commenting is achieved by seeking to highlight silent voices, hidden viewpoints, unknown stories, and different slants.

The digitally driven media environment may be far from a level playing field. Yet the policed boundaries of editorial control exercised by newspapers, TV, and radio are being challenged through a new cohort of bloggers, cable channels, Web surfers, and free papers. These new mediums can be employed strategically to offer intelligent and humane perspectives that would otherwise be lost. Critical in this changing media arena is the crossover between what would once have been sharply differentiated "alternative" and "mainstream" outlets.

In the United Kingdom and beyond, two big stories in this regard were those concerning Norman's supposed "ingratitude" toward his SAS freers, and repeated accusations that the peace activists had irresponsibly put the lives of military personnel at risk. In both these instances, the dominant narrative, while remaining the most widely circulated account by definition, turned upon itself by virtue of small interventions which Ekklesia and others were able to make.

The "ingratitude" story emerged very shortly after the three men's release was announced on March 23, 2006. On a day of much confusion, CPT's immediate response, at a time before their spokespeople had had any opportunity to talk with the released captives, was to thank God for their freedom and to reiterate the organization's core messages about an end to occupation and detention within Iraq. As CPT's Doug Pritchard subsequently remarked, while the media wanted instant response, no one had any real idea what had happened or who had done what. It simply wasn't possible to attribute specific thanks at the earliest stage. Moreover Norman's first comment was (understandably) one of relief and joy at his freedom and concern for his family. Later that day, CPT posted a statement on the Web thankfully acknowledging the soldiers' for role in the (nonviolent) release. It also became clear that the men themselves had expressed gratitude to those with whom they had been in touch. When Norman arrived back in Britain a little later, he expressed his thanks publicly—while making it clear that he still did not believe military force was the way to resolve Iraq's many problems.

Many commentators and reporters had already decided their story in advance of determining these facts. Indeed the idea that peace activists would be naturally reluctant to thank soldiers seemed so obvious and the notion that military action had proved "superior" to nonviolence was so ingrained that the conviction that this in fact happened took instant root— with little regard for what was actually said or done. Perhaps the catalytic moment in the United Kingdom was when the then-head of the British Army, the charismatically bullish Gen. Sir Mike Jackson, went on Channel 4 television News on March 24, the day before Norman arrived back in Britain but the evening after CPT's statement of thanks on March 23.

In that interview, General Jackson declared, "I am slightly saddened that there doesn't seem to have been a note of gratitude for the soldiers who risked their lives to save those lives." He went on to say that if an expression of thanks had been made, he was unaware of it. Ekklesia's Jonathan Bartley provided evidence to the contrary to the same program the next day. They chose not to use that excerpt, but Bartley was able to make a rebuttal on a range of BBC programs over the next few day. However, the response of the wider media to the British Army chief's comment had been instant. It was taken as gospel, and the note of qualification was immediately eliminated, as any good PR realized it would be, given the trend toward simplification in transmission.

At that stage, I phoned a press officer at the Ministry of Defense (MoD) to clarify why General Jackson had gone on record in this way and what his sources were for this (inaccurate) remark. The person I spoke to was pleasant but uninformative. He ventured that Sir Mike had "obviously not realized" that a thanks had been offered by CPT and Norman Kember to his releasers and that he was "apparently unaware" of what was on the Christian Peacemaker Teams' website. Other than that he had "no further explanation" or comment. I politely asked whether it was usual MoD or British Army policy to send their most senior figure onto a national TV news program to comment on events that neither he nor they appeared to have researched. Rather expectedly, no answer was given. It seemed an ironic failure of "military intelligence."

Nonetheless Ekklesia was able to run a story on March 28, indicating that the "Army chief spoke without knowledge on alleged Kember ingratitude." This was then picked up by several news agencies and as a footnote to the saga by two British newspapers. It was fairly widely syndicated on the Internet as well. As a footnote, the week before he retired at the end of July 2006, Jonathan Bartley bumped into General Jackson at a Lambeth Palace reception hosted by the Archbishop of Canterbury. The general had little recollection of what he had said or of the whole incident. The truth is that the dominant narrative does not have to struggle to assert itself. It is the accepted, commonsensical viewpoint that becomes the received account, such that it no longer requires justification. This is why the subversive footnote and the well-documented counter-fact remains important. It is in this way that a wedge is maintained through which truth can seep, feeding the hope and reason of those who would do and see things differently.

Similarly Ekklesia, small though it is in the grand scheme, played a part in the unraveling of the "script" that blamed the CPT-Iraq team for the alleged risk of the rescue operation. Speaking on the Jeremy Vine BBC Radio 2 program on March 27, a leading counter-terrorism and security analyst, Col. Mike Dewar, inadvertently poured scorn on the idea—by then widely circulating—that Norman and his fellow CPTers had caused any danger to British service personnel by their actions. He has also defended CPT's right to be in Iraq.

Colonel Dewar is a vigorous supporter of the Iraq War and a practicing Christian. During the interview he made clear his contempt and distaste for nonviolent campaigners, and he dismissed Christian peacemaking as "fundamentalism." He mocked the idea that prayer could thwart dictatorship and described weapons as God's "tools" for use "in the real world." The colonel told CPT dismissively, "If you want to send back more teams, that is entirely your business."

In response, Jonathan Bartley explained that CPT were concerned about the welfare of coalition soldiers as well as Iraqis and that this is why they had categorically said that they did not want the lives of military or civilian operatives endangered through military rescue, should their volunteers be captured.

At this point, Dewar exclaimed angrily, "You needn't worry, Mr. Bartley, about putting troops in danger. It's part of a soldier's job to be in danger, so we don't need your worries, thank you very much, about putting us in danger. British troops are out there in danger on a daily basis. And in fact they were extremely glad to be able to rescue them."

Once again, the curious attempt to blame peace for war had turned in upon itself, proving that, even in the face of overwhelming odds, it is worth the patient attempt to illicit overlooked facts and those more nuanced interpretations of events that affirm the "underside of history" in the face of often-jaundiced first drafts of the public record.

Tim: The scandal of a committed peacemaker

Jan Benvie, then a CPT reservist, found herself a focal point for journalists after the hostages' release. Jan is from Inverkeithing, Scotland, and joined CPT as a part-time member in January 2005. She spent six weeks in Iraq in the summer of 2005. On the day after the hostages' release, she told journalists that she was moving forward with plans to leave her job as a special needs teacher to work full time with CPT. Furthermore she expressed willingness to spend time in Iraq if asked to go there.

The Telegraph, Guardian, Scotsman, and BBC News, all ran quotes from her, playing her plans as a mini-scandal. How could anyone consider doing peace work in Iraq after what had happened? For a few days, Jan found herself inundated with calls from journalists. As with Maureen, the Scotsman gave Jan the most space to explain herself in their article on Saturday, March 25. "In general we allow adults to make their own decisions about their lives," she said. "Despite the dangers I believe, as Christian Peacemaker Teams believe, that it is vitally important that we go and try to make peace."[22]

The Telegraph ran the same quote in its article, but with only the first sentence, giving Jan an almost adolescent defensiveness.

The Guardian, the Telegraph, and the Scotsman played quotes from Jan off against quotes from Terry Waite, famous for the time he spent as a hostage in Beirut and later as a hostage negotiator. He gave a mixed opinion in the Telegraph article, supporting CPT's motives but questioning their tactics: "The first thing I would say is I applaud the motives of anyone who wishes to work for peace. …The situation in Iraq is dreadful, the ordinary civilian population are suffering terribly and it is something to be commended to go and stand alongside such people. I question, though, the tactic because I think the situation in Iraq is so vastly different to when I was negotiating 20 years ago."[23]

Waite went on to say that he was concerned that the CPTers tactics "involved other people in the situation." He wasn't clear on what other people might be involved, but the implication was that CPT was putting soldiers at risk, a concern echoed by many journalists throughout the crisis.

The Guardian was the only paper that ran Jan's suggestion that the responsibility for the soldiers lay with the government, not the CPTers. "We make it clear that if we are kidnapped, we do not want there to be force or any form of violence used to release us," she told GMTV. "If the

---

[22] Source: thescotsman.scotsman.com/index.cfm?id=463752006.
[23] Source:
www.telegraph.co.uk/news/main.jhtml?xml=/news/2006/03/24/uwaite.xml.

government or military commanders choose to do that, that is their responsibility."[24]

Both the Scotsman and the Telegraph seemed to defer to Waite as expert on Iraq, despite the fact that Jan had been to Iraq, while Waite apparently had not visited Iraq recently, if at all.

"The media had the story they wanted to tell," Jan said, reflecting back on the coverage seven months later. "Their story was about whether or not Norman or CPT had appropriately thanked the military and my willingness to return to Iraq if CPT decided to remain there. The story of the ungrateful, reckless peaceniks. They were not interested in reporting the horrendous daily living conditions caused by the war in Iraq, of which I had first-hand experience. They selectively used anything I said to tell their story."

The media spotlight had effects beyond the pages of the newspaper, however. On Friday, March 24, 2006, the same day the Telegraph article came out, Jan opened her door to discover that two police officers had been sent to try to dissuade her from going back to Iraq. It took her five months, with the help of her Member of Parliament, to find out who had requested the visit.

Two weeks after most of the hubbub had died down, The Guardian ran a feature story on Friday, April 7, interviewing Jan on her work with CPT and her convictions. It also gave her an opportunity to share, in more depth, her perspective on the media hubbub and why CPT was in Iraq: "Speak to the Iraqis we work with and ask them. That's what we use as a measure of whether our work is worthwhile. They do say so. For me, as long as people are saying what we do is worthwhile, then we will keep doing it," she said.[25]

On Sunday, June 11, the Scotland on Sunday, sister paper of the Scotsman, published a feature article on Jan. Like the Guardian article, it looked more deeply at her motivations. "Benvie's anti-war stance is philosophical, but it's also practical. ...War robs the living as well as the dead. ...For Benvie's grandfather life changed when his son failed to come back from Salerno [in World War II]." Unlike other press coverage, this article reported something of her first-hand experience of "an injured country, war ravaged, where schools and hospitals are in ruins, where sewage runs in the streets."[26]

---

[24] Source: www.guardian.co.uk/international/story/0,,1738793,00.html.

[25] Source: www.guardian.co.uk/women/story/0,,1748972,00.html.

[26] Source: scotlandonsunday.scotsman.com/spectrum.cfm?id=854052006.

Simon: Experiments in hope

The most important lesson I learned from interactions with the media during the CPT-Iraq hostage crisis is that no matter how remorseless the media juggernaut—efficient in rapidly disseminating information, but often at some considerable cost to accuracy and understanding—it is always worth engaging. In an era of corporate power and mass consumption, cracks in the system, viewpoints from the grassroots, truth from the margins, and wisdom from the outsider are the concrete ways in which a new kind of gentle energy can be nurtured and sustained.

Again and again, the dominant narratives of our time, most especially what theologian Walter Wink calls "the myth of redemptive violence," assert themselves in such a way as to write peace and peacemaking out of the script. This is only to be expected. The appropriate response is not despair or collusion, but the cultivation of what the late Archbishop Helder Camara once called "small-scale experiments in hope."

Such experiments arise from the constructive but vulnerable witness of persons like those who serve with Christian Peacemaker Teams in situations of seemingly intractable destructiveness—and above all in the local people whose ongoing resistance to the powers that be is the only final source of alternatives, when attempts to impose external "solutions" by force inevitably break down. To be effective, however, alternatives need to spread. To spread they must be heard. And to be heard they must be re-inserted into the script, written out of it (in the sense of inscribed within and inscribed without)—not written off or written away. This is the task to which we continue to be called.

Tim: Epilogue

Six months after the hostages were freed, I asked Pat Gaffney, Bruce Kent, Maureen Jack, Jan Benvie, and others to reflect on some of the things that worked in relating to the media, and things that didn't.

Pat Gaffney felt that the press coverage for the most part helped to create a human connection with the hostages and what they were doing, and it made Norman and the others a household name in the United Kingdom.

Bruce Kent compared the experience to his previous experience with the press as director of the Campaign for Nuclear Disarmament. "During the eighties, we had endless hostile media on the issue of alleged support of CND of the U.S.S.R.," he said. "The press was very hostile about everything we did on the ground. They said we were communist sympathizers, neutralists, and defeatists. ...We were very good at defending ourselves."

Bruce felt the media attention given the hostage crisis provided a real opportunity for friends and supporters of Norman to present nonviolent alternatives to war through interviews. "We were able to share about the middle ground between going to war and sitting on our hands and doing nothing, and to tell about those helping families of prisoners and doing mediation," he said.

Bruce was particularly inspired by the collaboration with Muslim Association of Britain. "That opened up a door we'd never been through before, and those relationships have continued," he said. "Anas Altikriti's bravery was really quite astonishing."

Al Jazeera's consistent coverage of the situation throughout the crisis was also key. Bruce did a number of interviews with Al Jazeera. "They deserve a big thank-you because they got our message out to places we would not have been able to reach," he said. "We still don't know what effect that may have had."

Despite these positive experiences, Bruce also had concerns about the handling of media, concerns that he and others were making it up as they went along due to lack of information. He admitted, "Norman's supporters were clearly not prepared for a kidnapping or what might come."

Bruce felt there was a strong need for a full-time, senior CPT staff person to help those in the United Kingdom answer questions and coordinate their responses. Although this was requested by the group meeting in London in February, CPT did not have the resources to respond beyond the CPT-UK volunteers already working in the United Kingdom. As a result, they were very grateful for the support they received from fellow U.K. peace organizations.

Bruce was frustrated by the media environment that met Norman when he returned to the United Kingdom. "The media become almost savage before Norman even arrived home." Bruce said. "I felt that CPT was a bit unaware of general public opinion [in the United Kingdom] and gave critics an excuse to be hostile very quickly."

When I talked with CPT co-director Carol Rose in July 2006, she explained that in the days immediately following the release CPT was not just concerned with public perceptions in North America and Europe. They were also concerned for the contacts and allies of Christian Peacemaker Teams in Muslim communities. As CPT responded to the media they had to keep in mind the impact their statements could have on their partners. If CPT's statements were seen as supporting the U.S. military, these partners could be targeted for collaborating with an organization perceived (however wrongly) to be supporting the military occupation of Iraq.

Maureen Jack felt there were significant differences between the situation for CPTers in the United Kingdom and those in the United States. "In Toronto and Chicago there are CPT offices, from which official CPT statements were issued. We have nothing like that in the U.K., which I think put additional pressure on us as individuals. As the crisis wore on, we increasingly liaised with one another, but perhaps, in retrospect, it might have been better if we had empowered one of us to take on a coordinating role. This would have enabled us to be more proactive, issuing statements rather than simply responding to the media's agenda."

CPT-UK is continuing to get the story of the missing peace out in the United Kingdom. On December 8, 2006, Norman, Harmeet, and Jim were reunited in London for the first time since they left Iraq. In a press conference organized by Ekklesia, they issued a joint statement in which they discussed the upcoming trial of their kidnappers in Iraq (see the chapter entitled "Joint Statement of Forgiveness").

Simon Barrow is co-director of Ekklesia, a U.K. Christian think tank. A theologian, writer, ecumenist, and current-affairs journalist, he has been involved in peace and justice causes and has worked for a range of churches and nongovernmental organizations.

Tim Nafziger is a member of CPT Reserve Corps who has served in Colombia. He worked to coordinate and organize CPT-UK with a focus in London from 2004-2006. He is currently a freelance Web designer.

16

A Trip of Miracles

Ehab Lotayef

I don't recall the exact time, but it was early in the morning of March 23, 2006. My radio/alarm-clock must have repeated the word *hostages* several times before it grabbed the attention of my half-sleeping brain. I sprung up and listened attentively. A few minutes later, I was on the phone with Sheila Provencher affirming, "Yes, yes, I am sure." I needed to repeat the words a few times before she and I could move to congratulating one another—or whatever one would call what we said.

Where did I meet Sheila, and why was she the first person I called about news of the release of Norman Kember, Jim Loney, and Harmeet Singh Sooden?

Our connection began in the fall of 2005.

Early in October, Mary Foster, a long-time friend and Montreal social-justice activist, invited me to meet Greg Rollins, a CPT member who had been in Iraq a few months prior and who was planning to return shortly. Greg, who is from British Columbia, was visiting Montreal as part of a cross-Canada tour to share his experience and raise awareness about the situation in Iraq. I'd had an interesting conversation with Greg comparing the situation in Iraq as he last saw it to how it was when I was there, in December 2003.

A few weeks later, I heard that Greg was in Amman, Jordan, having difficulties getting into Iraq due to changes in Iraqi visa regulations. Iraqi authorities now required Canadian citizens to obtain a visa ahead of time, rather than at the point of entry as in the past.

Another few weeks passed before the world heard the shocking and sad news of the CPT members kidnapped in Baghdad. CPT was one of the last independent groups still operating in Iraq. The numerous hostage-takings and mounting dangers in Iraq had forced or scared out most other nongovernmental organizations. In the few days after news of the kidnapping broke, since the names of the hostages were not yet made public, I thought of Greg. I assumed he must have reached Baghdad and was one of the hostages. I felt the situation touched me personally, for although I did not know Greg well, he was someone I had met, talked to, and shared a meal with only a few weeks earlier.

Activists in Montreal started wondering how to help. As a Muslim and Arab-Canadian who has contacts with many leaders and organizers in the Muslim and Arab communities, I was sought out to contact the Canadian Islamic Congress, the Canadian Muslim Forum, the Muslim Council of Montreal, and Parole Arabe, among others, asking them to issue statements in support of the CPT hostages.

Right away I began making contacts and talking to activists and leaders in the Muslim and Arab communities. All the while I had a thought I could not make practical sense of: "Maybe I should travel to Iraq to help." I kept it mostly to myself. Whenever the thought came, I asked myself, "How would that help?" And I found no answer.

Shortly thereafter, the names of the hostages were made public and I knew that Greg was not among them. Nonetheless, I still felt a strong connection.

Statements of support began to flow in from organizations and groups across Canada and the world, commending CPT and its members for their great work of supporting the oppressed and needy worldwide, statements asking the abductors to free the CPT hostages who were in Iraq with nothing on their minds but the good of the country and its people. Statements came from Christians, atheists, Jews, and Muslims; from anarchists and politicians; even from behind prison bars: a statement of support was issued by three Arab Muslim detainees held in Canada under Security Certificates, in support of whom CPT members had campaigned and still are campaigning. All of this was encouraging and uplifting. Still I could not stop myself from asking, "How much of this support and how many of these testimonials are reaching the abductors or those with influence in Iraq?"

Everything suddenly changed on Saturday, December 3, 2005. I was checking my e-mail before leaving home when I came across a short note from Mrs. Wahida Valiante, the vice-president of the Canadian Islamic Congress (CIC). She confirmed that the CIC would issue a media communiqué regarding the hostage crisis the following morning, and in closing asked if I would be interested in traveling to Iraq.

I had been in Iraq two years earlier, in December 2003, nine months after the invasion. During that trip, I spent three weeks traveling across the country, witnessing and documenting the situation of Iraq under occupation. In addition, I had lived in Iraq many years earlier as a child— between 1968 and 1970. At the time my mother was teaching at the University of Baghdad. Thus I had reasonable knowledge of the country and customs, and familiarity with the current situation there. I am also a native Arabic speaker. That said, it was well known that there were no certainties about anything, let alone security, in the Iraq of December 2005.

As I joined the March Against Climate Change that afternoon, I could think of nothing but Wahida's question: "Would you be interested in going to Iraq?" Within a few hours I had made up my mind. I called her and confirmed my willingness.

The hostage takers had just announced a deadline: December 8. Though I didn't give much credence to the deadline (deadlines come and go in these situations, as similar incidents proved), it made sense to try to get to Baghdad before it passed. Come Monday, things became clearer. I decided to leave within twenty-four hours (though I had not yet made travel arrangements).

Although I was going to Iraq as a CIC envoy, it was crucial to coordinate my efforts with CPT. Thus I contacted Doug Pritchard, the CPT co-director who works out of Toronto, and discussed my plans. I then contacted the Muslim Association of Britain and managed to contact their envoy, Anas Altikriti, who was already in Iraq. Most important, I was introduced to and managed to contact someone in Baghdad who is both efficient and experienced in working with independent foreign journalists. He committed to helping me make my trip as productive and safe as possible.

Before Monday's end I had managed to book a ticket for Tuesday evening.

Things were moving ahead on many fronts but obstacles remained. Greg's experience a few weeks prior proved that entering Iraq had become more complicated for Canadians than the last time I'd visited. The ticket I booked was to Amman, since booking tickets to Baghdad could be done only from connecting cities (mainly Amman, Beirut, and Damascus). Iraqi parliamentary elections were coming up soon (announced for mid-December) and there was talk about closing the borders during the elections. Furthermore, I still did not know what I would do in Baghdad.

I had no option but to act without a clear plan, one step at a time. I informed the CIC of the possibility that I would not even reach Baghdad, and we agreed it was worth the risk. Another thing was clear to us: I was not going as a negotiator or to attempt to contact the hostage takers, which is, unfortunately, how some in the media portrayed my intent.

Exhausted, I went to sleep late Monday night. I hoped for a good night's rest that would prepare me, at least physically, for what lay ahead. But very early in the morning, I was awakened by a phone call—a Canadian Broadcasting Corporation (CBC) producer asking about my trip. I had no knowledge that information about the trip had been communicated to the media, since communicating such information at this point was not in the plan. When I asked the producer how he knew about my trip, he said he heard about it from Mr. Altikriti in Iraq. Ah! So now I would have to spend

155

a large part of my day dealing with the media rather than working on preparations for the trip. Who knows, I told myself, maybe it's all for the best. Maybe media coverage in Canada would bring Arab and international media attention to my efforts. Perhaps it would help get the word out to the hostage takers.

At Dorval airport on Tuesday evening, I was still being interviewed live on TV and photographed for the print media as I waited for my plane. But as soon as I boarded, I was alone in peace. I could finally focus on what lay ahead.

I was traveling Air France with a stopover in Paris, and thus would not reach Amman till Wednesday evening. Wednesday was still the seventh of December, and I could leave for Baghdad early Thursday morning— especially if I did not need a visa. Perhaps things were still under control. I made some phone calls from the airport in Paris to Amman and Baghdad but still received no definite information regarding my need for a visa to enter Iraq.

I reached Amman on Wednesday evening and headed directly to the al-Munzir hotel. In al-Munzir's modest but friendly lobby, with which I was familiar from a stopover two years earlier, I met with CPT members and other local and international activists. Discussion and exchanges throughout the evening confirmed that I would need a visa to enter Iraq and that there was no point in trying to head to the airport to board a plane the next morning. Without a visa stamped on my passport and an okayed ticket in my hand, I would be grounded. I also learned that I could not book a return ticket (Amman-Baghdad-Amman) from Amman and that tickets for the Baghdad-Amman flight could be booked only in Baghdad. Not having a confirmed ticket to leave Baghdad meant that I could get stuck in Iraq indefinitely.

In short, I had to spend Thursday in Amman working on getting a ticket and a visa so that I could leave on Friday. I would also have to make all arrangements for what I would do in Baghdad and try to coordinate with my Iraqi contact to buy me a Baghdad-Amman ticket so that—God willing—I would be able to get out of Iraq in reasonable time (that is, if I managed to get in).

Thursday morning I left the hotel for the Iraqi Airways office. I managed to book a seat to Baghdad for the next morning, but could not get a ticket without the Iraqi visa stamp on my passport. Friday is the weekend in the Muslim world, so in many cases Thursday is a short workday. When I reached the Iraqi Embassy at eleven a.m., the guard at the door told me without hesitation, "Come back on Saturday; we are closed for the week."

Is this the end of my trip? I wondered.

Knowing Arab bureaucracy, I thought this could well be the case. I had to convince myself that miracles happen. I pulled out a letter I had asked the CIC to fax me for no particular reason before I left Montreal, stating that I am a CIC official envoy to Iraq. As I passed through the door, I confidently handed it to the guard, telling him to deliver it to the consul personally, informing him of my presence.

The time I spent in the waiting room among people who obviously had worries and anxieties of their own, waiting for a verdict from the consul, felt like eternity. I had no expectations and knew I could do nothing to influence the situation. I spent my time making "theoretical" plans for the press conference I may hold in Baghdad.

When a clerk called my name and told me I should have my visa by one o'clock, I felt, in a strange way, that I had received help from somewhere beyond my comprehension. Although a practicing Muslim and a believer, beyond doubt, in God, I usually reject the inexplicable, refusing to believe that God intervenes in our lives in the direct way many people believe He does. Was I about to change this conviction?

As I sat waiting to get back my passport, I asked myself, "Why did I accept being 'pulled' into a photographer's shop a few steps before reaching the embassy door to get my 'visa' photos taken?" Without those photos, which I had no idea were needed for the application, the visa process would have been even harder.

On my way back to the Iraqi Airways office, I again called my contact in Baghdad. I asked if he had managed to book a Baghdad-Amman ticket for me. When he confirmed that he had, I asked him to buy it and pay without delay. Back at the Iraqi Airways office, I got my ticket within an hour but not without having to leap a couple of small hurdles. The clerks first doubted the authenticity of the visa I had miraculously obtained in under three hours, which required some convincing. Then they insisted that I pay in Jordanian dinars (JDs)—which I did not have—after originally quoting me in U.S. dollars. I had to quickly find an exchange bureau, buy JDs, and get back to the office before it closed.

At this point I knew there was a good possibility I would get to Baghdad. Still I had no clear plan what I would do when I got there, though the idea of a press conference had started to take shape in my head. As soon as I was back at al-Munzir hotel, I was on the phone and e-mail. I communicated with Montreal, where Mary was online and in contact with a media work-group in Hebron, Palestine; with Wahida in Toronto; and with my contact in Baghdad, trying to plan a press conference and communicate information to the media.

Holding the press conference at the Baghdad Airport—a naïve idea—turned out to be impractical due to the access and security restrictions around the airport, restrictions no journalist would want to battle. Other ideas were likewise shot down, one after another. Finally, as the sun was setting in Amman, my Baghdad contact informed me that he had contacted Sheikh Abd es-Salaam al-Kubaisi of the Muslim Scholars Association in Baghdad who agreed to hold the press conference at the association's headquarters, at Um al-Qura mosque, following the mid-afternoon (Asr) prayers on Friday. It would be a joint conference with him and me. This was beyond our best expectations.

I wrote a press release announcing the conference and e-mailed it to the CIC and to Mary. Finally, I could breathe. The press release was sent out from Montreal and Toronto, and I was able to sit down with the CPT team, among whom was Sheila Provencher. We shared a light meal and discussed the details of my upcoming trip. As may be expected, I slept little that night.

Only security-authorized taxis can reach the arrival and departure gates at Baghdad airport. These taxis take passengers to the publicly accessible point a few kilometers away. I got out of the cab and found my contact waiting for me in his car. "Everything ready?" I asked. Everything seemed to be. The press conference was set for 3:30 p.m., and it was now mid-morning. We would go for Friday prayers at the mosque where Sheikh al-Kubaisi delivers the Friday sermon, stop to make copies of the press kit Mary Foster had prepared for me, check me into a hotel, have something to eat, then head to Um al-Qura mosque for Asr prayers before the press conference began. I couldn't get the question off my mind: "Will there be media coverage?"

We made it to Friday prayers. The mosque was crowded but orderly, yet the Friday sermon was delivered by someone other than Sheikh al-Kubaisi, whom we had expected to hear. This was a first-hand introduction to the maneuvers people, and especially public figures, have to make to escape danger and stay safe in Iraq. Like many others, Sheikh al-Kubaisi had to regularly alter his plans and avoid being in public places where he was expected to be. As I listened to the sermon, fatigue caught up with me. I could barely keep my eyes open.

Only by God's grace did things fall into place. The photocopier at the one shop we found open on Friday afternoon delivered our copies, but only after showing serious signs of malfunction. We had no time to eat and had to maneuver our way to avoid checkpoints and roadblocks. But by three p.m. we were finally at the heavily guarded gates of Um al-Qura mosque, the headquarters of the Muslim Scholars Association. As we entered and pulled into the parking lot, I felt relieved. At least a half-dozen media vehicles were already there. Perhaps my trip would achieve something after all.

I prayed Asr with the congregation, then proceeded to a small auditorium where the media cameras and microphones were assembled. Within a few minutes, Sheikh al-Kubaisi arrived.

I spoke first. I started in Arabic, pleading with the kidnappers to release the CPT hostages, assuring that CPT is an independent organization that neither aims to convert people nor is linked to any government. I reminded whoever would listen that I was testifying as a Muslim and as an Arab who knows and has worked with CPT, and as someone who has witnessed and heard of their work in Iraq and Palestine as well as Canada. I closed by pleading with the kidnappers to give those courageous Christian friends, those supporters of oppressed people all over the world, the opportunity to spend the upcoming Christmas holidays with their families and loved ones.

At the request of the journalists from Canadian and other international media, I summed up in English what I had said in Arabic. Sheikh al-Kubaisi spoke after me, directing his words to the kidnappers. Without mincing words, he told them that if they are working under the guidance of Islam, they should release the hostages without delay; this is the only action Islam would condone. However, he continued, if they are acting under the guidance of something other than Islam, they should come clean and leave Islam out of it. Following our presentations, I gave a few interviews and had a short private conversation with Sheikh al-Kubaisi, thanking him for his help and support. Again, we were on our way.

My Baghdad-Amman flight was booked for Saturday afternoon, twenty-four hours away. At this point we had to decide if I should extend my stay in Baghdad or leave the following day. Weighing the pros and cons, we decided to stick to our original plan and try to achieve as much as possible in the time I had left.

I wanted to meet and talk to as many influential people in Iraqi society as I could, assuring that they heard, first hand, that the CPT hostages are innocent of any wrongdoing and deserve freedom. I believed this was the first step toward the hostages' safe release.

Perhaps the kidnappers really believed that Norman, Tom, Jim, and Harmeet were spies or evangelists. In this case the more people who knew the truth, the better the chances it would reach the kidnappers, and the higher the probability of the kidnappers releasing the hostages.

On the other hand, if the kidnappers had other motives, whatever those were, spreading the word about CPT's credibility would disarm the kidnappers, nullifying any false justifications they planned to use for harming the hostages.

My contact got on his cell phone and started calling people, only some of whom he knew. I forgot how tired and hungry I'd been earlier and felt energized to do more. That evening and the next morning—until I was dropped off at the security point on the airport road—I must have met a dozen people: politicians, party leaders, writers, and academics. To each of them, I repeated the same message and asked them to spread the word, even if they could do nothing more. Some of them got on the phone while I was still in the room and called acquaintances and tribal leaders in and outside of Baghdad, repeating what I had told them and testifying to the credibility of the CPT hostages.

Before arriving at my hotel on Friday night, I received a call on my contact's cell phone from a reporter with the Canadian TV channel CTV, requesting a personal interview. I told her that she was welcome to come to my hotel later that evening. She said she had to first check if my hotel was one of the "safe" places she was allowed to go to. Earlier, after the press conference, an Arab cameraman from the CBC had recorded an interview in which he asked me questions in Arabic and I replied in English. When I asked why the interview was being done in this way, he explained that the Canadian reporter would not come to the (unsafe) Um al-Qura mosque and would later add the questions in English to the "interview." These are but two examples of the shallow way in which international media covers Iraq. These anecdotes also reveal the importance of the presence in Iraq of independent media and grassroots activists, such as CPT.

On Saturday morning I visited the Iraqi Islamic Party where I was given a copy of the statement they had issued, days earlier, calling for the release of the CPT hostages. The party promised to continue their efforts, doing all they could to help. That morning we made a few other visits, though not as many as we would have liked, because a bomb had exploded near my contact's house and a limited curfew was imposed for two hours on his neighborhood, thus delaying the start of our day.

Such is life in Baghdad.

I left Baghdad for Amman on a plane carrying the Iraqi youth soccer team traveling to a three-team qualifier tournament in Amman. It was uplifting to see those seventeen-year-olds ready to face the world with confidence despite their personal sufferings. I say "personal sufferings" because the violence, killings, injuries, and destruction in Iraq affect every single individual. It would be rare if any of those youngsters had not witnessed a death or a serious injury within his immediate family. Add to this the fear and the lack of security, of which the greatest casualty can be young minds.

I reached Amman late Saturday evening and decided to spend a few days trying to keep my message alive in the Arabic media and helping the CPT team in Amman. One way I could assist was by translating material into Arabic and doing Arabic media interviews.

Working with Peggy Gish, Sheila Provencher, and Jenny Elliott, and continuing my contacts with Arab satellite TV channels, I helped keep the CPT hostage crisis on the news despite increasing competition with the approaching Iraqi Parliamentary elections. I never lost hope that people's efforts in support of the hostages would be fruitful.

After my return to Canada, I repeated, on many occasions, that "no news is good news" and that I gave myself no option but hope. Giving in to despair would only inhibit our work and decrease the probability of a positive outcome.

When I attended a CPT vigil in Toronto, I was met with much gratitude from the CPT members who were there, a gratitude I do not feel I deserve. I sincerely believe that I, and the whole world, owe so much to Norman, Tom, Jim, and Harmeet.

The tragic day when I heard of Tom Fox's death was, to say the least, a setback. Sheila had told me in depth about her trip with Tom accompanying Palestinian refugees across the desert from Baghdad to Syria, and how Tom had been a source of support and encouragement to everyone. I felt deeply saddened by his death.

Even after Tom's death, I continued to hope that the others would be freed safely. *Al-Hamd-u li-Allah* (thank God) it was not long before they were. When I heard the news, I felt that the first person I should tell was the person with whom I shared a large part of my experience, Sheila Provencher.

Though this crisis is behind us, it remains alive as an encouragement to me to fight for justice even when it is costly. I also came out of this experience with a clearer realization that without the support of our families, friends, and loved ones, we achieve little.[27]

My trip to Iraq had been full of miracles—a trip that took me to a higher level of belief in God, a trip that was a sort of coming of age for me, a trip for which I am grateful.

Ehab Lotayef of Montreal is a poet, photographer, essayist, playwright, and computer engineer at McGill University. More than anything, Ehab is a passionate activist who has traveled extensively in the Middle East. Born in Egypt, he lived in several countries before moving to Canada in 1989.

---

[27] I owe to the efficiency and commitment of my Iraqi contact and guide everything achieved in my trip. Without his contacts, planning, advice, and enthusiasm, little could have been done. I hide his identity only at his request and for his own safety. Also, I could not have done what I did without the moral support and encouragement of Tali Goodfriend (now my wife), my sons Youssef and Ahemd, and my ex-wife among many others. Last, but not least, I relied on the help, advice, and logistical support—every step of the way—from Mary Foster, Mohamed S. Kamel, and Wahida Valiante, although they never left Canada. Without them I wouldn't have been able to make it.

17

A Great Hand of Solidarity:
Jim Loney and Canada's Secret Trial Detainees

Matthew Behrens

A great hand of solidarity reached out for us, a hand that included the hands of Palestinian children holding pictures of us, and the hands of the British soldier who cut our chains with a bolt cutter. That great hand was able to deliver three of us from the shadow of death. I am grateful in a way that can never be adequately expressed in words. There are so many people that need this hand of solidarity, right now, today, and I'm thinking specifically of prisoners held all over the world, people who have disappeared into an abyss of detention without charge, due process, hope of release, some—victims of physical and psychological torture, people unknown and forgotten. It is my deepest wish that every forsaken human being should have a hand of solidarity reaching out to them.
—*Jim Loney, March 27, 2006*

Saturday, September 12, 2004, was the kind of day that reminded Toronto climate-change watchers there's still such a thing as change of season. Pleasantly warm and sunny, the leaves were beginning to turn, providing a colorful display that can make Ontario a visual delight.

There was another colorful display that day, organized by CPT and the Campaign to Stop Secret Trials in Canada. Designed to draw attention to the links between the illegal and indefinite detention of people in Canada, Guantanamo Bay, Afghanistan, and Iraq, the Multifaith Walk to Set Captives Free proved a striking visual procession as it made its way from the Toronto offices of Canada's spy agency, Canadian Security Intelligence Service (CSIS), to the U.S. consulate, the Federal Court, and the headquarters of Canada's ruling Liberal Party.

At each stop, caged doves were released, and peacemakers who had been at the gates of Abu Ghraib joined with those who have lived through the pain of Canada's own version of Guantanamo Bay to address the hundreds of participants.

Among the many memorable moments that day was the sight of a "soldier," prop machine gun in hand, leading hooded, shirtless "Iraqi detainees," their hands behind their backs in plastic handcuffs, up the ramp to the entrance of the U.S. consulate. Another was the constant presence of five individuals wearing prison-orange shirts and carrying jail bars with the names of Canada's secret trial detainees.

As with similar demonstrations before and since, this September multifaith gathering of hundreds of Jews, Christians, and Muslims was a morale builder for the men detained in Canada under secret hearing "security certificates." Any non-citizen in Canada can be arrested under these security certificates, detained without charge, and held indefinitely on secret "evidence" that neither the detainee nor the lawyer is allowed to see.

Though no evidence has been shown to support the accusations against them, the brush of "terror suspect" has been used to tar five Muslim men who, as of April 2008, have been detained both behind bars and under draconian house arrest control orders a collective 33 years, the threat of deportation to torture hanging over their heads.

Given the manner in which most people tend to scatter in fear when the word *terror* is uttered, there have been few people in Canada willing to take a public stand against this injustice. Hence, any public gathering of supportive spirits has proven cathartic for families who, isolated in their own communities, have been forced to go it alone with a handful of dedicated supporters to raise funds, publicize the cases, attend the very limited public portions of the hearings, and act as advocates for men who've been indefinitely locked up.

One of those advocates and an organizer of the September procession is Jim Loney, a member of the Toronto Catholic Worker community and CPT, who was that day doing double duty as emcee and as the one charged with caring for the caged birds before they were set free at each location. No one could have dreamed that a photo of Jim from that day—one of Jim helping a young woman wearing hijab release one of the doves—would be flashed around the world some fifteen months later, as part of an international effort to convince those in Iraq holding him and three CPT comrades that the four men were in Iraq to help Iraqis, in solidarity with those suffering under the terror of the U.S.-led occupation.

The young woman in the picture, Afnan Jaballah, knows something about terror. Her father, Mahmoud Jaballah, was forced to flee Egypt with his family after being arrested, but never charged, on seven different occasions. Having survived years of incarceration and torture, Jaballah came to Canada with his loved ones seeking a peaceful life. But it seems that when he applied for refugee status, Canada's spy agency, the CSIS, checked with Egyptian authorities. Despite the bias against Jaballah by Egyptian officials, who had harassed him so often without charge and despite the fact Egypt is known for its record of corruption, deception, and torture, CSIS appears to have based its response to Jaballah's application on information from Egypt's blood-stained security apparatus. CSIS admits that its private relationship with overseas "intelligence" agencies trumps an individual's right to know the details of his or her case. This veil of secrecy allows for an untold number of possible violations, as in Jaballah's case.

As Jaballah's refugee claim was held up, CSIS officers began arriving at his small apartment late at night in 1998 for "interviews," in which Jaballah was asked to spy on his community. Jaballah refused, and the agents threatened him with jail and deportation to torture. A few short weeks later, in the spring of 1999, Jaballah and his daughter Afnan were in an underground parking lot when he was suddenly surrounded by heavily armed agents of the Royal Canadian Mounted Police, thrown to the ground, handcuffed, and whisked away, leaving a screaming five-year-old Afnan behind.

Afnan and her brothers and sisters had grown up with the fear of such treatment in Egypt and now faced it in Canada. In a curious twist of fate, though, their father was saved by the intervention of his then twelve-year-old son, Ahmad. During the session when CSIS agents threatened Jaballah, Ahmad placed a tape recorder in the hallway, unbeknownst to CSIS. When this tape was produced in the open portion of the hearing, it contributed to a judge's conclusion that the case against Jaballah was not credible. He walked free after seven months behind bars.

Then in August 2001, CSIS had Jaballah arrested on an unprecedented second certificate, despite admitting that they had no new evidence against him—only a new interpretation of old evidence already dismissed as not credible. Jaballah was detained another six years until his release on the most draconian house arrest conditions in Canadian history.

It was this second arrest that caught my and others' attention, and thus the Campaign to Stop Secret Trials in Canada was born. The campaign began as a series of walks and educational sessions about an issue virtually no one in Canada had heard of. The events of September 11, 2001, also raised awareness, though by that time security certificates had been in use for more than a decade.

Numbers at our events have never been large. Therefore it is easy to remember the few faces who consistently show up at the entrance to the prison, at the courthouse, or at the vigils at CSIS. Jim's has been one of those faces, as have other members of CPT.

When another of the Canadian detainees, Hassan Almrei, a Syrian refugee who spent a total of forty-nine months in solitary confinement, most of that time in an unheated cell, went on a hunger strike for heat, Jim was there at Metro West Detention Centre (dubbed "Guantanamo North") with a large sign that read, "Equal Rights for All." A picture of Jim holding that sign, along with many other snapshots, was sent to Hassan, a reminder that there were people in Canada who cared for him.

The hunger strike caught national attention and brought the reality of Kafkaesque detentions based on secret evidence and no charges to the attention of many Canadians for the first time. Such detentions were happening smack in the heart of Canada's largest city.

As our campaign grew, so did the knowledge of the massive rise in "security" detentions in Iraq. Al Slater, a CPTer who had slept out with us in an all-night protest at a jail in Toronto and who had joined a long-distance walk to publicize the plight of Canada's detainees, returned from Iraq with the first public reports of abuses at Abu Ghraib. As Jim headed back to Iraq for another journey in the fall of 2005, few of us realized how strong the connections between CPT's work in Iraq and our work in Canada might prove to be.

The moment news of Jim's and the other CPTers' captivity hit the headlines, a familiar phone voice came from the echo chamber that had been his solitary confinement home for four solid years. (Despite being in the hole, the man behind that voice had a remarkable capacity to learn both local gossip and global newsbreaks faster than most on the outside!)

"Good morning, brother," Hassan's voice echoed. His tone was solemn, absent the usual merriment that remarkably came with his daily calls. "I think I know this man whose picture is in the paper," he said.

"Yes," I replied, "Jim is a friend, and he has demonstrated many times for your rights."

"Then we must do something," Hassan replied.

Then we must do something. With those five words, Hassan summed up a spirit of survival and resistance that has somehow carried him and his fellow detainees through the bleakest of times. Though their bodies are definitely broken—the years of hunger strikes as long as 155 days, the lack of fresh air and sunlight, the terrible muck that passes for jail "food," the denial of touch visits with families, and so many other physical depredations—the detainees' spirit and faith has carried them this far. Also keeping the detainees going from day to day has been the hand of solidarity extended to them by hundreds of people across the country who have prayed, fasted, and demonstrated, mailed cards and letters, sent books and magazines, and received long-distance collect phone calls from the jail.

And so one of the least powerful and most isolated men in Canada, sitting in his nine-by-twelve-foot cell with no physical contact to the outside world since October 2001, talked about how to aid Jim Loney and the Christian peacemakers held in Baghdad. There would have been no point in suggesting to Hassan he was powerless. Hassan would have laughed. He would have asked why we had no faith.

Physical confinement proving no barrier to his imagination, Hassan said he would call later that day if a friendly guard was on night shift—and he did. Calls also came from the two other detainees held in Toronto: Mahmoud Jaballah, and Mohammad Mahjoub, held since June 2000 and also in solitary confinement. Both men expressed similar concerns and wanted to do something to help Jim. Every call I received from the detainees over the months of Jim's confinement started with questions of concern for him, a man they had never met but who elicited their deepest compassion despite their own daily difficulties.

And what difficulties! The detentions of individuals in Canada on security certificates are not unlike detentions without charge in Iraq, Afghanistan, or Guantanamo Bay. When the picture of an Iraqi man being dragged through Abu Ghraib flashed around the world, it struck a chord with Mahjoub, who had been treated in a similarly degrading fashion after requesting medical assistance for severe pain. During one emotional court appearance, Mahjoub held up the photo and declared, "This was me!" What separates the Canadian detentions is the facade of "due process" by which an individual named in the certificate is given a "reasonable opportunity to be heard." But given that security certificate detainees are unaware of the case against them, which is kept secret, how are they expected to respond? It is the unknowing that can drive a person mad.

But despite the potential for becoming immersed in their own situations, these men downplayed their troubles. They reached out.

After I'd first talked to him about Jim, Hassan, who had learned to speak English in solitary confinement by listening to the guards and who was slowly learning to write in English, immediately drafted a letter. He had worked on it through the night, writing it first in Arabic, then translating it word by word. If he dictated it to me, would I share it with Mahjoub and Jaballah? Hassan had no access to either man, but when Mahjoub and Jaballah called me later in the day, I went over Hassan's draft with both of them, incorporating their input and suggestions.

The plea was finalized and an open letter to those holding Jim and his CPT comrades was released on December 3. "In the name of Allah, the Most Gracious and Merciful," the letter explained the plight of the three men, noting, "Allah is witness to our innocence of these allegations. We are suffering a great injustice here in Canada because the government stereotypes Muslims and because of our strong faith and daily attendance to mosque. We have been suffering innocently."

The letter continued, "Many Canadians have heard of our injustice and have been supporting us in our fight for freedom by contacting politicians, by holding demonstrations in front of the jail, by writing letters to authorities and spreading the word all over Canada by way of media. James Loney of the Christian Peacemaker Teams is one of thousands of people who have been fighting to right this wrong. He is a person who has organized and motivated people to participate in this struggle for what is right. We have recently seen a photo of him in the newspaper and it has saddened our hearts to learn that he is being held captive in Iraq.

"This is the same James Loney who has traveled to Iraq on more than one occasion to help the people of Iraq. This is the same James Loney who has reached out to the families of the Abu Ghraib prisoners. This is the James Loney who was against the U.S. invasion and is against the U.S. occupation of Iraq.

"It pains our heart to know that a person of this caliber is being held captive. We care about his freedom more than we do our own.

"If you love Allah, if you have goodness in your heart, please deal with this matter as righteous Muslims and not let these kind, caring, compassionate and innocent people suffer. Prophet Mohammad, Peace be upon Him, said, 'If you do not thank the people, you do not thank Allah.' The Prophet, Peace be Upon Him, also said, 'If someone did a favor to you, try to return his favor.'

"We hope and pray to see these captives freed as much as we hope and pray for our own freedom here in Canada, a freedom for which James Loney has worked so hard."

Within minutes of the letter's release, national news media started calling. Could they speak to the detainees? Could they speak with someone at CPT? Arrangements were made for the men to call reporters and share their thoughts, though most in the media were less than charitable in their approach to this heartfelt plea.

Reporters interrogated the men about their *real* agenda. Surely, they were prodded, there must be *some* self-interested reason they had produced the statement. Were they hoping the letter would stand them in good stead in bail hearings? Were they linking their release to Jim's? After all, the reporters' tone implied, they are Muslims. They allegedly pose security concerns. How could they be trusted to have heartfelt concern for Jim's well-being? Did churches, labor groups, or others calling for the CPTers' release face such a grilling from reporters?

Jaballah told the press he could sympathize because he knew what it was like to be captured and held without a release date. Mahjoub, on hunger strike in solitary confinement, said Jim is a righteous man who speaks on behalf of people he has never met. This regard for the stranger is a theme running not only through Christian traditions, but through Muslim ones as well. Hassan eventually decided to refuse interviews because he did not want his and the other detainees' stories to eclipse Jim's. "Let the statement we made speak for itself," he said.

The letter from the Toronto detainees was a hand of solidarity reaching out to our friends in Baghdad and to those of us advocating for their release. We resided in a state of constant urgency in those days, straining to get the message out in the first days after the news broke.

The daily dread hanging over the heads of those who knew and loved the kidnapped CPTers gave us all a small sense of what it was like for Iraqi families whose loved ones were similarly held with no release date and for Canadian families experiencing the same torment.

But as the weeks passed and deadlines came and went with no word on the captives' fate, some of us experienced the "normalization" of a dire situation, something everyone in a crisis fears. It is physically and emotionally impossible to stand by a phone 24-7 or to operate in crisis-mode for extended periods without severe consequences. We all have family, friends, and work commitments we must meet. And so we have to weave the reality of the situation—the confinement of our friends—into the daily fabric of our lives. We head back to work, to school, to family functions, and we attend the prayer vigils for our friends.

The crisis becomes in an odd way one more item on our daily agenda. This normalization does not make the issue any less compelling or heartfelt, but is perhaps a survival mechanism that saves us from going mad. Allowing the situation to completely overtake every waking moment can eventually overwhelm and immobilize us. Yet, as one woman who writes monthly cards to the Canadian detainees points out, this normalization is also a disturbing sign of our ability to accept the existence of truly intolerable situations because it feels there is only so much we can do. It often feels this way working in solidarity with the secret-hearing detainees and their families, who must go to bed every night not knowing what daylight will bring.

However, we don't leave things there. Like nature in her seasons, we enter new phases that allow us to challenge the normalization of injustice. We are called to organize significant events or campaigns that affect us personally (while also affecting the public discourse on an issue), deepening our sense of resistance as we give an extra measure of ourselves.

This sense of needing to up the ante, to challenge ourselves while also attempting to prick the conscience of the country, was certainly part of the June 2006 Freedom Caravan to Ottawa—a ten-day journey through scores of communities en route to the Supreme Court hearings on security certificates. It took place after Jim and two of his comrades were released from captivity in Baghdad. When Jim heard about the caravan, he gave us a call and said he wanted to be part of it. He recalled that when he was first released in Baghdad, he called his partner, Dan, who told him of the letter the three Toronto detainees had written.

While gracefully handling the crush of media interest when it was announced he would be joining the caravan, Jim managed to get out of Toronto to join us. He was with us for three days in some of the smaller communities along the road to Ottawa. His first day on the caravan was a challenging one. We encountered counter-demonstrators screaming, "Kill all the Muslims and burn all the mosques," in the small town of Brighton. Jim tried to dialogue with them but it was difficult. At one point, one of the counter-demonstrators suddenly appeared shocked and turned to his pal. "Dawg," he said, "that's the dude who was held in Iraq!"

The temporary reprieve from yelling did not last long, unfortunately. Still, one can't help but wonder if a deeper impression was made in that moment of recognition than we will ever know.

The next day we made our way to the remote federal penitentiary at Millhaven, where a new unit had been constructed specifically to house secret-trial detainees. Jim led a group of some fifty Raging Grannies, students, and caravan members up the hill, singing freedom songs and ignoring repeated requests by federal marshals to vacate the property. As police vehicles gathered at the top of the hill, we slowly ascended, finally stopping at what we considered an appropriate spot for a few speeches and moments of reflection. There Jim reminded us of why he had joined this walk, telling those gathered that the detainees had written "we care about this man's freedom more than we do our own. They beautifully spoke up for me. Now that I'm free I have to speak up for them."

As we prepared to head back down the hill, Ahmad Jaballah, who had visited his father earlier in the day, announced that all three men were beginning another hunger strike to protest their conditions of detention. It was a reminder that although we were headed for the nation's top court, we still had a long road to travel.

When we eventually arrived in Ottawa, Jim joined a protest at the office of the prime minister, where Mahjoub's youngest children, ages six and eight, tried to make their way through a wall of RCMP officers to have a word with the leader of Canada. They were turned away. When Jim spoke, it was impossible to find him, surrounded as he was by national and international media.

The next day, Jim's open letter to members of Parliament appeared in the national newspaper *Globe and Mail*. "While I was held by a band of insurgents subject to no law but their own, these five men are being held under legislation passed by men and women who sat in the same chairs you currently occupy," he wrote, noting that in both cases, the detentions were marked by no fixed release date. Jim also pointed out that Canadian Foreign Affairs Minister Peter MacKay had spoken up for a Canadian-Iranian being held in Iran, urging that he either be charged or released. "While I am grateful for Mr. MacKay's principled stand," Jim wrote, "I can't help but wonder how he would respond if the foreign affairs minister of Iran were to point out that Canada has been holding five men without charge for between four and six years."

Certain media pundits came out swinging, saying Jim had no

business getting involved in the issue. But former Liberal cabinet minister and Deputy Prime Minister Sheila Copps, writing in the *Ottawa Sun*, praised Jim for speaking "from the heart about his own fears and how important it was that we, as Canadians, did not visit his private hell on others."

While he was in Ottawa, Jim met with politicians, many of whom were interested in what he had to say about his own ordeal. However, Jim refused to let these meetings be solely about him, insisting that they address the issue that had brought him to the nation's capital: abolition of the secret trial security certificate.

While at the court, we received daily calls from the detainees. They were thrilled to see on the national news clips of Jim joining the caravan and our Camp Hope at the Supreme Court steps. Jim was returning the great hand of solidarity from one of the many places it had come to help him regain his freedom. Three months later, Jim testified in court, offering bail money for Mr. Jaballah.

Since that time, a great deal has happened. The Supreme Court declared security certificates unconstitutional in February, 2007. Four of the five men have been returned to their families, but under onerous, humiliating control orders that require, among many draconian deprivations, government approval for a walk to the corner store to buy some milk. And the government has passed a new secret trials bill that virtually mirrors the old one, threatening to prolong for many years into the future the suffering of the detainees and their loved ones.

As we gathered in October, 2007, in front of CSIS for what felt like the millionth time, urging the government not to bring in the new law, Jim was there once again, as he has been and will continue to be for the long haul. It was a grim day as we struggled with the notion that seven years of work to end a human rights crisis were beginning anew. But it was also a hopeful day, for the familiar hands of solidarity that attach to faces like Jim's and the rest of the small, dedicated crew who have committed themselves to this issue held on to each other in a solidarity circle whose message was clear: with these hands we will continue to deflect, defuse, and disarm the forces of injustice that separate families from their loved ones, whether it be in Canada, Kabul, Basra, Guantanamo Bay, or sites unknown.

Matthew Behrens is the Toronto coordinator of Homes not Bombs (www.homesnotbombs.ca). One of the group's projects, The Campaign to Stop Secret Trials in Canada, works with the men detained on security certificates and their families. Matthew has had the privilege of knowing Jim Loney since the late 1980s.

18

An Interview with Harmeet Sooden

Sahar Ghumkhor

This chapter is an edited version of an interview that appeared on July 23, 2006, in Craccum, *the weekly magazine of the Auckland University Students' Association of the University of Auckland, New Zealand, where Sahar Ghumkhor and Harmeet Sooden are both students.*

Sahar Ghumkhor: Upon arrival in Baghdad, what was your first impression of the city?

Harmeet Sooden: In Amman, Jordan, on the way to Baghdad, I met a three-year old girl, Alaa'—she ran up to me and gave me a big hug, just like my niece. Except she couldn't really see me—her face and legs were peppered with micro-fragments of shrapnel.

In May of 2005, her older brothers, aged four and five, were killed when a tank shell or rocket fired by the U.S. military hit their home in the city of Al Qa'im in Iraq near the Syrian border. Three of her cousins were also killed. Alaa' and about eight others, mostly children, were injured. Her mother lost an eye. They were having a party.

Alaa's father asked her to lift up her shirt. She complied obediently to reveal a large scar and hernia resulting from a crudely treated shrapnel wound. He turned to me and said: "Is this democracy?"

I've just heard from Alan Pogue, from Veterans for Peace. He's been trying to get the family to the U.S. for treatment. He says that when her father returned home from work on the day of the incident, Alaa's condition was so poor that a doctor on the scene had prioritized treating the other wounded children instead of Alaa'. Her father refused to give up and drove her for a couple of hours to get medical help. The doctor he found just sewed her intestines back together to placate the father. In Alan's words, "That Alaa' lived actually is a miracle."

This is the story of just one Iraqi refugee out of hundreds of thousands who have fled into Jordan over the past few decades, escaping one horror or another. I have relatives that have been living in refugee camps since 1947 in Kashmir. It's not a pleasant experience.

We were greeted by the presence of blue-uniformed Gurkha guards at the Baghdad International Airport reminiscent of the depravity of the British Empire in India that my grandparents used to describe to me.

There were passengers at immigration control. Some of them were security contractors—highly paid mercenaries. Quite a few New Zealand soldiers have gone to Iraq as mercenaries. There were second-hand American Bradley vehicles lining the notorious Airport Road, each sporting a freshly painted Iraqi flag in an apparent display of Iraqi sovereignty, and kids squatting in a looted department store. All this had a veneer of normalcy in a city of blast walls.

As Norman [Kember] said, I think it's the people of Iraq we should be listening to. If we care to look, that information is readily available.

SG: You were in Iraq for only a short time before you were kidnapped. What did you witness among ordinary Iraqis?

HS: Well, being captives did not prevent us from being witnesses. We, like the Iraqi people, suffered from lack of food, an inadequate supply of electricity and shortage of kerosene during the cold winter. Our delegation actually went to the power-generating facility in Al Dura to interview managers and employees before the kidnapping. The power plant was severely damaged in 1991 by American bombing—a war crime. Baghdad's power infrastructure has not been operating at full capacity since then because of the U.S./U.K.-initiated UN sanctions. This stopped spare parts for public utilities and medical supplies reaching the people of Iraq for twelve years.

Much of the construction in Iraq has been U.S. military facilities, concrete blast walls, and oil extraction facilities. This is not really helpful to the civilian populace. One reason the U.S. has for the construction and reconstruction is to serve U.S. companies, like Bechtel, which has been given a contract to rehabilitate the Al Dura power plant. Essentially this is a way to relocate American tax dollars to the private sector—the U.S. public footing the bill. It's an assault on the American people. Another reason is for the U.S. to be able to sell its client government to the Iraqi people. This has not worked, so far, because of the extremely insecure environment of occupied Iraq. So the U.S.'s help is basically reduced to forcing compliance by violence.

The occupation is also economic in character, forcing the client government to sell off state-owned assets to privateers, easing legislation governing corporate behavior and impoverishing the people as their resources flow out of the country.

Many Iraqis I spoke with believed the United States had invaded their country for its oil. Certainly this is the first time the U.S. has had troops in the center of the foremost energy-producing region in the world, giving it greater control over other economies like the EU and China.

We visited a women's human rights group called Iraqi Al-Amal. They have mobile clinics that travel throughout the country providing medical services as well as healthcare education to mainly women and children—groups that are always the first to suffer in war. They sponsor an income-generating program for widows and legal seminars on women's rights amongst other things. So the people are mobilizing themselves, as there is limited help from state agencies.

SG: News reports have implied you are a delusional Christian missionary. What is your relationship with Christian Peacemaker Teams and your reasons for going to Iraq with them?

HS: Friends and family don't consider me a Christian although I could identify myself as such if I wish. Some consider me a Sikh, some an atheist; others prefer to think of me as possessing secular values.

Anyway, in this case, a description like "delusional Christian missionary" is a form of ignorance and an attempt to ridicule and dismiss the work of organizations like CPT without understanding their work. In this instance, my religious identity is irrelevant.

First of all, I'm not a member of CPT. I joined a short-term delegation to Iraq. CPT's delegations have proven to be an extremely effective tool in raising awareness in the West of the reality of occupation. I wished to acquire a greater understanding of the nature of the conflict and to learn various nonviolent conflict-resolution techniques. My role was to bear witness to the suffering of Iraqi people living under a harsh military occupation and to provide this narrative, based on humanitarian interpretations of events, to a wider audience, and as a westerner to offer a sense of solidarity to the Iraqi people and human rights groups. CPT felt I had the required training and experience.

I was working as a software engineer for Oscmar International, a U.S.-owned company based in Auckland that produces simulation and training equipment for "defense" forces. Oscmar had been awarded a contract to supply the Israeli Defense Force. Shortly after I resigned, a New Zealand peace organization revealed that it had received leaked documents showing that although the N.Z. government had denied Oscmar an export permit, Oscmar, undeterred, tried to fulfill the contract by electronically transferring the completed design to the U.S. for manufacturing. This exposure forced a rather reluctant N.Z. government to open an investigation. The N.Z. government's final decision was that there was no case to answer and therefore no further action would be taken. No further explanation was given. There were student demonstrations outside Oscmar's facilities. Sadly the N.Z. government continues to support companies like Oscmar and weapons or weapons-related research and production. So, that's another motivation for me.

You know, my great-grandfather was a soldier in the British Indian army. He was killed in Basra in 1916. Now, a century later, not much has changed.

SG: Many would criticize Christian groups like CPT for exploiting the suffering of others—in this case the Muslim world—by taking advantage of a vulnerable environment and spreading Christianity. Could you comment on that?

HS: Christianity informs the internal structure of CPT drawing upon centuries of Mennonite, Brethren, and Quaker peacemaking tradition. Proselytizing is strictly beyond CPT's mandate. Aside from being potentially immoral, it would render CPT's work virtually impossible.

CPT's Iraqi working partners and welcoming bodies know that CPT doesn't evangelize or provide any material humanitarian aid. It works ecumenically with other faiths. CPT assisted in the creation and training of the Muslim Peacemaker Teams, a predominantly Shi'a group based in Karbala. CPT joined MPT in a carefully planned program cleaning the streets of the largely Sunni city of Fallujah, after it was devastated by U.S. forces in November 2004.

SG: Based on the reports made by CPT, how extensive is the problem of the coalition violating the civil liberties of Iraq? How accurate is the impression we have here in the West?

HS: The occupation includes the actions of the Multi-National Force-Iraq, the client government, and the insurgents. And one thing I'd like to make clear is that the crimes that stem from the occupation are the responsibility of the occupiers. That's common sense.

The impression we are getting in the West does not reflect the reality of the situation in Iraq. Western media is generally confined to the safety of the Green Zone and other fortified compounds and doesn't get to see the suffering of the ordinary Iraqis. But CPT is part of the local community living outside the Green Zone. Let's just take New Zealand, specifically New Zealand media's message, which is basically gleaned from international media outlets. There are a few central themes. One is racism. The other is Islamophobia. There's a business-orientated bias. What opinions we adopt are mostly up to us.

SG: Paul Buchanan from the political studies department claims in his article "Paying for the rescue of Western Martyrs" that you and your colleagues suffer from the same "Martyr complex" as that of "Islamic Jihadists and Iraqi resistance fighters." What is your response to those who believe you put yourself and others who helped in your release in harm's way?

HS: I will comment, but with reluctance, only because Mr. Buchanan's misconceptions are common misconceptions.

From what I remember, he wrote that we found ourselves in a predicament because we have psychological problems and we're naïve enough to confuse the U.S. occupation of Iraq with the Israeli occupation of Palestine. And that legislation should be enacted that would require survivors who ignore expert advice to reimburse the government for costs associated with rescues to deter mercenaries, thrill-seekers, and manic peace activists, lest they be infected by our example.

Pop psychology terms such as "martyr complex" are like any cultural trend: they appear and disappear and don't require much thought. I'd rather live and I don't like conflict zones. It can't be said that firefighters want to be martyrs solely on the basis of their profession. What about soldiers? Mr. Buchanan believes the "Stockholm syndrome" doesn't apply in our case, because we were "sympathetic" to our kidnappers long before our capture. Yes, in a way as sympathetic as we are to U.S. soldiers suffering in Iraq. But again, he employs "psychology" to draw parallels between resistance fighters and us. Such exercises carry no information.

CPT and its working partners are in a very good position to assess the conditions in Iraq, simply because the conditions are affecting them directly. The specific work of any CPT project, like Columbia, Palestine, or Iraq, varies according to the nature of the conflict and the needs of the community in question. The thing all have in common is gross human rights violations.

Mr. Buchanan suggests we pay for the costs incurred by governments as a result of our captivity. That principle must also apply to governments for their crimes—the U.S. government should pay due reparations to the Iraqi people (although that could never replace what they have lost) and compensation to U.S. soldiers and aid workers. There are plenty of sources of funding, such as war profiteers. CPT's presence in Iraq was sanctioned by the U.S., the Coalition Provisional Authority, and the Iraqi interim government.

The American Academy of Arts and Sciences estimates that over ten years, the war could cost as much as two trillion dollars. The October 2004 Lancet report estimated one hundred thousand excess deaths since the U.S. invasion in 2003. Violence accounted for most of these excess deaths and air strikes by coalition forces accounted for most violent deaths, and most individuals reportedly killed by coalition forces were women and children.

You can see now how the use of language serves to distract us from the real issues at hand. We've already spent valuable time talking about diversionary trivialities. I find the article, by an academic of Mr. Buchanan's caliber, to be irresponsible. I'm not sure what else to say.

Foreign soldiers are under continuous threat of harm simply by virtue of being present in Iraq—that too on the basis of lies. These soldiers have my sympathy. I want them to be home and safe with their families.

SG: There were claims made by those who helped in your release that you and your colleagues showed little gratitude. Could you clarify this?

HS: CPT and the captives were vilified by sectors of the media, public, and various officials by being called naïve, foolish, ungrateful, ineffective, uncooperative, inexperienced, untrained, and so on.

It doesn't take much effort to expose such things as false. I've already talked about the CPT's work. In particular, I was astonished to read that Norman was accused of "not thanking the troops." We are grateful to all those who worked to secure our release. But, we wouldn't have been kidnapped in Iraq—we wouldn't even be in Iraq—if not for the actions of these soldiers' employers.

We cooperated and continue to cooperate with British and Canadian authorities to promote human rights and conflict resolution. Governments are also CPT's working partners.

Again, such disparaging remarks have the effect of drawing one's attention away from the real issues at hand. The UNAMI [United Nations Assistance Mission for Iraq] chief of the Human Rights Office and the deputy head of the Red Cross Iraq Delegation both acknowledged the important and valuable role CPT plays in Iraq.

SG: Clearly CPT has not let your kidnapping and other possible dangers hinder their work in Iraq as they have already sent another group into Iraq. Do you agree this is a wise decision considering Tom Fox's death? And if given another opportunity, would you go back?

HS: Members of CPT chose to remain in Baghdad during the hostage crisis. CPT is in constant dialogue with Iraqi NGOs and other advisers about its work in Iraq, including its continued presence. After our release, based on these discussions, they decided to leave temporarily, because of security concerns, and then reevaluate the situation. CPT has now returned to Iraq to a location outside Baghdad.

I would like to continue to work for peace; commitment, not necessarily location, is what's important.

19

Christianity Is a Radical Call to Peacemaking

Norman Kember

Published in the *Daily Telegraph* newspaper, London, December 12, 2006

This week I had the great pleasure of meeting up again for the first time since March with Jim Loney from Canada and Harmeet Singh Sooden from New Zealand. One year ago we were companions in kidnap and held in close confinement in Baghdad, where we had gone as members of a Christian Peacemaker Teams delegation. Two weeks into that captivity, that is, at this time last year, and in spite of repeated promises of release, it was becoming evident that we were likely to be held until after Christmas and this was a source of extreme sadness—no, rather deep depression. I was painfully reminded of those days as we sang our Advent hymns in church last Sunday.

Advent is the time when we re-encounter Mary's song—the Magnificat—and we are made to recall the radical nature of the Christian faith. "He has brought down rulers from their thrones but has lifted up the humble, He has filled the hungry with good things —and sent the rich away empty." Impossibly idealistic? Certainly not realized in our everyday experience as the powerful continue to oppress the powerless and the wealth gap between the rich and poor across the world, gets ever wider. The vision of the Magnificat is hardly that of the world of business, commerce, and party politics.

Now I confess to conforming to the accepted British way of life for most of the time and live comfortably on my university pension with my wife in Pinner—the quintessential middle class suburb. I also use my car regularly to drive to church and cheerfully go abroad on holidays by plane in spite of the effects on global warming—but I do get twinges of conscience—it was such a twinge that took me to Iraq.

Part of my understanding of the radical nature of Christianity affects another aspect of our common life. I see in Jesus' teaching and example a revolutionary approach to the manner of dealing with conflict and wrong-doing. I believe with Gandhi that Jesus' way is that of nonviolent resistance to evil. Many others have followed in that way, for example Martin Luther King Jr. and the little-known Muslim Badshah Khan (1890-1988). I have always been an admirer of the German theologian and pastor Dietrich Bonhoeffer, who was executed in 1945 for his opposition to the Nazi regime. He wrote: "There is no way to peace along the path of safety, for peace must be dared, it is in itself a great venture, and can never be safe. Peace is the opposite of security. To demand guarantees is to mistrust, and this mistrust in turn brings forth war. To look for guarantees is to want to protect oneself. Peace means giving yourself completely to God's commandment." This is hardly the view of the establishment—even the church establishment—and certainly not since the time of Emperor Constantine, who in AD 312 brought about the marriage between church and state. In following this radical view of the teaching of Jesus I have been opposed to war as a method of bringing lasting peace and have celebrated the many victories of nonviolence. I believe that Christians should abandon the outdated Just War theory and advocate the discovery of new ways of bringing about reconciliation without resort to armed violence.

Now I have long held these views as an armchair theorist but have been a "cheap" peacemaker in practice. For most us it is easy in Britain to be a conscientious objector, to demonstrate and write letters to government. It was when I heard about the work of the Christian Peacemaker Teams—seeking to bring reconciliation in conflict situations, that is, in risky conflict situations, that I felt that twinge of conscience.

I therefore signed up for a modest trip to Iraq—just 10 days—with modest aims: to meet Iraqi people, to learn how Christian Peacemaker Teams worked in practice and to show that at seventy-four I was not "past it" in adventures in Christian peacemaking.

The rest is history. I was asked recently in a radio interview if I considered myself lucky to be alive. No, I am not lucky—my release was not due to luck but to the painstaking investigative work done by police and foreign office staff in Iraq and the U.K. and to the bravery of the SAS group that acted on that intelligence came and released us. I am constantly thankful to all those people.

The great tragedy for us was the death of our fellow captive, the American Quaker Tom Fox. Tom was the most compassionate peacemaker of the four of us, praying for the victims of each bomb explosion that we could hear from our "cell." Tom was separated from us, murdered, and his body dumped by the roadside. But the great tragedy for the people of Iraq is that such kidnapping and deaths are common daily occurrences. The violence of the war against Saddam has released such a tide of violence in its wake that, at present, no one seems to know how to stop it. The heavy-handed pursuit of peace by the coalition forces after the invasion has proved a disaster. It has been costly in the waste of resources for

178

reconstruction and much more tragically in the lives of young soldiers and Iraqi citizens. In this I was surprised to find common ground in a recent statement by General Dannerts and, this week, from the American "Iraq Study Group."

Returning to my experience, whatever the rights and wrongs of my original decision to go to Iraq, the misadventure has had some remarkable and unsuspected results.

The worldwide fellowship of the church was clearly demonstrated by the support given to my wife, both locally in practical ways and around the nations through prayers, vigils, and messages of solidarity. It has not been possible to thank all those people, many unknown to us.

The Muslim community gave remarkable testimony to our witness for peace and our desire to bring reconciliation to Iraq and to oppose any human rights violations by whichever side in the conflict. The Muslim leaders made clear that the kidnapping of those who work for peace is against the true spirit of Islam. They also took part in many of the vigils that were arranged in cities across the country so that bridges were built between Christian and Muslim communities. Long may they continue to be strengthened in mutual respect and understanding.

Then my notoriety has given me and other members of the peace movement the chance to share and explain our views to some new audiences—even to the extent of a woolly liberal being invited to write for the clear-minded readers of the *Daily Telegraph*!

I am expected to say something about my attitude towards those who captured us. Within the strict limits of our confinement we were, in general, treated with humanity and the occasional act of compassion. All three of us are united in our offer of forgiveness to these men. We do not condone what they did to us but believe that forgiveness is in short supply in Iraq and there is no hope for that country until the communities seek mutual reconciliation rather than endless cycles of revenge.

We believe in restorative, not punitive, justice. If these men are brought to trial we would ask, if convicted, that they be treated with clemency. We do not wish for retribution but ask that they accept our forgiveness by changing their lives from violence to nonviolence. Although we are all absolutely opposed to the death penalty we do not have, at present, enough information about the working of the Iraqi court system to discover if we can best help these men by refusing to testify and asking for clemency outside the court system or by agreeing to take part in the trials and ask for clemency within the court process. The CPT are seeking to retain an Iraqi lawyer to act in court on behalf of these men.

Our experience has not brought about a change in our belief in the need for and efficacy of nonviolent solutions to conflicts. The best way to peace is not to prepare for war—as the old saw has it—but to work for

179

justice. A world war against structural and economic injustice is not the quick fix that the politicians seek, but it is our most certain long-term defense against terrorism.

20

Tom Fox:
A Profile of an Ordinary Man's Calling to an Extraordinary Life

Selby McCash and Johannes Williams

First came the clarinet. God arrived much later. Each, in turn, became a consuming focus in the 54-year journey of Tom Fox from his coming of age in Tennessee, to his decades as a professional musician and later an organic grocer in the bustling Washington, D.C. metro area, to his final days advocating peace and providing care in violence-ridden Iraq.

Tom took up the clarinet at age 9 or 10. This was all family and friends remembered him saying about a fateful moment that determined much of his life.

Music brought Tom growing recognition, including all-star status within his high school band in Chattanooga. The band not only served as an outlet for playing his instrument of choice. The band was a refuge where the quiet, socially awkward youth found kindred friends and temporarily escaped from a home life that was nurturing on one hand and on the other stressed by his parents' financial hardships and chronic illnesses. He earned bachelors and masters degrees in music. He courted and married classmate Jan Echols, a flautist, while studying for his first degree at George Peabody College in Nashville, now part of Vanderbilt University. His skillful, technically proficient playing landed him his first fulltime job with "The President's Own," the elite Marine Corps band based in Washington, D.C.

While living near the nation's capital Tom encountered the Religious Society of Friends, more commonly known as Quakers.

During his college years, and for a considerable time thereafter, Tom defined himself as an agnostic who questioned the existence of God and the potential of religion to reveal the purpose of life. Yet in spite of these well-considered doubts, he joined his wife in searching for a spiritual environment compatible with the couple's views about peace, equality and compassion. As a consequence of Jan's curiosity, they ended up visiting an unprogrammed Quaker meeting for worship in Alexandria, Virginia, George Washington's hometown a few miles south of the District. Tom's connection with the community was immediate.

According to Jan, 31-year-old Tom appreciated the ecumenical community where members and attenders sought the truth within themselves through silent introspection and collective inspiration without the intercession of clergy, dogma, or prescribed theology. Always a prodigious reader, Tom began to study the works of spiritual thinkers exhaustively. He also listened to basic Quaker expressions of faith, and engaged in social activism, especially youth work. Through reasoning and mystical intuition, he acquired an unshakeable conviction that God, personified by Jesus' ministry of love and good works, exists within everyone.

Life's purpose now became clear: to "help create God's peaceable realm," as he expressed it.

Thomas William Fox was born on July 7, 1951, the son of Henry Melvin Fox and the former Virginia Sylvania Thomas. His mother was approaching 40, and his father in his mid-fifties. "Tommy," as he was known until he started calling himself "Tom" in grade school, would be their only child.

At the outset, the family of three resided in the rural southeastern Tennessee community of Graysville, just outside Dayton, a town that attracted national and even international attention as the site of the 1925 Scopes evolution trial. When he was about five, the family moved a few miles further southeast to Chattanooga, where they settled into a small house in a lower-income inner city neighborhood. This was home to Tom until he finished high school 12 years later.

Tom lost his father while in college and, soon after, his mother. By his early adult years, he had few surviving roots. Although he seldom talked about himself, what is known about his youth comes mainly from recollections he shared with people close to him. He was raised in a loving home, he said. But, he confided, it was also dysfunctional.

Tom's father, an engineering graduate of Drexel University in Philadelphia, suffered from emphysema, and his increasingly debilitating condition forced him to retire in mid-career. The elder Fox had served in combat as a Marine during World War I. Family speculated that his illness may have resulted from exposure to poison gas on a smoky battlefield. Although no proof existed, Tom grew up thinking war may have caused his father's suffering.

His mother, long employed by a Chattanooga beer distribution firm, was the family's sole wage earner for a number of years. She had grown up in disadvantaged circumstances, and financial pressures in her married life likely weighed heavily on her. She was also sight-impaired, making life all the more difficult. Tom believed she succumbed to alcoholism, although she managed her drinking enough to keep her job.

The family was never without food, shelter, and other necessities. Tom's father always owned a car, leaving his last one to his son. But the family's financial struggles were sometimes evident to outsiders. As a teenager, Tom occasionally appeared for his private clarinet lessons without money to pay the modest fee. When this happened, his instructor waived the fee.

If his parents could not provide material things beyond the essentials, they did everything possible to encourage educational and intellectual pursuits during Tom's formative years. His mother loved the arts and encouraged her son's interest in music, taking him to concerts and other artistic performances. By all accounts his father was an erudite individual, a voracious reader who sat with his son for extended readings and discussions on a wide variety of subjects including philosophy, history and religion. His father, who was not religiously active, and his mother, a devout Episcopalian, were remembered as Southern "progressives" who favored civil rights and the teaching of evolution.

Fortunately for Tom, the nearest public high school was Chattanooga High, unofficially called City High, well known for its excellent band program. Not only was he taught by the school's music teachers, he was taken under the wing of Jay Craven, for many years the first clarinetist for the Chattanooga Symphony and Opera Orchestra and a noted figure in the area's music scene. Craven tutored at Chattanooga schools under a special citywide program and offered private lessons to advanced young musicians who demonstrated a willingness to work hard. Tom studied under Craven from his early teens until his high school graduation.

When Tom's photograph appeared in a newspaper following his abduction, Craven instantly recognized his former pupil. It had been some 37 years since he had last seen Tom. But the image that Craven saw in his mind was that of the gangly young man wearing horn-rimmed glasses who never had much to say and who always appeared for his lessons on time, well prepared, and eager to learn.

Everyone who knew him as a child and as an adult described Tom as quiet-mannered. Whether in groups or one-on-one conversations, he characteristically listened attentively and said little.

Yet now and then Tom revealed a probing mind and poetic voice. He often joined late-night student bull sessions without saying a word for long periods. Then he would chime in with an especially insightful remark, recalled Michael Hime, a contemporary at Peabody who later served on the Vanderbilt faculty. Tom once introduced a woman from a farming background to a Quaker gathering by describing her work-worn hands with such eloquence that it surprised Lauri Perman, then clerk of the regional Quaker association called the Baltimore Yearly Meeting. She thought of Tom as someone more comfortable doing than talking. His blog as a peace worker, which would eventually be read by countless thousands, is full of eloquently expressed emotions and incisive analysis.

In the words of John Stephens, a young Quaker who worked under Tom's supervision in the organic grocery business, "he talked about small things but was thinking big thoughts."

Many people who knew Tom believed he was the most laid-back person they ever knew, someone who maintained a calm demeanor in the most trying situations. He was an anchor to other peacemakers in Iraq, including the three colleagues abducted with him, who said Tom never stopped reaching out to comfort them—or their abductors. Yet, while outwardly unflappable, he internalized intense feelings—for music, for his spiritual quest, for the political and social issues he confronted, for his children.

Tom had a romantic nature, as reflected in his enthusiasm for virtually all kinds of music from Bach to the Beatles. He was also intensely analytical, guided by realistic logic as he saw it.

He was both a loner and someone who was socially engaged. As a youth, he spent much of his time in solitary pursuits and likewise as an adult. He read, played solo clarinet or recorder, meditated, rode his bicycle and hiked. He averaged about four miles a day hiking, usually alone, in his neighborhood, at nearby green spaces or, when time permitted, his favorite walking venue in the mountain ranges southwest of Washington, D.C. He often retired to the rooftop of his apartment building in Iraq to mediate, play the recorder, or walk a figure-eight pattern in the limited space. "I miss hiking more than anything," he emailed friends at home.

At the same time, Tom sought the company of other people throughout his life, always taking part in collective social activities of groups with which he was involved, gradually becoming more comfortable socially as he grew older. Later in life he could even be the hit of a party—like the time he impersonated maverick presidential candidate Ross Perot at a Quaker Halloween bash. He was never at ease doing public speaking—but he did it. The dictionary defines an "introvert" as someone wholly or predominately concerned with one's own self. This misses the mark with Tom. An "introspective" person is defined as someone who reflectively looks inward. This fits.

Tom had a sense of humor and an easy-going nature. Quakers said he was almost always quietly cheerful, displaying a "lightness of spirit." His humor tended to be dry and laconic among adults and playful among young people. Once, while home between Iraqi sojourns, he was asked what the U.S. should do about the devastating insurgency then erupting in Iraq. "Apologize," he said. With youngsters, he could be as zany as they sometimes were.

This is not to say he was immune from anger. Tom confessed to struggling with bitterness over the carnage in Iraq. But he never vented his anger in emotional outbursts—only in succinct and pointed arguments and unbending resistance.

For the most part, Tom was exceptionally open and yielding with respect to other points of view. Yet at times people found him astonishingly stubborn, rigidly standing his ground even when his intransigence strained relationships with colleagues, other Quakers, or his marriage partner.

After graduation from City High in the spring of 1969, Tom enrolled in Peabody College that fall. Student loans and some scholarship funding made this possible. As his musical promise grew exponentially, he found a number of jobs in musically-vibrant Nashville, subbing for two years with the city's symphony orchestra, playing in stage bands at Opryland, home of the Grand Ole Opry, and once joining the pit band for road performances of "Fiddler on the Roof."

This was a turbulent time in U.S. history. The civil rights movement and the war in Vietnam were at the forefront of current events. The beat generation was sweeping the country, challenging America's mores. One popular songwriter envisioned the dawning of a new age of love, freedom, and peace. But if the age fell short of its hype, the epic events of the 1960s and early 1970s influenced the thinking and shaped the lives of many in Tom's generation.

Tom did not participate in the campus anti-war protests organized by a small minority of the student body. His fervent commitment to social and political activism came later. While Tom opposed the war and supported racial justice as a college student, his focus was preparing for a career as a musician. It was also on Jan Echols.

The pair met when both were selected for a regional high school band program, and they started going together while freshmen at Peabody. They were married the summer prior to their senior year in a ceremony attended by a few family members and a handful of friends at a chapel on the grounds of the Hermitage, Andrew Jackson's home near Nashville.

As college graduation approached in 1973, Tom's preferred choice of employment was playing in professional bands maintained by the armed services for ceremonial and promotional purposes. Music students were well aware of the opportunities in the military for well-trained young musicians. The bands were highly professional and many featured a diverse repertoire of classical, jazz and popular forms of music. The pay and benefits were decent. Moreover, military musicians lived more like civilians than soldiers, with little military discipline imposed on them other than wearing well-shined shoes and sharply pressed uniforms while on duty.

Tom didn't have to worry about the draft. The high number he had drawn in the lottery-style draft in effect at the time placed him well beyond the draft's reach. But he would have noticed that many of his peers were being sent to Vietnam, with many dying or returning permanently disabled. By joining up as a military bandsman, he could serve the country, as his father had done, without firing a shot in a war he considered morally and rationally wrong.

Tom auditioned for Navy and Marine Corps bands and was selected for the Marine band that regularly performs at the White House and makes appearances throughout the country and the world.

Washington was an up-tempo experience for Tom and Jan with its many artistic and cultural offerings. Tom regularly played at glittering White House functions. He toured the world. For some years, his job and life proved to be exciting and rewarding. He continued his musical education, earning a masters degree from Catholic University, an institution with noted arts programs located near Capitol Hill.

Tom and Jan's children were born during these years—Katherine, called Kassie, in 1980, and Andrew in 1984. No one could have loved his children more, Jan said. Tom found ways to interact with them at all ages. On a personal information form for his Quaker meeting, he entered just one listing under accomplishments and awards: "parent of two exceptional human beings."

Tom and Jan divorced in 1990. The cause of the break-up remained private. But while Jan said they never quarreled, never exchanged a harsh word, there were times when Tom's quietly stubborn nature wore on those around him. After 17 years, Washington's excitement had dimmed and Jan and Tom had grown apart. Tom moved into a townhouse in the northern Virginia suburb of Springfield about a mile from where his former wife and his children continued to reside. Most days when not traveling he found time to visit Kassie and Andrew, often keeping them overnight on weekends and taking them on trips to nearby places of interest.

Along with fatherhood came Tom's spiritual leading. In 1983, thanks to Daisy Newman, Tom and the Quakers converged.

The late Daisy Newman was a Quaker who wrote prolifically about Quaker life in a series of romance novels and historical works. Which of the five Daisy Newman novels Jan happened to read would escape her memory. But whether or not it was enduring literature, the integrity of the Quaker community portrayed in the book encouraged Jan, and subsequently her husband, to check it out.

With no clergy standing between him and a Supreme Being, with both mysticism and scientific logic a direct part of the experience, Tom's spiritual path shifted from agnosticism to the fundamental Quaker testimonies of community, equality, simplicity and truth, all culminating in the testimony of peace. Said one-time Earlham College professor and president, D. Elton Trueblood, the Quaker peace testimony "is cherished not for the sake of a doctrine and not even for the sake of Quakers. It is cherished for the sake of the world."

For Tom, the peace testimony simultaneously supported and opened the door to his work as a peacemaker in hostile parts of the globe. The Quaker testimonies and Tom's deeply held belief in making the world a better place, in seeking to will into existence the biblical concept of the peaceable kingdom, fit together like the gears of a fine watch.

Early on, Tom had an experience he regarded as a milestone in his pursuit and understanding of God's message. An elderly woman rose to break the silence of a Quaker meeting for worship and said simply, "In all things, we need to keep to Jesus."

Like many others, Tom participated in Quaker affairs as an "attender" for years before he applied for membership. In 1994, he submitted his application, soon accepted, stating, "the most powerful structure is not the individual Friend, rather it is the corporate body of seekers, the Monthly Meeting. Jesus was very clear when he said it was where 'several' are gathered 'in my name' that the Spirit would be born."

For seven years Tom attended the meeting in Alexandria where he had started with Jan. Then, following the divorce, Tom transferred to the nearby Langley Hills Meeting in McLean, Virginia, where he remained for the next fifteen years.

At both meetings, Tom actively contributed. At Langley Hill, he edited the newsletter, served on a series of committees, and served a term as the meeting's presiding clerk. His angular frame became a familiar fixture at Sunday worship as he sat in different seats around the meeting house each week in an "orbit" he said helped him experience the "inner light." He became a leader of youth activities for the BYM regional Quaker association. He regularly set aside a part of each summer to serve as the volunteer kitchen manager and cook at the Opequon Quaker Camp for young people near Winchester, Virginia, one of the last things he did before returning on his final trip to Iraq.

Nothing was more important to Tom than his relationship with young people, and his bond with the young was widely recognized among Quakers. He was constantly involved with his own children, with various Quaker youth activities, as a Little League umpire. Young people of all ages, he said, made him feel "real." He listened to the young, enjoyed their company as they enjoyed his, and mentored them in understated ways.

He often shot the bull with youth groups at Quaker gatherings. On his last trip home from Iraq, he stayed up until 2 a.m. with about 50 teenagers at the annual BYM conference, making "pizza bites," answering questions about his experiences in the Middle East, and exchanging thoughts about everything the teens wanted to talk about. Youngsters at the Hopewell Centre Quaker Meeting near Clear Brook, Virginia in the Shenandoah Valley, a retreat for Tom, jokingly called him "Foxy Tom," a nickname that spread.

His BYM friend Lauri Perman recalled Tom's last day at Quaker camp before returning for his final trip to Iraq. None of the campers wanted him to leave, and one young lady ran to him and said she wished he wouldn't go. Tom smiled, gave her a hug, and said, "I'm leaving, but we have the memories, and we're here together now."

For the most part, Quakers also regarded Tom as an effective adult leader. Doug Smith, Tom's successor as Langley Hill's presiding clerk, said Tom proved in time to be a committed and capable meeting clerk. But his term was not without controversy. He got off on the wrong foot with some at Langley Hill who thought he breached Quaker tradition when, as a member of the nominating committee, he suggested himself as the meeting's next clerk. Tom was eager to implement some ideas, and he believed his record of service qualified him for the position. In spite of the grumbling, the committee and the meeting at-large eventually agreed he was the right choice. If projecting himself in this way was uncharacteristic of the self-effacing Tom Fox, it was not necessarily so for the Tom who could be headstrong about things he felt were logical and right. This "stubbornness" at times created backlash. But no one denied that Tom brought energy and ideas to the meeting.

One of these ideas was the "Experiment with Light" process developed by British theologian and Quaker Rex Ambler in the mid-1990s. As widely as Tom read about Quakerism and religion in general, it was inevitable he would hear about a process that seeks to recreate the "inner light" experience of early Quakers through readings and meditation. By 2000, Tom had learned enough about "Experiment with Light" to lead sessions at Langley Hill. He would continue to explore the process for the rest of his life.

In 2003, Tom attended a five-day "Experiment with Light" retreat at Pendle Hill, a Quaker center located near Philadelphia, at which Ambler himself was present. The Christian Peacemaker Teams (CPT) and its mission of seeking nonviolence in violent places came up for discussion among those attending the program. Diana Lampen, a British Quaker and widely known peace worker who was present, believed this is where Tom first began "to hear God's calling to join CPT."

Another turning point occurred earlier in Tom's life, in 1993. After 20 years, he decided to retire from "The President's Own." He told friends he was tired of the musical repetition, though considerable variety existed in the band's performances, and was weary of the travel. Many of the bandsmen he started out with had left. He might also have been feeling the effects of his pacifist views that, as they became more pronounced, might well have rankled some in the line of command. Tom had grown increasingly conflicted over military service considering the kind of wars waged by the U.S. in the post-World War II years. At some point he refrained from buying discounted products at military commissaries.

Cooking had been a passionate pastime for years, and Tom thought about turning a pastime into a profession. A year before his retirement he entered L'Academie de Cuisine, a culinary school in nearby Bethesda, Maryland, receiving a professional culinary certificate. Some of his fellow Marine bandsmen had moved on to other jobs in music when they retired from the military. But Tom sold the several clarinets he owned. Although he would play the recorder alone, in a meditative way, in the years ahead, his decision to turn in a new direction was decisive.

Tom was hired by Whole Foods, a grocery chain specializing in organic food. He started as a baker and rose to chief of a bakery team and finally to assistant manager of an outlet near his Springfield townhouse. His second career as an organic grocer would last ten years.

Around 2000, Tom's friend from the Alexandria meeting, Barbara Ginsburg, bumped into him one day while shopping at Whole Foods. She discovered then he was thinking of ways to get more involved in promoting peace and justice. Friends believe his desire to work for peace became even more intense following the 9/11 terrorist attacks and the U.S. military responses to them. After attending the retreat with Rex Ambler in 2003, Tom specifically focused on the possibility of joining CPT.

He did not act immediately. He was still working hard at Whole Foods, still committed to the organic food business. Then something unexpected happened—something that put him on a collision course with management and triggered an immediate decision.

Whole Foods had offered Tom a higher supervisory position, but on the condition he adopt a more demanding approach in handling employees under his supervision. From Tom's perspective, this meant treating those under his authority in a less understanding and tolerant way, and this he was not prepared to do. He could only continue to lead by example and positive persuasion, he told his employers. He must have known this candid response would cause concern. Yet his commitment to truthfulness made it the only possible response.

If this was his decision, replied management, he would have to relinquish a supervisory position and take a pay cut. This, Tom said, was God giving him "a kick in the seat of the pants." He would delay no longer.

Tom weighed CPT service from all angles. He questioned what the impact would be on his children, deciding his fulltime presence in their lives was not as critical now that they were out of high school. He considered how long he could financially and physically serve on the frontlines of CPT projects, and figured it would be up to six years. He also prepared himself by studying. In addition to undergoing intensive CPT training, he squeezed in a course on strategic nonviolence at Eastern Mennonite University in Harrisonburg, Virginia taught by Lisa Schirch, who described him as an exceptionally quiet and serious student who wrote first-rate papers.

Before first contacting CPT in the summer of 2003, he convened several Quakers in the library of the small, whitewashed former country church that served as the meeting house for Langley Hill Friends to seek their advice. This group became the nucleus of a five-member support team that advised and assisted him throughout his CPT service, doing everything from providing moral and spiritual support to checking on his mail and dealing with the town house he rented out and eventually sold.

Tom would later write on his blog, "While I knew very little about Christian Peacemaker Teams, at the time I had a clear sense that I wanted very much to pull us out of the darkness and move the world (even if it was the movement of one human being) towards the light." His supporters would explain that following 9/11 he "came to the understanding that this was an especially important time for people of good will to act" and CPT had "given voice to his hope for offering fruitful nonviolent alternatives to war."

The U.S., the United Kingdom, and a smattering of other allies had just deposed Saddam Hussein and begun a prolonged occupation of Iraq. President George W. Bush had proclaimed "mission accomplished." A widely published photograph showed U.S. forces helping topple a statue of Saddam and, in the foreground, an American soldier gazing quizzically into the camera as if to say, "now what?" For Tom, the mission was about to begin.

Over a period of about a year and a half, from September 24, 2004 until March 9, 2006, he would serve nearly eight months of CPT duty on six trips to four countries. Trips to Canada, Palestine, and Jordan would be for training and learning purposes. His three trips to Iraq would be as a full-fledged team member and coordinator.

Tom would chop wood on freezing days in Canada, where he would briefly train as part of a CPT project supporting Natives attempting to save forest resources threatened by a massive logging operation. He would stand up to Israeli bulldozers threatening to destroy olive trees in Palestine. With temperatures sometimes reaching 130 degrees, he would grapple with depression, fatigue, and fear in Iraq, where he would spend endless hours documenting human rights abuses, searching for missing family members, escorting refugees across dangerous countryside, and providing comfort and care to families who had lost homes and loved ones.

190

Along with other CPTers in Iraq, numbering two to four during his three tours of duty there, he would live openly among the Iraqi people and travel around the city and country unarmed.

Tom and his teammates would hear gunfire and explosions from their Baghdad apartment building. Scores of people would be killed and injured in separate bombings near their living quarters. A mortar shell or rocket would slam into the rooftop of CPT's apartment building where CPTers often went for exercise and fresh air, shattering windows on several floors.

Early in his Iraqi service, CPT would carry out a discernment process to evaluate whether the project's goals justified the risk. Tom's supporters would respond that the mission was too dangerous and would urge all the CPTers to return home. Tom would have known without asking that this is what his children wanted. But Tom and CPT would choose to stay the course.

Tom expressed his outlook in communicating with his support group: "I feel I can speak for all of us in saying that we have no interest in being either martyrs or heroes. Both are ego-driven attitudes. We are searching for God's will in the matter and will continue that search daily no matter what decision we finally make."

"We are throwing ourselves open to the possibility of God's grace bringing some rays of light to the shadowy landscape that is Iraq," he later said on his blog. "We are letting ourselves be guided by something that is beyond rational, intellectual analysis. ...[The] people of Iraq need to let their Light run before them as they bring redemption to those in power who are seeking to rule from a place of fear, violence and shadows. That truly would be the highest achievement."

He would meet an Iraqi Christian on that first trip, a member of the Dominican Order, who would tell him, "I am prudent. I try to be wise. But I have no fear." Commented Tom, "fearless, prudent, and wise. We in CPT need to work to find a balance among all three of these character traits."

When Tom arrived in grim, war-ravaged Iraq in the fall of 2004, abductions were escalating. Many of the kidnappings were apparently motivated by ideology. Others seemed to be motivated by money. On one of his periodic visits home, Tom told Langley Hill Quaker Walter Brown that Iraqi criminals might have emerged as an even bigger threat than the religious extremists.

Shortly before his arrival, the soaring danger level had prompted CPT and every known care agency stationed in Iraq to pull out. Three weeks later CPT was one of the few to return. CPT co-director Doug Pritchard said a number of the CPTers' Baghdad neighbors thought it would be safer for everyone if the team left. Iraqis had become increasingly concerned that any foreign presence would attract danger, even those providing humanitarian service.

But when the CPTers returned to Iraq, they were welcomed, Pritchard said. As many care organizations withdrew, the need for CPT's presence greatly increased.

About a month after Tom came to Iraq, Margaret Hassan was kidnapped and killed after about a month in captivity. A British citizen married to an Iraqi citizen, she had lived for many years as a fulltime resident of Baghdad, where she had long been involved in care work. She had assisted CPTers in Iraq, giving them inside advice and helping them adjust. Tom had not met her in person, but had talked with her several times by telephone. Once he called her to ask if a scheduled visit by CPT observers should proceed as planned. "Under no circumstances," he quoted her as saying. It was too dangerous.

Of Margaret, Tom wrote on his blog, "She lived a life of courage in the midst of fear. We are called to do the same, no matter what the consequences."

Tom and the only other team member then serving in Iraq, Matthew Chandler of Springfield, Oregon, adopted the following "Statement of Conviction" on October 7, 2004:

> We reject kidnapping and hostage-taking wholesale. If any of us are taken hostage, absolutely no ransom will be paid. ...CPT will work against journalists' inclination to vilify and demonize the offenders. We will try to understand the motives for these actions, and to articulate them, while maintaining a firm stance that such actions are wrong. If appropriate, CPT will work with diplomatic officials from our representative governments to avoid a violent outcome.
>
> We reject the use of violent force to save our lives should we be kidnapped, held hostage, or caught in the middle of a violent conflict situation. We also reject violence to punish anyone who harms us. We ask for equal justice in the arrest and trial of anyone, soldier or civilian, who commits an act of violence, and we ask that there be no retaliation [against] their relatives or property. We forgive those who consider us their enemies. Therefore, any penalty should be in the spirit of restorative justice, rather than in the form of violent retribution.
>
> We hope that in loving both friends and enemies and by intervening nonviolently to aid those who are systematically oppressed, we can contribute in some small way to transforming this volatile situation.

After three months, Tom was due to fly home for a period of rest and relaxation. Instead, at his request, he traveled to Palestine to observe the CPT project centered in Hebron. During his short stay he helped save threatened Palestinian olive trees and escorted Palestinian children who feared harassment while walking to school on a road adjacent to an Israeli settlement. After a couple of months at home, he resumed his Iraq work in April of 2005, this time as team coordinator.

First he flew to Amman, Jordan, for several weeks of Arabic study, then on to Baghdad. At first, his hopes were raised.

"In many ways Baghdad is a different place from when I left," he reported in an email to supporters. As he visited different parts of the city, he sensed "there is less tension and more optimism than last fall." Children were playing in parks that were previously abandoned and more people were coming and going on the city streets. Violence was still widespread. But security seemed more prevalent and it appeared city life might make a comeback.

Tom's optimism did not last long.

Several weeks later, Tom quoted seventeenth-century philosopher Thomas Hobbes as saying the ultimate nightmare of society would be "the war of all against the all." That, Tom now believed, was the state of existence in Iraq. "I have not heard one person say that Saddam was a wise or revered leader," he noted. "But I have heard many people say that while they lived under the threat of violence with Saddam they prefer that life to the bloodshed, chaos, and anarchy that surrounds them now."

Tom would describe his second tour in Iraq as a "roller coaster," physically and emotionally. Sleeping and working were difficult with temperatures rising well above 100 degrees during the day and falling only into the 90s at night, especially with electricity to run electric fans available only a few hours a day. The roaches infesting their apartment building were a small annoyance. Of much greater concern was the overwhelming workload. So was the danger that was never far away.

But the CPT work went on. Typical was the help Tom and his team provided for an Iraqi father who could obtain no accurate information from U.S. authorities on the whereabouts of his two missing sons. The CPTers were able to confirm that both were being held at Abu Ghraib prison. While this was hardly good news, the parents were relieved to know their sons were alive. Countless similar cases were coming to their attention. The CPTers could provide real help for some, but could do little or nothing for many others, and that was taking an emotional toll.

Tom and other team members traveled to embattled Fallujah six times on his second tour in Iraq to assist Iraqis who had suffered losses in fierce U.S. anti-insurgency attacks. He called Fallujah "ground zero of the U.S. oppression of the Iraqi people," adding that "not a day goes by that I don't have the images of destruction... and images of the many people I got to meet. I feel Fallujah inside of me. It is painful, but it also gives me a stronger sense of determination to continue the work, both here and in the States, to raise the consciousness of the American people."

Toward the end of his second tour, a Baghdad neighbor ominously warned the CPTers to be on guard. Although the team made friends with many Iraqis, the neighbor told them a rumor was going around that they could be foreign spies.

With a two-month summer break coming up, Tom shared his homecoming plans with his support group. He would fly from Baghdad to Chicago to meet with the staff at CPT's U.S. headquarters, then onward to Des Moines to serve as CPT's representative at the Friends United Meeting Triennial, something he had volunteered to do. Then he would go to Camp Opequon in Virginia to spend a week cooking for the campers and counselors as he had often done before. Next he planned to attend the BYM annual session to serve as an adult presence with high schoolers as he had also done many times. He was also committed to making as many speaking appearances on behalf of CPT as he could fit in.

In spite of his jam-packed schedule, he also planned to pack up and leave the Washington area where he had lived for thirty-two years.

With the help of his supporters, Tom put his Springfield townhouse on the market and moved into an upper-story room of a former farmhouse adjacent to the Hopewell Centre Quaker Meeting House in Clear Brook, Virginia, located less than an hour and a half drive from Washington. He told friends he was ready to live in a less fast-paced and material-minded area. The old house next to the Hopewell Centre, which had been converted into a youth center for the Quaker meeting, had served as a retreat for Tom in the past, and the people at Hopewell were pleased to rent the room to him for the summer before he returned to Iraq.

The Hopewell Centre Meeting House stands resolutely in the verdant rolling countryside of the northern Shenandoah Valley, surrounded by ancient trees and a historic cemetery where weathered tombstones mark the graves of early Quakers and the native Americans they befriended.

The house where Tom stayed and the second-story room where he slept are stoic—in keeping with the Quaker testimony of simplicity. Among the few belongings he brought with him were his computer and a shelf of books including a Bible and Koran. From his window, he could view the distant profile of the Blue Ridge Mountains. His favorite hiking spot, the Massanutten Mountains, was not far away. Downstairs was a spacious kitchen enabling him to practice his joy-giving and joy-bringing hospitality for others.

No one knows exactly how much time Tom spent at Hopewell Centre. He was coming and going. But this would be his final American home, the setting where he hoped to someday settle for good. After learning of Tom's death, the Hopewell Centre Quakers placed a small hand-lettered sign against a vase of dried flowers in the upstairs room where Tom stayed. The sign simply reads, "Tom's Room."

During his stint at nearby Camp Opequon that summer, Tom modeled a small abstract clay bust and brought it to Bob Pidgeon, a potter and member of the Hopewell Centre meeting, asking him to fire the piece. The face on the bust resembled the tormented figure in the iconic painting "The Scream" by Norwegian artist Edvard Munch. Although Tom gave no explanation, those who knew him had no doubt it reflected his feelings about the violence that had surrounded him in Iraq and would soon surround him again.

Early in September of 2005, Tom rejoined CPT in Baghdad after an exhausting trip. His plane had been diverted to Basra, some three hundred miles to the south, because of an attack, or the threat of one, at the Baghdad airport. When he finally reached Baghdad, Tom found that "much of the life here in the middle of the country seems to be drifting back to the bad old days of Saddam, with the addition of an insurgency movement that seems to operate with a large degree of impunity even with the massive U.S. and Iraq military and police forces seeking them out."

Within a month, Tom and the team turned their attention to the Palestinian community in Iraq, which had become a target of both the new Iraqi government and unknown armed groups. Saddam had invited Palestinians into Iraq and given them favorable treatment in order to elevate his prestige among Sunnis in the Middle East. But the Palestinians were resented by many Iraqis. In early October, a CPT contingent consisting of Tom and team members Beth Pyles and Sheila Provencher, a member of the Muslim Peacemakers Team CPTers had helped organize, and a Palestinian translator traveled as escorts with nineteen Palestinians. These refugees, including five children ages one to thirteen, were fleeing to the al Wahid border in a bus in hopes they would be admitted into Syria. Eventually they were. A few weeks later Tom contacted a Palestinian leader who lived in Canada, setting in motion a process that would lead to the Canadian immigration of some of the families he helped. It was a happy ending Tom did not live to see.

Authorities at the U.S. embassy became aware of the CPT excursion to the Syrian border, and it evidently served as a wake-up call. They contacted the CPTers and asked them to arrange a meeting with some of the remaining Palestinians to discuss ways to protect them from what looked like a threat of cultural "cleansing." The meeting was held at a high-security hotel catering to foreign visitors outside the fortified Green Zone where the embassy was situated because the Palestinians were reluctant to enter a site many Iraqis associated with the occupation. The embassy officials arrived, Tom noted on his blog, accompanied by some fifty soldiers and security contractors in four Humvees and four armored SUVs.

Out of the meeting came a promise of increased U.S. pressure on Iraqi authorities to prevent unwarranted raids, beatings and arrests of Palestinians. CPTers continued to visit Palestinian families to monitor their treatment.

On November 18, Tom reported to supporters that he was scheduled to host a visiting delegation of CPT observers for ten days. Among the delegates would be Norman Kember, Jim Loney, and Harmeet Singh Sooden from England, Canada and New Zealand.

On November 25, Tom raised this question on his blog: "Why are we here? If I understand the message of God, his response... is that we are to take part in the creation of the Peaceable Realm of God. Again, if I understand the message of God, how we take part in the creation of this realm is to love God with all our heart, our mind, and our strength, and to love our neighbors and enemies as we love God and ourselves."

On November 26, Tom responded to an emailed invitation to speak during his next trip home at William Penn House (WPH), a Quaker educational and social service center located near the U.S. Capitol. In a message back to WPH Executive Director Byron Sandford, he said, "I will be happy to put something together in terms of bio material. We are busy with housecleaning today, in that a mortar round landed on the roof of our apartment building two days ago. ...No one was injured but the blast blew out many of the windows and made one big mess on the roof. It landed directly on one of the huge water tanks folks use here and I think that acted as a 'cushion' to the blast. If folks at WPH would like me to share some experiences (some more positive than a mortar landing on the roof) I would very much like to be there."

Several hours later, Tom and the three visiting CPT observers left their apartment and drove across Baghdad to meet with a Muslim cleric to discuss efforts to assist families of imprisoned Iraqis. En route, armed men forcibly stopped their car and the four were taken captive. The abductors later identified themselves as the "Swords of Righteousness," an unknown group. The four men would be held as hostages for more than three months. All but Tom would be found alive.

On March 9, 2006, authorities discovered the body of Tom Fox near a residential neighborhood in western Baghdad.

This is what Tom said when he first came to Iraq: "I am to stand firm against the kidnapper as I am to stand firm against the soldier. ...Does that mean I walk into a raging battle to confront the soldiers? Does that mean I walk the streets of Baghdad with a sign saying 'American for the Taking?' No to both counts. But if Jesus and Gandhi are right, then I am asked to risk my life, and if I lose it to be as forgiving as they were when murdered by the forces of Satan. I struggle to stand firm but I'm willing to keep working at it."

Mere hours after the news of Tom's death became public, the Langley Hill Friends Meeting issued the following statement:

It was an act of courage for Tom to travel to Iraq, to live in an ordinary Baghdad neighborhood, and to try to give voice to the concerns of ordinary Iraqi people with friends and family members in prison, out of sight, and with no avenue for communication. The loss of Tom is personal to those of us... who knew him and loved him. We need to remember that personal loss has also happened to thousands of Iraqis—indeed to tens of thousands of families around the world—who have lost loved ones in acts of violence just in the past year. Tom's story is being shared widely; the stories of these other losses are not. We at Langley Hill will honor Tom's courage by ensuring that the work to which he was dedicated continues, and that all stories of loss—not just Langley Hill's—are told.

Tom Fox was a soft-spoken person doing what he believed God asked him to do, someone so unassuming he would have been surprised by the outpouring of sympathy upon his death, said Langley Hill Quaker David Boynton.

Tom and the other three abductees were "doves of peace" who should have been rewarded rather than imprisoned, said Abdel-Salam al-Qubaisi, a spokesman for the Association of Muslim Scholars, an organization tied to Iraqi opposition to the U.S.-led occupation.

He was courageous, said Cindy Sheehan, a leading American peace activist whose son was killed while serving in the military in Iraq.

He was strengthening. "This is very difficult for my brother and me," wrote his daughter, Kassie, at the time of the kidnapping. "We want to be with our dad again. I didn't want him to go to a country where his American citizenship could potentially overshadow his peaceful reason for being there. But this is who my father is, and I am strengthened by it."

He was God-centered, someone who listened to others, loved and accepted others, and "lived Jesus' example in everything he did," said Lauri Perman.

To some in the media and public, Tom Fox was naïve and driven by a martyr complex.

But to his family and friends, Tom was not a saint nor naïve nor someone who had a wish for martyrdom. They knew him as someone who

197

was knowledgeable and realistic about the dangers he and other peacemakers faced, and who was aware of the limited amount of good a handful of care-givers could provide in the midst of overwhelming chaos and destruction. They knew him as someone who wished nothing for himself other than to someday return to his children, his many friends, and the mountains of northern Virginia.

To them, he was an ordinary person called to do extraordinary things.

Selby McCash was a newspaper reporter and public television commentator for twenty-five years and congressional aide for twenty-two years. He attends Friends Meeting of Washington (FMW) and is a member of the board of directors for William Penn House (WPH).

Johannes Williams received a JD degree from Georgetown University Law Center in 1985 and also serves on the board of the WPH. An attendee of the FMW since 1999, he has been on a spiritual sojourn at Langley Hill Friends Meeting since Tom Fox and three other CPTers were kidnapped in Baghdad.

21

Practicing Peace

Elizabeth Pyles

I spent seven weeks with Tom Fox on the CPT Iraq team in Baghdad. We lived and worked together. Along with Sheila Provencher, we accompanied a group of nineteen Palestinian refugees seeking to flee the persecution in Iraq. We worshiped and prayed and ate together. We laughed together. We talked. But seven weeks is no time at all in the life of a man.

Shortly after the kidnapping became public knowledge, CPT members around the world were deluged with media calls. I remember standing in the living room during a conversation with a newspaper reporter from Los Angeles, looking out at the peaceful street where my mother lives and being struck with the irony and tragedy of the situation. I told the reporter it felt strange to be speaking "for" Tom when he is fully capable of speaking for himself. "But he is unavailable by phone just now," I said.

My flip tongue concealed the truth I wanted to convey: at that time, and even now, it felt as if Tom, Jim, Norman, and Harmeet had become iconic, something other than the very real human beings they were and are. Speaking "for" someone is always dangerous business—so I tread lightly.

"Tom's dead."

This is what I wrote in my journal days after learning that Tom's body had been found near railroad tracks in a neighborhood in western Baghdad.

In speaking with some soldiers about Tom a day or two later, I said, "Tom was killed." It took several more days before I could say, "Tom was murdered." Such a harsh word and reality, and so hard to believe, even after my attempt to accompany Tom's body home.

The CPT team in Iraq made a commitment that whenever one or all of our kidnapped friends were released—healthy or sick, alive or dead—we would accompany them home. As I was the team member scheduled to leave Iraq next, I was chosen to accompany Tom's remains.

A problem quickly developed: though Tom was a civilian, the United States government required that his remains be taken by military transport to Dover, Delaware, for an autopsy. I received initial permission to accompany him, but got only as far as Anaconda Air Force Base in Balad, Iraq. There I was turned back two days later—permission denied.

In the meantime, I stayed on the base with the Army Reserve Mortuary Unit that received Tom's body and would transport him home. The unit treated me with kindness and respect, and we spent time together in conversation during my vigil. Though it was decided I could not accompany Tom's remains back home, I was allowed to walk with these soldiers onto the transport plane.

At predawn, my new friends bear Tom's casket draped with an American flag. The flag surprises me; Tom was not a soldier (although he previously served in the Marine Corps Band). For the soldiers, it is an act of honor and respect, and I am touched. I even smile a bit at the irony.

The soldiers load Tom's casket into a van, and I ride along as it is transported to the cargo plane. The plane is gaping and immense. Entering its empty hold feels like stepping into the Close Encounters spaceship. For me, it is alien territory, made more surreal by the droning engines, which drown out all other noise.

The soldiers carry Tom's body to the front of the airplane as I follow. They set the casket on the floor and stiffly salute. I stand at the front and read the beginning of John 1, which says of the light: "and the darkness did not overcome it."

When I return to the tarmac, soldiers approach with the remains of another— an Iraqi detainee. (All detainees who die in U.S. or coalition custody are taken to Dover for an autopsy). Displaying the same respect that was paid to Tom, minus the flag and salutes, the soldiers pass. I start to recite "Bis'm'allah . . ." then "Allah Akbar . . ." but cannot recall the words. Stumbling, I recite a part of Job 1, both for Tom and the unknown detainee: "Naked I came into the world, naked I will depart. The Lord giveth, the Lord taketh away, blessed be the name of the Lord." Laughter mingles with my steady tears. Even in death, Tom accompanies an Iraqi safely to his destination.

Such a fitting end: Tom and an Iraqi detainee side by side in death, ministered to by young soldiers from Tom's home. No more anger, no more fear, no more violence; only kindness and peace. How many more will die before moments of peace for the dead are transformed into a lasting peace for the living?

As we leave the cargo plane, I look to the sky. The bright morning star shines like a blessing.

Back in Baghdad, the CPT team wrestled with how to honor the life and memory of our friend in a way that would promote peace and reconciliation. We dreamt of planting a date-palm grove, each tree a living memorial to those who have died in Iraq: Sunni, Shi'a, Christian. It is the dying that unifies. All return to the same earth. Perhaps the living would come together in peace in the date-palm grove to honor the dead. We dreamt and hoped.

Never much of a poet, I struggled to express my own prayers about the manner of Tom's death, prayers for an end to suffering, prayers for redemption amidst the evil of such violence. I e-mailed the following to family and friends:

To the Kidnappers of Tom

If there was a life he begged for,
it was yours.

If he wept when you killed him,
he wept for you.

If I would have anyone know about Tom, it would be this.

In response to my and others' e-mails, friends and strangers poured out their grief, their love, and their prayers.

A Palestinian friend in Amman wrote, "Some fifty years ago a child was born who grew up to be a correct and moral man. A man of deep respect and passion for human life; a hero in the most basic sense of the word. This hero did many good things: helping the poor, giving hope to the despondent, and drying the tears of the sad. He dedicated his life's work to helping those less fortunate than he. He made his work putting himself in harm's way. This hero was a friend to all people: rich, poor, Muslims, Christians, Jewish, old and young. . . . We commend CPT for continuing to *get in the way*; there is no better way to honor his memory. Though his name may one day be forgotten, his deeds will live on forever!"

Perhaps the most surprising response was the condolence we received from a Muslim religious school in Iran, from people we have never met who wrote to us with words of comfort from the Qur'an, "We are made for God and we return to God." It is the traditional condolence in Islam. Having been taught for so long in the West to view Iran as an enemy, we were humbled by the outreach of kindness across so many divides. This condolence is what we placed on the black banners we commissioned, in keeping with the custom in Iraq. The banners with this message, along with a message of forgiveness, were hung near the place where Tom's body was found.

Yet for all the meaning we find in Tom's death, it is his life that bears the true mark of Tom Fox. And it is his life that will have the last word. Following a discussion of Tom's life at the Baltimore Yearly Meeting of Friends on August 4, 2006, the Friends shared their memories of Tom.

One woman from the Langley Hill Friends Meeting said, "I am not called to make peace in this world. I am called to practice peace."

I can think of no more fitting words to sum up Tom's life: he practiced peace.

May we all heed the call to practice peace in our time and place. "For once you were darkness, but now in the Lord you are light. Live as children of light" (Ephesians 5:8).

Beth Pyles is a Reserve Corps member of CPT who works with CPT's Iraq Team. She lives and works as a Presbyterian pastor in McDowell, Virginia.

22

No Greater Love

James Loney

No one has greater love than this, to lay down one's life for one's friends.
                                                                    —John 15:13

As I begin this writing, it was 224 days ago that Tom's body was found, wrapped first in a sheet and then in plastic, near a school in the Andalus district of Baghdad—not far, it appears, from where we were first held.

I write these words almost as if to give myself a pinch. Yes, it is true. Tom was murdered. It really did happen: six bullet holes, six murderous instructions to an index finger, six separate emissaries of a singular intention to kill; mind steadying the hand, eyes directing the bullets that ripped through Tom's emaciated body, releasing his soul into light. Though I say it, though I see the words written by my own hand, still I cannot quite get my head (or is it my heart?) around a fact that seems as far away, as remote and impossible as the kidnapping itself.

That's how it was. Things were just facts. *Look, four men have hijacked our vehicle. Now they are pointing guns at our heads. Now they are searching, handcuffing, blindfolding us. Now I am riding in the trunk of a car, being taken God knows where. Now there is a man facing me with a video camera. He's telling me I must plead for my life. Now I am hungry. Now I am excruciatingly bored.*

Things were possible to manage this way, stripped down to bone and picked clean of emotion. When something is a fact, there is only response—things to do, or not do, according to the measure of the fact, and the field of possibility around it. Facts are things you can observe, walk around, kick the tires of, make decisions about. Feelings, on the other hand, are dangerous, volatile, unpredictable. You're too much inside them—or they inside you. They leave you burning, shivering, raw-wide-open, falling helpless into helplessness.

That's what February 12 was, the day Tom was taken away from us—another fact in a series of cold hard facts. *Now Tom's hands are being handcuffed behind his back. Now they are gathering up his little bundle of clothes. Now he is saying, "Well, I guess this is goodbye." Now we are exchanging hugs. Now they are leading him away.* A fact I watched from another room, from another body. A fact I did not dispute.

Greg Rollins, a full-time Iraq team member from Surrey, British Columbia, happened to mention that he had laundry to do. It was a complaint against time. As the logistics coordinator for the delegation (Harmeet Sooden, Norman Kember, and me), Greg was scheduled to accompany us for a full day of meetings the next day, and then travel with us to Kerballah the day after that. When would he have time to get his laundry done?

(In Iraq, laundry is an all-day affair. You wash it by hand in the morning and hang it on the rooftop clothesline to dry. By nightfall it's ready, cured in the aromas of Baghdad's smog.)

The team was setting the table for supper. Tom said, "I don't have anything planned for tomorrow. Why don't I take the delegation for the morning meeting and you can get ready for the trip to Kerballah?"

"Are you sure?" Greg asked.

"Yup, no problem," Tom replied.

The plan was thus: Tom would accompany the delegation to our ten a.m. meeting with a senior Shi'a cleric at the Khadimiya shrine; we'd return to the CPT apartment for a quick lunch; Greg would then take us, along with a different translator, to our two p.m. meeting with the human rights officer of the Muslim Scholars Association.

But of course, in Iraq nothing ever happens according to plan: the meeting didn't start until eleven, it went longer than expected, we were too polite to interrupt. When the meeting finished, there was no way we could negotiate Baghdad gridlock, get back to the apartment, make the switch, and be on time for our appointment. We had a quick lunch in the Khadimiya market and then drove to the Muslim Scholars Association—a Sunni organization located in the Umm al Qura mosque in Ghazaliya.

I first met Tom in August 2004. He was fresh from training in Chicago and was beginning a three-year term as a full-time CPTer. I had just been appointed to the role of Canada coordinator, a job I was to share with an old friend, Rebecca Johnson, with whom I had trained in the summer of 2000. Tom and I were beginning our work in CPT at a biennial full-timer's retreat.

During that retreat, I heard Tom mention that he had been in the Marine Corps. I was immediately intrigued—how does a former Marine become an activist, pacifist, violence-reduction Christian peacemaker? He even looked like a soldier: tall, lean, conservatively dressed, his demeanor often remote.

I posed my question to him the first opportunity I got. Our conversation proceeded in fits and starts. I would ask a question, he would answer in terse, two or three-sentence paragraphs that often ended abruptly. If I wanted to know more I had to ask a further question.

Yes, he explained, he had been in the Marines, but he was a musician, not a soldier. He played the clarinet in the Marine Corps Band. He didn't know how to use a gun. The Marine Band was the only military band in the world that didn't take basic training. That's because during the Civil War the Marine Band was made to fight and the result was a disaster—they all got killed, or got those around them killed.

A professor told him he should try out for the band. He was among eighty people that auditioned, and much to his surprise, he got the job. When he retired in 1993, he sold all his musical instruments. He was an artist, and art was something you gave yourself to completely, or not at all. He trained to become a baker and started work in a large organic food chain where he eventually became a manager.

Led by a mutual spiritual curiosity, Tom and his wife at the time, Jan Stansel, begin to explore Quakerism in 1983. A spiritual awakening during his transition out of the Marine Band led him deeper into the practice of Quaker spirituality. With 9/11, he saw the landscape of American life take a hard turn toward unlimited global warfare. He needed to do something. He began to research options on the Internet and found CPT's website. He didn't rush things. He learned as much as he could, tested the Spirit's leadings, got his affairs in order. He went on a delegation and took training. Now, finally, his work was about to begin. He was leaving for Iraq in three weeks.

I asked him if he had any family. Yes, two children, a son named Andrew, nineteen, and a daughter named Kassie, twenty-four. "How do they feel about your decision to work in Iraq," I asked.

"They're worried, of course," he said in his matter-of-fact way, "but I explained to them this was something I had to do." He felt they were ready now, both of them living on their own, though he was a little worried about Andrew, who was just starting in the work world as a young adult. Perhaps because he felt they really had to face the possibility he might not come home, he warned them to prepare for the worst. "Armies expect casualties when they go to war. Those working for peace in war zones have to expect the same." I remember thinking there was something uncharacteristically stark about that statement. It strikes me now as something a soldier might say: Tom's military background showing itself.

Especially in the beginning of the captivity, Tom was our stalwart anchor and in-house expert. He knew all about Iraq's kidnapping industry, how the field was played by both criminals and insurgents, how they were organized in a hierarchical network of power and influence, how hostages were put up for auction and sold up the ladder until the highest bidder secured the rights to extort princely ransoms—or execute their ideological prey on grainy videos—things he'd learned during a previous team crisis when a CPTer's name had appeared on a kidnap list and had to immediately leave the country. He knew a great deal about Iraqi culture, history, politics. Even more important, he knew crucial Arabic words, like *hamam* (bathroom), *my* (water), *mumkin* (could I please), *la* and *nam* (no and yes), the numbers, the days of the week, various references to time. His knowledge and unflappable calm were invaluable resources for our survival.

During those first days of relentless, terrifying, excruciating uncertainty, where we had no idea of anything, not even of how our bodies and minds were being affected by the unending hours of immobility and lack of stimulus, Tom dove into prayer the way a warrior might charge into battle. He turned his captivity into a sustained, unbroken meditation. The chain that bound his wrist became a kind of rosary, or *misbaha* (the beads Muslims use to count the names of God). He would picture someone: a member of his family, a member of the Iraq team or CPT office, one of the captors, whomever he felt needed a prayer. Clasping the chain, he would breathe in and breathe out, slowly, so that you could hear the air gushing in and out of his lungs. With each breath, he would pass a link of the chain through his thumb and index finger. In his first breath he would mind-say, *with the warmth of my heart*. In the second, *with the stillness of my mind*. In the third, *with the fluidity of my body*. And in the fourth, *with the light of my soul*. At the end of each cycle of four breaths, he would pause, and simply rest in the Light with the person he was praying for.

Tom's vigilance in prayer was astounding. I sometimes felt ashamed. My mind would wander helplessly in a wilderness of self-preoccupation. His unrelenting focus called me back to prayer again and again, almost as if someone had suddenly taken hold of my shoulders, was gently shaking me, telling me, "Wake up! Come back to your senses."

Tom would exhort us to live in the present moment. The past and the future did not exist, he would say, we only have the now. He would remind us, despite assurances from our captors that release was imminent, that we could be held for months, even years.

Though I often thought of it, being the official delegation leader and all, for some reason (which I still don't understand) I could never bring myself to articulate the idea to the group. Tom did. He suggested that we begin to think of ourselves as a team and conduct ourselves accordingly. On December 23, Day 29 of captivity, we began the practice of a daily check-in (where team members share how they are doing physically, emotionally, and spiritually) and worship service. Tom also introduced our first *de memoriam*, Bible-less Bible study. The format was simple. The leader would recall as best he could a Bible passage and then we would reflect together on it according to a series of four questions: What is the main point of this passage to me? Is it true in my experience? What is difficult, challenging or confusing about the passage? How might this passage change my life?

We set up a schedule and took turns leading these diurnal team disciplines. It was thus that the days became more like days. There were tasks, responsibilities, decisions to make (when shall we have worship today—before or after lunch?), a little structure to mark our progress through the endless gray-wash of time. And perhaps most important of all, through our prayer together we could reach outside the paint-peeling walls of our second-story dungeon, reach with our hearts and our souls to all those imprisoned by despair, poverty, and violence. It was a way for us to counteract the creeping self-absorption that inevitably accompanies captivity.

Tom's prayers were profound. They brought our suffering into dialogue with the vast suffering of the world. Again and again his prayers brought other prisoners to us—security detainees in Iraq, illegal combatants in Guantanamo, the lost and forgotten souls in American penitentiaries. And every time we heard a bomb explode, near or far, Tom would stop to pray for those whose lives had just been changed. Every time, without fail.

I remember asking him during that first week if he was afraid they might find out he had been in the military. I wanted to know because I had my own secret to protect: the fact that I was gay and in a long-term relationship with a man. Early on, the captors said they would release us after they checked our backgrounds. As it was, I found it hard to explain why I wasn't married. All they had to do was Google my name, and references to things I had written about being gay would pop up on the Internet. Iraqi attitudes toward homosexuality were not exactly accepting: Ayatollah Sistani, for example, had issued a fatwa that men who had sex with men should be killed in the worst possible way. I worried the same fate awaited Tom if they found out he had been in the Marine Corps.

Tom's answer was characteristically unadorned. "No," he wasn't afraid, he said. "That's beyond my control. Whatever happens, happens. I'm just trying to stay in the present moment."

His answer seemed impossibly detached. How could he not be afraid? Maybe he wasn't. Or maybe he was trying to protect us. You could never tell with Tom, what he was thinking or feeling. His face was an imperturbable mask. Later on he would call it his "poker face." It was only as I got to know him better that I realized this was his way of coping, keeping vulnerability at bay.

On Day 8, the Saturday following our abduction, the captor we called Medicine Man paid us a visit. He earned that name when he brought blood pressure medication for Norman. Medicine Man announced that we were going to be moved, one by one, in the trunk of his car: Tom first, then Norman, then me, then Harmeet. We would be separated and held in different locations.

Though my mind was perfectly clear, my body began to shiver uncontrollably. I hated when fear possessed my body and my mind was helpless to disguise or control it. Tom redoubled his meditations. Then, just before they took him, he said, "I've been preparing for this for a year—thinking about it, praying about it, meditating about it. The way I feel now, I could do this forever." I turned in my chair to look at him, astonished that he could say such a thing. Serene determination illuminated his face. "Be strong," he said to us as they led him away, blindfolded and handcuffed.

Tom always took the hardest place. You couldn't argue him out of it. It was part of the fierce stubbornness that kept him going. Take our pillow collection, for example. We had five of them—three that were sufficiently comfortable, and clean, to rest your head on, and two that were so flat and grimy with human body oils they were hardly fit to use underfoot (which we did, day and night, to protect our feet from the greedy, heat-sucking cold of the tile floor). Norman, Harmeet, and I each had the luxury of our own pillow—only because Tom insisted on using his sweater as a makeshift headrest. From time to time we would check with him. "Tom, are you okay with not using a pillow? We can easily take turns."

"No," he would say, "I'm fine. I'm actually very comfortable with what I'm doing." I didn't believe him, but I didn't argue: one, there was no way of winning, and two, I *loved* my pillow and was secretly pleased I didn't have to share it.

And then there was the matter of blankets. There weren't enough of those either. The one blanket we had, a fire-engine red, double-lined fleece monstrosity (it had to weigh fifteen pounds!), was just big enough to cover three of us, as long as someone on an end didn't pull an unfair portion of the covers in their direction. This meant someone had to sleep outside the communal blanket. Our ever resourceful captors, seeking an immediate solution that didn't involve spending money, yanked two, dust-infested, ceiling-length curtains off the wall and thrust them into Tom's arms. One of the curtains looked like a bridal train. Without blinking an eye, Tom fashioned them into a makeshift mummy bag he could slide into. Again we would check. "Tom, are you sure you're okay? Why don't we share sleeping in those things."

"No, no," he'd say, "really I'm okay. I'm a hot sleeper and I've got myself a system here that's working really well." But when the nights got cold in January and as our metabolisms slowed from lack of food, Tom found it impossible to keep warm. The lack of sleep began to take a visible physical and psychological toll. Still, the course had been set, and Tom was going to keep to it.

"You know, last night I had this dream. I want to tell you about it." It was Tom's turn for check-in. "I was dreaming that we were sitting here in the room and Junior [the nickname given to the youngest captor] came in. His face was a mask of evil. He said somebody has been sold. One of you has to go. He had a gun in his hand. We looked at each other. Nobody moved. 'Come on,' he said, 'one of you must decide.' Then I stood up. 'I'll go. I'll be the one.'

"That's when I woke up. My heart was pounding and I couldn't get back to sleep. I began to think, over and over in my mind, could I do that, could I really do that? And it struck me, these guys are my friends. Yeah, I could do that, I said to myself. I really think I could do that."

How can I explain my reaction? Was it shock? Repulsion at the ugliness of having to make such a decision? I felt like somebody had punched me in the gut. It was, in fact, a scenario I had secretly tested in my own imagination. Filled with cold burning shame, I forced myself to admit that I was probably incapable of the same gesture.

No one spoke. A spring-loaded silence filled the room. Not wanting to catch his eyes, I stole a look at Tom from the corner of my eye. His face was open, searching, reaching. He wanted someone to respond.

I think it was Norman who eventually coughed and changed the subject. Our silence felt like a betrayal. We were captives indeed.

We ended up calling him Uncle. Norman christened him so, at the end of that second week of captivity when we were reunited after being separated for a week—Harmeet and I at the "first house," Tom and Norman at the "second house." I wanted to call him Big Foot because Uncle truly had the biggest, thickest, slab-of-meat feet I'd ever seen, and he hated wearing shoes. The others resisted, feeling this was disrespectful.

"He's kind of like an uncle," Norman declared, referring to the humane treatment Uncle extended to them during our week of separation. "Let's call him Uncle." And so we did.

It was New Year's Day. Uncle had been away on captor leave. As usual, the power was out and our nightly ritual of being unlocked, setting up the communal bed, being let one by one to the bathroom, and then being locked up again lying on our backs had to be conducted by lantern light. In the middle of the routine, Uncle limped into the room nursing his left foot. He eased himself into a chair and we could see that his ankle had swollen to the size of a cantaloupe.

"What happened?" we asked. He pointed to his ankle, decorated in painful-looking hues of yellow and purple, and said, "Football, football." He had twisted his ankle playing soccer.

"Doctor? You see doctor?" we asked. It looked pretty bad.

"Iraqi doctor *mozane,*" he said, unable to hide his contempt. He seemed to have an irrational hatred of Iraqi doctors. We tried to explain, in our handful of Arabic words, how one might treat a sprain. Harmeet was something of an expert, having had a couple of bad sprains himself. The one idea we seemed able to communicate was that he should rest it—for at least two weeks—which you'd think the pain would naturally force someone to do, but you never knew with Uncle. He wasn't the brightest light in the Christmas tree.

Tom got down on his hands and knees and gently wrapped his hands around Uncle's ankle. The room got very quiet. Uncle and Junior looked down at Tom, looked at each other, and then looked at me. Their foreheads and brows were knit with confusion.

"*Schoo?* What this?" Junior asked.

I pointed to my ankle, folded my hands under my chin as if I were saying a prayer, and then pointed to Uncle. "He is praying," I said, pointing toward heaven. "Allah. For *sadeeki.* Your friend."

Junior, suddenly understanding, nodded. He said something in Arabic to Uncle.

When he was done, Tom stood up, eyes blinking rapidly as if returning from a trance. "Sometimes . . . sometimes I can draw the pain out," he said. "I was trying to draw the pain out." Junior and Uncle looked bewildered, unsure what to do.

Upon my return from the bathroom, Harmeet, Norman, and Tom were all handcuffed and chained in their nocturnal stations. I lay down between Norman and Harmeet and waited for Junior and Uncle to handcuff me to them, but they said good night and left the room, waving cheerily and laughing, completely forgetting their custodial duty.

Maybe this is how God opens prison doors.

Between Christmas and New Years, something shifted in Tom. Perhaps it was the protein his body craved, the absolute lack of solitude (a cross indeed, as any introvert will know), or the relentless cold. Perhaps it was his inability to sleep, the burden of fear that came with his citizenship, or the oceanic boredom. Perhaps it was the accumulating deprivations of captivity (sunlight! exercise! choice! mental stimulation!), but Tom was losing his ability to cope. It was almost as if he had hit a wall. The intransigent strength and unflagging leadership of those first weeks evaporated. He asked for a sedative to help him sleep, and the captors obliged.

Tom took one, then two pills each day and still complained of being unable to sleep. His mind lost its suppleness. He seemed to be more fixed on his own ideas, less able to incorporate new information. His perceptions grew rigid. We would frequently have to repeat things. He was either stone silent or helplessly garrulous. His emotional life, which he once carefully guarded, became an open book. "You know," he once said, "I've shared more with you guys than I have with anyone else in my life." Sometimes his sharing sounded more like verbal floundering.

We started to worry. Tom no longer seemed himself. Something had to be said. As if on cue, he voluntarily cut back to one capsule a day. He felt the medication was pulling him deeper into a vortex of depression. "I don't like what it's doing to me," he said. I was relieved because it saved us from a confrontation.

Of course, none of us was at our best. Each of us, in our respective struggles to cope with the interminable confinement, fear, and hunger, took turns carrying, and being carried, by the others. While our coping styles inevitably clashed from time to time, the capacity to cope itself seemed to be dissolving in Tom, a process I felt was related to this unyielding interior battle to keep his mind and body "healthy" and every kind of "negativity" at bay. He was determined to "hit the ground running" when our release came. If only he could meditate harder, and meditate better, and do more exercises during the day, he'd manage it. It was a matter of hard work and applying himself in the right ways. I felt this was a hopeless and unrealistic strategy.

Sometimes, when we wanted to give each other a bit of advice, we'd couch it in the first person. Tom and I were the main culprits in this department. We'd say, "In my experience," or "What I try to do is," or "What I've learned about such and such is," when really we were trying to say what we thought someone else should do.

I wanted to tell him that it was impossible, that it was simply beyond human ability to try to will one's way through this nightmare. Though it drove me crazy to receive advice this way, I didn't know how else to do it. I didn't want to undermine his capacity to cope or for him to feel I was judging him.

At the end of a check-in one day, I embarked on a carefully prepared speech. "Early on, I figured out that there's no way I can defeat this boredom. It's just too big, too vast. It doesn't matter how many mental puzzles I do, how many prayers or mediations I say, there's just no way to win against it. I don't have enough will, or enough strength, or enough creativity, or enough of whatever it takes to control or moderate what we're going through, or my reaction to it. It's just too big. If I'm going to get through this, it's going to have to come from something outside of me, something beyond me. It'll be because God carried me, and not because of anything I did."

Tom's theology was unfamiliar to me. I felt rather old-fashioned and orthodox in comparison, believing that Jesus is the Son of God, the unique incarnation of God's love; that we are destined to live in communion with a God who loves and knows each of us by name; that the place (or state of being) where that happens forever is called heaven; and salvation is an unmerited consequence of God's unconditional love.

For Tom, God was a kind of nonpersonal energy, an energy of love, perhaps best described as Light that suffused and imbued everything. There was no limit to this energy, this light. It could—and wanted to— grow and expand infinitely. We each had a little bit of that light. Or, as Quakers say it, "there is that of God in everyone." While not the Son of God, Jesus had a unique and privileged understanding of his connection to God. This spiritual connection was accessible to all of us, but Jesus perfected that connection by going all the way in the spiritual life. Our task was to follow the example of Jesus by working to perfect our connection to God and thereby increase the amount of love energy in the universe, so that one day everything would be transformed into love. This task required tremendous effort, sacrifice, and hard work. It was effort, not grace, that seemed to animate Tom's ceaseless spiritual quest.

It's my hunch Tom was haunted by a dread fear that the stresses and privations of captivity would irrevocably sever his connection to the divine, that he would eventually succumb to the temptation to hate and dehumanize his captors, and thus lose everything he'd worked so hard to achieve in the spiritual life. In our desperate circumstances, his answer was to strive harder, to hold fast with every last ounce of strength lest he fall helpless into the abyss of negativity.

It pained me to watch him in this struggle. I wanted to tell him, "You don't have to fight. God loves you more than you can possibly imagine. You don't have to *do* anything. Your connection with God is permanent and irrevocable. You cannot not be in the Light."

At Tom's suggestion, we told each other our life stories, one of several projects we undertook to "kill time." Telling life stories is a tradition on CPT teams and constitutes part of our training. We began somewhere around Christmas, once we had determined that there would be no dramatic Christmas release and we had accepted we were going to be in this for the long haul. Here's some of what I recall from Tom's story.

Tom was born in Graysville, Tennessee, in 1951. At the time of Tom's birth, his mother was forty and his father was fifty-five. He was to be their only child. They moved when he was very young to Chattanooga, Tennessee. His grandparents, on both sides, had died, and there was no extended family to speak of. They moved into a racially mixed neighborhood just as the white people were beginning to move out and ended up being the only white family on their street.

His father, a World War I Marine, suffered from emphysema and couldn't work. Preoccupied with the study of an obscure philosopher, he spent his days reading and exchanging letters related to his philosophical interest. Tom said his father never played with him. He couldn't because of his health.

His mother was an alcoholic. She started to drink as soon as she got home from her working-class job in a beer-distributing company. Tom would come home after school and spend a half-hour visiting with her before the alcohol kicked in. He used to love that time with her. Then he would take off to a friend's house and return late in the evening. He was forever arranging things so that he'd have somewhere else to be.

They must have been dirt poor. And suffocatingly isolated.

Tom's street dead-ended onto a woods. He found refuge there, spent countless hours wandering, exploring, playing. He loved the trees, the creek, the sun dappling through leaves. It was where he truly felt at home, the only place where he was free.

He also took solace in the clarinet. He practiced endlessly in his room, and sure enough had quite a flair for it. Though he never said it, it became the instrument of his escape from the closed horizons of his childhood. It got him a scholarship to college, and thereafter a job in the Marine Corps Band.

Tom told his story without emotion. It's just what happened, the facts as they are. I wanted to cry, hold him tight, undo what could not be undone.

There was something different about Tom that morning. Though more quiet than usual, he seemed buoyant, alert to everything.

"I had this strange experience last night," he said once the captors had locked us up for the day. "I don't know what it was exactly—it wasn't really a vision, or a dream—it was more like a voice. I don't know how to describe it." He stopped speaking for a moment, self-conscious, unsure if he should continue. We encouraged him to go on.

"You might think this is strange, but I want to tell you because you're my friends. The most amazing thing happened. I couldn't sleep. I was just lying there, meditating, when I heard this voice. I don't know where it came from, but it was clear and unmistakable, almost as if it were a real voice. It said, 'I am here . . . I am here . . .' And I felt this incredible sense of peace. Total peace. Everything melted away, the worry and the fear and the handcuffs—everything. And the voice just kept repeating, over and over, 'I am here.'"

He looked at us, his face shining. "It was God's voice saying I am here. I don't know how long it went on but I just keep meditating on those words, 'I am here.' I've never felt more at peace."

There was a long silence. I looked over at Tom, smiled, and then bowed my head. I listened, and thought I could hear it too, the same voice resounding in my own heart.

They set it up two days before. "News good," they told us. "Big Haji will come and [you] go. *Schwaya schwaya* [a little bit of time] and [you] go." With a whooshing sound, Uncle rubbed one open palm against another and then lifted it skyward, following the trajectory of a jet taking flight: body language for freedom.

Big Haji, or Medicine Man, was the intermediary between the invisible "political leaders" who were deciding our fate and the guards (Nephew, Uncle, and Junior) who supervised us. His visits were always an occasion. He spoke English, he determined the conditions of our captivity, and he was the source of whatever news they wanted us to have about the outside world.

Medicine Man came on Day 78. The news was good. "We will take you, one by one in the trunk," he explained. "It is not a problem. You do this before. We will take you back to the first house. You will have some shower, we will take some picture, we will prepare you for release. Then we take you to a mosque—I think you know this place. It is where you are taken from. It is the safest place. We will take you all together, no blindfold, in a car. We will let you out and you will walk to the mosque. Your negotiators will come and meet you in five minutes. I will go now to see if the road is safe, no checkpoint." He turned and left the room.

We were excited. Here, for the first time, were specific details, a place and a plan. Finally! we told each other, finally!

"I'll go last," Tom declared. Harmeet objected. "I was last the last time. I don't mind. I'll go last this time." Without any of us having to say it, we all agreed that the worst thing was to be left to the end.

"No, I'm going last," Tom said.

"We could at least talk about it," Harmeet countered, but Tom's resolve was incontestable, and Norman and I weren't going to argue the point.

Then, for the first time in captivity, Tom told a joke. "What's the difference between a Marine and a mushroom?" he asked. We thought for a moment and then gave up. "Nothing," he said, grinning like a little boy. "They're both kept in the dark and fed bull s - - t."

The next day, Junior came into the room wearing a pink shirt, natty suit jacket, pressed trousers, and an irrepressible smile. He was hardly recognizable without his grubby tracksuit. We guessed that Medicine Man had taken him shopping.

He unlocked our handcuffs, gave us each a kiss and then, pointing to each of us in turn, told us he would take Tom first, then Norman, then me, then Harmeet. He told Norman and Tom to gather their clothes together and be ready to leave. Nephew took Tom's clothes and Junior held out a pair of handcuffs. Tom turned to us. "Well, I guess this is goodbye," he said. His words stabbed like a knife.

Norman shook his hand. Harmeet and I gave him a hug. There was nothing left to him, his body was all hardness and bone, the consequence of our miserly diet. "Goodbye, Tom," I said. "Be strong; God is with you," I wanted to say, but didn't. Junior handcuffed his hands behind his back and led him out of the room.

Looking back, it's clear now what Tom's separation meant. Deathly clear. It wasn't at the time. Our captors told us the British and the Canadians were willing to negotiate for ransom, but the Americans absolutely and categorically would not.[28] Instead arrangements were being made with the Americans for a prisoner exchange. "This very very secret. They never admit to this. They will say this is normal—we always release some prisoner every month. But no,"—pointing at Tom—"They make this release because of you."

There was in fact a big prisoner release in January. We saw it on the news. They also demanded that the last two of six women be released. (I learned later that four Iraqi women had been released at the end of January.)

Who knows what the truth was? In retrospect, our captors may have been stringing us along, spinning stories from the news to keep us compliant. For a while we believed that Tom had been released, the negotiations on his behalf having been concluded.

The morning after Tom was taken, the commonplace routine of folding away our bed and arranging our chairs against the wall for the long day of sitting changed forever. Now, instead of four chairs, we needed only to get three.

---

[28] According to the captors, their goal in abducting us was to secure ransoms from our respective governments in order to finance their war against the occupation. It is CPT's policy that it will not pay ransom under any circumstances. Our release was an "intelligence-led" military rescue operation undertaken by Canadian, British, and American governments. In my view, speculation about ransom is unhelpful as it only places westerners traveling and working abroad at unnecessary risk.

A great hole opened in our lives. It was like the soul had gone out of our group. We laboured through the day in a collective stupor. None of us wanted to acknowledge the horrible implication of his departure.

I remember going into the bathroom and seeing only three toothbrushes. I always enjoyed looking at them. There was something complete about them standing together in their square, grungy Tupperware container, each a different colour (chosen purposely by Medicine Man so we wouldn't confuse our toothbrushes—red and green and blue and purple—there was so little colour in our lives!). They somehow represented our individuality. But now the purple one, Tom's, was gone. For just a moment, grief broke through. That little forest of toothbrushes I loved had been decimated.

Check-in, worship, and Bible study ceased. After a handful of days, I suggested we resume check-in. After another handful of days, we returned to daily worship. Neither were ever the same. It always felt to me like we were merely going through the motions. As for Bible study, without Tom it was impossible.

We had to find out how to be a group again. And because we had no other option, we just kept on going. Emotion was not a luxury we could afford. We lived in facts, and clung half-heartedly to the hope that he had gotten home.

On March 7, Day 102, Medicine Man made a house call. "Do you have any news about Tom," I asked.

"Yes, he is still at the other house. We have some problems so we separate him. You know his government will not negotiate for him. The CIA is trying to prevent the negotiation. They do not want the [prisoner] exchange to happen so the negotiations are going very slow. We will make some announcement that we kill him—to separate your case. They do not know he is still alive. But we not kill him—he will be released with you. We make this announcement to the media, to put pressure on your governments, but we not kill him."

I said nothing. I looked at Medicine Man, nodded, received his news with a blank face. A poker face.

The next clue came four days later, on March 11. We were watching TV in our captors' living quarters. It had become something of a routine—they would unlock us around seven p.m. (after Junior returned from "work"), take us downstairs, and feed us supper. That was nice because we could eat with our hands free, like regular human beings. If we were lucky they'd have a pirate-edition DVD for us to watch. Otherwise it was an evening of Arabic channel surfing. At ten they'd return to us our room and lock us up for the night after we brushed our teeth.

216

We were watching TV when we saw it, a preview of the day's top new story, a poster-board with each of our pictures, a close up of Tom's picture, a cut to the last, ghostly video image of Tom in captivity. Then a road under construction, a piece of heavy equipment in the background, a close-up of a particular spot on the ground. That was all we saw before they changed the channel. I involuntary shivered. Harmeet asked the captor we called Nephew why Tom was on TV. "Oh, this is normal," he said. "They are showing about your life on the news. Every night a different one of you. Tonight they are showing Tom." We knew he was lying. We stopped asking about Tom after that.

We didn't know for sure until the day of our release, fourteen days after Tom's body was found. It was the first question I asked the British soldiers who busted us out. "Where's Tom? Is he free or has he been killed?" I still clung to the hope that he might have been released.

"No, he was killed." The voice was hesitant, apologetic.

"Are you sure? Did they find his body?"

"Yes. They found his body."

"They found his body? You're sure?"

"Yes, they found his body."

We were in the Green Zone, in the British ambassador's house. Norman had already left. Harmeet showed me his notebook. "Look," he said. "It's the only thing Tom wrote in my note book." He pointed to two fractions, 3/4 and 4/4, large figures sprawling lazily across the page. "He wrote them when he was teaching me about musical timing—3/4 time and 4/4 time." Harmeet was searching my face. I was failing to understand something.

He covered the 3/4 fraction with his finger. "First we were this— 4/4," he said. Then he covered the 4/4 fraction. "Now we're only 3/4. Sad, isn't it. It's the only thing he wrote in my notebook."

"Martyrdom is the supreme witness given to the truth of the faith; it means bearing witness even unto death. . . . [A martyr] endures death through an act of fortitude."
—*Catechism of the Catholic Church,* 2473

After the supper table was cleared away and the dishes were done, Tom sat down to his computer. He stopped to think for a moment, and then typed, "Why Are We Here?" Had the question been on his mind all day? Had it been percolating for weeks, or had it simply seized him, the way Tom could be seized by a thing, this time while putting leftovers away in the fridge?

217

Why *are* we here? It's the ultimate question, really. Whether we're cleaning up after dinner or facing a captor's gun, the earth turns, the sun rises and sets, the seasons come and go. We have all to find our way through, to somehow make sense of the turning, the rising and the setting, the coming and going of our lives, whatever the "here" is that we've been given to live. It's the task God has breathed into us.

On this Tom was clear, as he tried to be about anything that was important. Clear in the sense of being open, seeing, paying attention, pushing the clutter away. Clear in the sense of letting the Light within him shine. He answered the question in 417 direct-and-to-the-point words. He wrote them on November 25, 2005, the evening before he was kidnapped.

The answer, he wrote, is "that we are to take part in the creation of the Peaceable Realm of God," a realm we help create when we love God, our neighbors, even our enemies, "with all our heart, our mind and our strength." In the context of Iraq, where "dehumanization seems to be the operative means of relating to each other," and where U.S. forces kill innocent Iraqis in "their quest to hunt down and kill" those they've dehumanized as "terrorists," Tom defined love positively as "a profound respect for all human beings simply for the fact that they are all God's children," and negatively as "never thinking or doing anything that would dehumanize one of my fellow human beings."

"The first step down the road to violence," he said, "is taken when I dehumanize a person. . . . As soon as I rob a fellow human being of his or her humanity by sticking a dehumanizing label on them, I begin the process that can have, as an end result, torture, injury and death."

"Why are we here?" he asked again. It was not a rhetorical question. "We are here to root out all aspects of dehumanization that exist within us. We are here to stand with those being dehumanized by oppressors and stand firm against that dehumanization. We are here to stop people, including ourselves, from dehumanizing any of God's children, no matter how much they dehumanize their own souls."

Every time I read these words—the last words he wrote as a free man—shivers ride up and down my arms. Amplified by their uncanny timing, these words were his last will and spiritual testament. His will, fierce and indomitable, to root out all aspects of violence within himself, was the unceasing struggle of his captivity. His testament, the why of his "why are we here?" was what he called the Peaceable Realm of God, where the lion lies down with the lamb, every division is healed, fear is banished from every heart, and the rich feast with the poor at God's banquet table. That vision was what the arc of Tom's life pointed to, the Light that guided him.

You were emerging from the scars of a hardscrabble childhood. You had your own mind about and your own way of doing things that could be endearing or exasperating, depending on the mood of whoever was affected. Your judgment was sometimes compromised by an incorrigible stubborn streak. Your remoteness could be perplexing for those getting to know you, and painful for those who loved you. You could be difficult to live and work with—whether in freedom or captivity. Who could not say the same of any of us?

But, of this, I have no doubt: Tom, you are a saint. Not the saccharine, holier-than-thou, piously perfect, super-extraordinary kind that floated through life on white virgin wings, but the rough-and-tumble, fall-down-and-pick-yourself-up, everyday ordinary kind that struggled and yearned to grow into the swan that God created you to be. In any case none of that matters now. You're among the heavenly host, singing and playing your clarinet, rejoicing in the presence of God. You are a saint because you have joined your light to the Light. You are among all those who live now in the bosom of God, face to shining face.

You are a martyr. Not the passive, doormat, too-good-to-be-true kind whose eyes roll heavenward and leave behind empty white sockets, but the kind that thought for himself, gnashed against chains, and rolled up his sleeves; the kind that loved the Massanutten Mountains and the street-cleaning boys of Fallujah and the dreams of your children so much that you were compelled to live for their future. You are a martyr because God gave you the grace to stand and bear witness, even unto death, to the one truth authorities can't bear and those in despair forsake, that things do not have to be as they are. Your life is witness that a different world is possible.

You are an icon. Not the two-dimensional, up-on-a-pedestal, holy-card kind that one visits once a year, or once a life, and lights a candle before in a vaulted cathedral shrine, but the flesh-and-blood kind that points with his life to that which is before and beyond him. You are an icon because you are a face of the living God.

Dearest Tom, we have a privileged way of seeing you now. We can see how you lived in the light of how you died. Your death, and the life that led you to that death, is a revelation of God for us. My friend, you laid down your life for us, the human family. You laid down the sword, again and again, in your thoughts and words and deeds. You set your face like flint against the war machine. By your wounds you are healing the world. The punishment you accepted brings us peace. You are the suffering servant face of Christ.

You were a son, a husband, a father, a friend, a disciple of the light. You loved and were loved deeply. You are missed more than words, or tears, can tell.

You taught us to sing this in captivity. May I sing it for you now? Here goes:

Go now in peace
Go now in peace
Let the love of God surround you
Everywhere
Everywhere
You may go

Saint Tom, pray for us.

James Loney, 43, has been a member of CPT since 2000. He has served on CPT projects in the West Bank, Esgenoopetij (Burnt Church, NB), Asubpeeschoseewagong (Grassy Narrows, ON), Kenora and Iraq, and as the Canada program coordinator (2004-2007). He was kidnapped in November 2005 by Iraqi insurgents and held for 118 days before being rescued by British soldiers. James is a founding member of Zacchaeus House, a Catholic Worker house of hospitality for people who are homeless located in Toronto. Originally from Sault Ste. Marie, ON, he currently lives in Toronto with his partner Dan.

23

Joint Statement of Forgiveness
December 8, 2006, London, England

Norman Kember, James Loney, and Harmeet Sooden

We three, members of a Christian Peacemaker Teams (CPT) delegation to Iraq, were kidnapped on November 26, 2005, and held for 118 days before being freed by British and American forces on March 23, 2006. Our friend and colleague, Tom Fox, an American citizen and full-time member of the CPT team working in Baghdad at the time, was kidnapped with us and murdered on March 9, 2006. We are immensely sad that he is not sitting with us here today.

On behalf of our families and CPT, we thank you for attending this press conference today.

It was on this day a year ago that our captors threatened to execute us unless their demands were met. This ultimatum, unknown to us at the time, was a source of extreme distress for our families, friends, and colleagues.

The deadline was extended by two days to December 10, which is International Human Rights Day. On this day, people all over the world will commemorate the adoption of the Universal Declaration of Human Rights by the UN General Assembly in 1948 by speaking out for all those whose human dignity is being violated by torture, arbitrary imprisonment, poverty, racism, oppression, or war.

We understand a number of men alleged to be our captors have been apprehended, charged with kidnapping, and are facing trial in the Central Criminal Court of Iraq. We have been asked by the police in our respective countries to testify in the trial. After much reflection upon our traditions, both Sikh and Christian, we are issuing this statement today.

We unconditionally forgive our captors for abducting and holding us. We have no desire to punish them. Punishment can never restore what was taken from us.

What our captors did was wrong. They caused us, our families, and our friends great suffering. Yet we bear no malice towards them and have no wish for retribution. Should those who have been charged with holding us hostage be brought to trial and convicted, we ask that they be granted all possible leniency. We categorically lay aside any rights we may have over them.

In our view, the catastrophic levels of violence and the lack of effective protection of human rights in Iraq is inextricably linked to the U.S.-led invasion and occupation. As for many others, the actions of our kidnappers were part of a cycle of violence they themselves experienced. While this is no way justifies what the men charged with our kidnapping are alleged to have done, we feel this must be considered in any potential judgment.

Forgiveness is an essential part of Sikh, Christian, and Muslim teaching. Guru Nanak Dev Ji, the first of the Sikh Gurus said, "'Forgiveness is my mother," and "Where there is forgiveness, there is God." Jesus said, "For if you forgive those who sin against you, your heavenly Father will also forgive you." And of Prophet Mohammed (Peace Be Upon Him) it is told that once, while preaching in the city of Ta'if, he was abused, stoned, and driven out of the city. An angel appeared to him and offered to crush the city between the two surrounding mountains if he ordered him to do so, whereupon the prophet (or Mohammed PBUH) said, "No. Maybe from them or their offspring will come good deeds."

Through the power of forgiveness, it is our hope that good deeds will come from the lives of our captors, and that we will all learn to reject the use of violence. We believe those who use violence against others are themselves harmed by the use of violence.

Kidnapping is a capital offence in Iraq and we understand that some of our captors could be sentenced to death. The death penalty is an irrevocable judgment. It erases all possibility that those who have harmed others, even seriously, can yet turn to good. We categorically oppose the death penalty.

By this commitment to forgiveness, we hope to plant a seed that one day will bear the fruits of healing and reconciliation for us, our captors, the peoples of Canada, New Zealand, the United Kingdom, the United States, and most of all, Iraq. We look forward to the day when the Universal Declaration of Human Rights is respected by all the world's people.

Appendix

Persons and Groups who Issued Support Statements or
Appeals on Behalf of the CPT Four[29]

Mohammad Mahdi Akef, Muslim Brotherhood
Abdul Latif Humayem
Iraqi al-Amal Association
Sheikh Harith Al-Dari, head of Association of Muslim Scholars, Iraq
Iraqi Islamic Party
Sheikh Maher Hammoud
Mufti Mohammad Saleem Jalaleddine, Sheikh of Saida and the South
Women's Willpower Committee, Baghdad
Sheikh Mehdi Al-Karki
Sheik Dr. Abed Al-Latif Al-Humaum, general director of the Popular
    Islamic Conference
Muslim Detainees in Toronto
Palestinian Political Groups
Ikram al-Sabri, the head mufti of Palestine
Dr. Wasif Abu-Yousef, a representative of the National and Islamic Forces
    in Palestine
Ferial Abu-Hakil, headmistress of Qataba school, Hebron
Canadian Muslim Forum (CMF), a political public relations organization
United Church of Canada—Human Rights and Peace
The State of Palestine National and Islamic Forces
Northwest Yearly Meeting Board of Peace and Social Concerns
The Indiana Peace and Justice Network
Al Mezan
Bob Paterson-Watt, President, Baptist Peace Fellowship of North America,
    Toronto
Canadian Friends Service Committee
Reedley Social Services, Inc., Reedley, Calif.
Sojourners
The Justice Committee of the Congregation of St. Joseph (Catholic order of
    sisters), Cleveland, OH
Bert Newton, associate pastor, Pasadena (Calif.) Mennonite Church

---

[29] Though we made every effort to construct a comprehensive list, some letters
and/or statements may not appear. The importance and impact of every single
effort has not been overlooked.

Penny Eckert, Seattle, Wash.
>Hamilton Action for Social Change (HASC) and Fathers' Day
Coalition for Peace (FDC4P)
Dr Sayeed Syeed, head of the Islamic Society of North America
Sheila Musaji, editor of *The American Muslim*
Abdul Malik Mujahid, chair of the Council of Islamic Organizations of
>Greater Chicago; that council as a body
Anwar N. Haddam, elected Member of Parliament of Algeria (December
>1991), member, Executive Committee, Coordinating Council of
>Muslim Organizations of Greater Washington Area (CCMO)
Imad-ad-Dean Ahmad of Bethesda, MD
Muhammad Ali-Salaam of Boston
Abdul Cader Asmal, MD, PhD
Rev. Bob Edgar, general secretary of the National Council of Churches
Rev. Peter Laarman of Progressive Christians Uniting in California
Rev. Osagefyo Sekou, director of Clergy and Laity Concerned about Iraq
Lawrence S. Cumming, chairperson, Church Council, Southminster United
>Church, Ottawa
Rabbi Arthur Waskow, rabbinic director of The Shalom Center
The National Council on Canada-Arab Relations
TEAR Fund New Zealand
Bloomington Peace Action Coalition
Citizens for Public Justice
Church of the Brethren General Board News Services
Olympia-Rafah Sister City
Toronto Coalition to Stop the War
Saint Louis Monthly Meeting of the Religious Society of Friends
Peace and Justice Committee, Manhattan Mennonite Church, Manhattan,
>KS
Women's International League for Peace and Freedom
International Women's Peace Service
Peace Brigades International, USA
St. Patrick's Four
Islamic Association of Shenandoah Valley, Harrisonburg, Va.
Islamic Center of Shenandoah Valley
General Council of the Society of the Sacred Heart
Mennonite Church USA
The Muslim Council of Montreal (MCM)
Sheikh Yusuf Al-Qaradawi, chairman of Al-Quds International Foundation
Sheikh Faysal Mawlawi, secretary general of the Islamic Group in Lebanon
Khalid Mishaal, head of Hamas Political Bureau, Palestine
Musa Abu Marzuq, deputy head of Hamas Political Bureau, Palestine
Maan Bashur, secretary general of the Arab Nationalist Congress

Hasan Hudruj, Hezbollah, Lebanon
Mahmud Al-Qumati, Hezbollah, Lebanon
Father Antwan Dhao, Lebanon
Sheikh Abdulhadi Awang, Islamic Party, Malaysia
Professor Aleef-ud-Din Turabi, Kashmir
Dr. Mohamed M. O. Jamjoom, businessman, Saudi Arabia
Dr. Khalid Abdurrahman Al-Ajami, university professor, Saudi Arabia
Dr. Muhsin Al-Awaji, Islamic writer and thinker, Saudi Arabia
Dr. Abd Al-Quddus Al-Midwahi, Yemen
Muhammad bin Ali Ijlan, Yemen
Dr. Abdullatif Al Mahmud, Islamic Society, Bahrain
Abdulmunem Jalal Al-Mir, Palestine Solidarity Association, Bahrain
Dr. Muhammad Al-Sheikh Mahmud Siyam, former imam of Al-Aqsa
        Mosque, Palestine
Khalid Mahmud Khan, Pakistan
Dr. Zafrul-Islam Khan, India
Dr. Azzam Tamimi, Muslim Association of Britain, UK
Haitham Yassin Abu Al-Raghib, Jordan
Saud Abu Mahfuz, Jordan
Engineer Boulafaat Abdulhamid, Algeria
Muslim Peace Fellowship / Ansar as-Salam
Rick Ufford-Chase, moderator, 216th General Assembly, Presbyterian
        Church (U.S.A.)
Clifton Kirkpatrick, stated clerk of the General Assembly, Presbyterian
        Church (U.S.A.)
St. Louis Religious Society of Friends.
Council of Organizations of Civil Society
World Council of Churches (WCC)
Episcopal Peace Fellowship
Forum of Human Rights Workers of Barrancabermeja, Colombia
Canadian Centre for Victims of Torture (CCVT)
Canadian Friends Service Committee (Quakers) and Canadian Yearly
        Meeting of the Religious Society of Friends (Quakers), Toronto,
        ON
The Canadian Islamic Congress
Catholic New Times, Toronto
The Community of St. Martin, Minneapolis
The Citizens for Public Justice
Conflict Mediation Services of Downsview
The Congregation of St. Joseph Justice Committee Council of
        Organizations of Civil Society
International Women's Peace Service Toronto

The National Council on Canadian-Arab Relations and the Canadian Arab
    Federation
The Al Mezan Center for Human Rights, Gaza, Palestine
Northside Friends Meeting, Chicago
The Shalom Center
Southminster United Church Ottawa
The Toronto Catholic Worker Community
The Toronto Coalition to Stop the War
Week of Prayer for World Peace committee
The United Church of Canada
Women's International League for Peace and Freedom—Canadian Section
The World Council of Churches
Peter DeMott, Danny Burns, Clare Grady, and Teresa Grady
Christie Goering Schmid
Phil Jones, director of the Brethren Witness, Washington Office
Toronto City Council
Mennonite World Conference
Evangelical Mennonite Conference
The Congress of Arab American Organizations in Michigan (CAAO-MI)
Church of Scotland, Edinburgh
Oak Park Friends Monthly Meeting
Islamic Society of Greater Springfield
Dominican Sisters of Springfield
Peace Movement Aotearoa (PMA), New Zealand
Catholic Peace Fellowship
Toronto Monthly Meeting of the Religious Society of Friends (Quakers)
Mennonite Fellowship of Montreal
Muslims Students Association, University of Windsor, Canada
Shafici Mohyaddin Abokar, secretary general of Peace Maker and Research
    Group in Somalia (PRG) and president of Somali Sports Press
    Association in Mogadishu
Moazzam Begg
Huddersfield Interfaith Council
Mark Pelavin, associate director, Religious Action Center
Guirguis Ibrahim Saleh, general secretary of the Middle East Council of
    Churches
Prof. Dr. Hamed Bin Ahmad Al Rifaie, president of the International
    Islamic Forum for Dialogue
Muslim Association of Canada (MAC)
César García, presidente, Hermanos Menonitas de Colombia
September 11th Families for Peaceful Tomorrows
Seattle Mennonite Church, Weldon D. Nisley, pastor
Global Women's Strike

Witness for Peace, Sharon Hostetler
Wellington Palestine Group
Students for Justice in Palestine
Auckland University Students for Justice in Palestine
New Zealand Palestine Human Rights Campaign and Students for Justice in
        Palestine
New Zealand Council of Christians and Muslims
Keith Locke, MP, Green Party Foreign Affairs and Human Rights
        Spokesperson

1652880

Made in the USA